First World War
and Army of Occupation
War Diary
France, Belgium and Germany

29 DIVISION
86 Infantry Brigade
Royal Dublin Fusiliers
1st Battalion
1 August 1917 - 31 May 1919

WO95/2301/2

The Naval & Military Press Ltd
www.nmarchive.com
Published in association with The National Archives

Published by

The Naval & Military Press Ltd

Unit 10 Ridgewood Industrial Park,

Uckfield, East Sussex,

TN22 5QE England

Tel: +44 (0) 1825 749494

www.naval-military-press.com

www.nmarchive.com

This diary has been reprinted in facsimile from the original. Any imperfections are inevitably reproduced and the quality may fall short of modern type and cartographic standards.

© **Crown Copyright**
Images reproduced by permission of The National Archives, London, England, 2015.

Contents

Document type	Place/Title	Date From	Date To
Heading	WO95/2301-2 Battalion Royal Dublin Fusiliers 1918 May-1919 May.		
Heading	Southern (Late 29th) Divn 86th Infy Bde 1st Bn Roy. Dublin Fus. Jan-Dec 1919 1919 Jan-1919 May		
Heading	29 Div 86 Bde 1 Bn R Dublin Fus 1918 May 1919 May From 16 Division 48 Bde		
Heading	War Diary 1st Royal Dublin Fusiliers. May 1918 Vol 25		
War Diary	Batt H.Q. Papote. D.22.a.Sheet 36.A.	01/05/1918	01/05/1918
War Diary	Batt. H.Q. E 19.C. Sheet 36.A.	02/05/1918	09/05/1918
War Diary	Papote D 22.a.54	10/05/1918	15/05/1918
War Diary	Batt. H.Q. E.19.C. Nieppe Furest	16/05/1918	18/05/1918
War Diary	Batt. H.Q. E.19.C.	19/05/1918	19/05/1918
War Diary	Batt. H.Q. Grand Hazard D.14.b.	20/05/1918	26/05/1918
War Diary	Batt. H.Q. Grand Hazard	26/05/1918	30/05/1918
Operation(al) Order(s)	1st Bn. Royal Dublin Fusiliers. Operation Order No 26.	01/05/1918	01/05/1918
Operation(al) Order(s)	Operation Order No. 27 1st Bn. Royal Dublin Fusiliers.	02/05/1918	02/05/1918
Operation(al) Order(s)	1st Battn Royal Dublin Fusiliers Operation Order No. 28		
Operation(al) Order(s)	1st Bn Royal Dublin Fusiliers. Operation Order No. 29.	14/05/1918	14/05/1918
Operation(al) Order(s)	1st Bn Royal Dublin Fusiliers. Operation Order No. 30	18/05/1918	18/05/1918
Operation(al) Order(s)	1st Bn Royal Dublin Fusiliers. Operation Orders No. 31	26/05/1918	26/05/1918
Operation(al) Order(s)	1st Bn Royal Dublin Fusiliers. Addendum No. 1 Operation Order No. 31.	26/05/1918	26/05/1918
Miscellaneous	1st Bn Royal Dublin Fuslrs. Amendment No. 1 Operation Order No. 31	27/05/1918	27/05/1918
Operation(al) Order(s)	1st Bn Royal Dublin Fusiliers. Operation Order No. 32.	31/05/1918	31/05/1918
Heading	War Diary 1st Bn Royal Dublin Fusiliers to Month Of June 1918 Volume 39.		
War Diary	Petit Sec Bois E 7.b.9.7	01/06/1918	01/06/1918
War Diary	Batt H.Q. E.7.b.9.7 Sheet 36 A.	02/06/1918	04/06/1918
War Diary	Batt. H.Q. D6.d.9.7. (36 K. Sheet)	05/06/1918	09/06/1918
War Diary	Petit Sec Bois E 7 b 8.7	10/06/1918	10/06/1918
War Diary	Petit Sec Bois	11/06/1918	12/06/1918
War Diary	Le Trocadero	13/06/1918	14/06/1918
War Diary	D.9.a	15/06/1918	17/06/1918
War Diary	Batt. H.Q. Fettle Fm D24a.8.2	18/06/1918	19/06/1918
War Diary	Le Trocodero D.9.a	20/06/1918	24/06/1918
War Diary	Blaringhem B.16b.7.2 (Sheet 36 A)	25/06/1918	27/06/1918
War Diary	Papote D.22.	28/06/1918	29/06/1918
War Diary	Blaringhem B16b.	30/06/1918	30/06/1918
Operation(al) Order(s)	1st. Bn Royal Dublin Fusiliers. Operation Order No. 32.	31/05/1918	31/05/1918
Operation(al) Order(s)	1st. Bn Royal Dublin Fusiliers. Operation Order No. 33A	02/06/1918	02/06/1918
Map	Dispositions 1st R.D.F. 3/6/18		
Operation(al) Order(s)	1st Bn Royal Dublin Fusiliers Operation Order No 33.	02/06/1918	02/06/1918
Miscellaneous			
Operation(al) Order(s)	1st Bn. Royal Dublin Fusiliers Operation Order No. 34.	09/06/1918	09/06/1918
Operation(al) Order(s)	1st R. Dublin Fusiliers. Operation Order No. 35.	11/06/1918	11/06/1918
Operation(al) Order(s)	1st Bn R. Dublin Fusiliers. Operation Order No. 36	12/06/1918	12/06/1918
Operation(al) Order(s)	1st Bn Royal Dublin Fusiliers. Operation Order No. 37.	17/06/1918	17/06/1918

Operation(al) Order(s)	1st Bn Royal Dublin Fusiliers. Operation Order No. 38	19/06/1918	19/06/1918
Operation(al) Order(s)	1st Bn R. Dublin Fusiliers Order No. 39.	24/06/1918	24/06/1918
Operation(al) Order(s)	1st. Bn. Royal Dublin Fusiliers. Operation Order No. 40.	27/06/1918	27/06/1918
Miscellaneous	1st. Bn. Royal Dublin Fusiliers. Amendment No. 1 to Operation Order No. 40.	27/06/1918	27/06/1918
Operation(al) Order(s)	1st Royal Dublin Fus. Operation Order No. 41.		
Operation(al) Order(s)	1st R Dublin Fus. Operation Order No 42.	30/06/1918	30/06/1918
Miscellaneous		29/06/1918	29/06/1918
Heading	War Diary of 1st Bn Royal Dublin Fusiliers for month of July 1918 Volume 40		
War Diary	Campagne Sheet 27 S.30	01/07/1918	06/07/1918
War Diary	Campagne	07/07/1918	22/07/1918
War Diary	Noordpeene	23/07/1918	31/07/1918
Miscellaneous	Arrivals.		
Heading	1st Royal Dublin Fusiliers War Diary for August 1918. Vol 28		
Heading	1st Royal Dublin Fusiliers for Month of August 1918 Volume 41.		
War Diary	Noordpeene	01/08/1917	01/08/1917
War Diary	Hazebrouck V.22.c	02/08/1917	02/08/1917
War Diary	Batt H.Q. W.20b.6.9. Sheet 27	03/08/1917	04/08/1917
War Diary	Batt H.Q. E.10.b.3.9 Sheet 36 A.	05/08/1917	09/08/1917
War Diary	Batt H.Q.	10/08/1917	10/08/1917
War Diary	Batt HQ V.24.c. Sheet 27	11/08/1917	16/08/1917
War Diary	Batt H.Q. Curfew House	17/08/1917	18/08/1917
War Diary	Curfew Ho.	18/08/1917	21/08/1917
War Diary	Batt H.Q. War Stazeele Rly Station	22/08/1917	23/08/1917
War Diary	Batt. H.Q Near Stazeele Station F.N.B. Sheet 36.A	23/08/1917	27/08/1917
War Diary	Batt. H.Q. E4.C.5.2 Sheet 36 A.	28/08/1917	31/08/1917
Miscellaneous	1st Battn. Royal Dublin Fusiliers. Warning Order.	01/08/1918	01/08/1918
Operation(al) Order(s)	1st Battn Royal Dublin Fusiliers Operation Order No. 2	02/08/1918	02/08/1918
Operation(al) Order(s)	1st Bn. Royal Dublin Fusiliers. Operation Order No. 3.	04/08/1918	04/08/1918
Operation(al) Order(s)	1st Bn. Royal Dublin Fusiliers. Operation Order No. 4	07/08/1917	07/08/1917
Miscellaneous	Strength 31.7.18 45 Offers., 932 of Ranks	31/07/1918	31/07/1918
Operation(al) Order(s)	1st Bn Royal Dublin Fusiliers. Operation Order No. 5	09/08/1918	09/08/1918
Operation(al) Order(s)	1st Bn R. Dublin Fusiliers. Addendum to Operation Order No. 5.	10/08/1918	10/08/1918
Miscellaneous			
Operation(al) Order(s)	1st Bn. Royal Dublin Fusiliers. Operation Order No. 6	15/08/1918	15/08/1918
Miscellaneous	Strength 7.8.18. 43 Offs. 911 of Ranks.	07/08/1918	07/08/1918
Operation(al) Order(s)	1st R. Dublin Fusiliers. Operation Order No. 7.	21/08/1918	21/08/1918
Operation(al) Order(s)	1st Bn R. Dublin Fusiliers. Operation Order No. 8	23/08/1918	23/08/1918
Operation(al) Order(s)	1st Bn R. Dublin Fusiliers. Operation Order No. 9	24/08/1918	24/08/1918
Operation(al) Order(s)	1st Bn R. Dublin Fusiliers. Operation Order No. 10	27/08/1918	27/08/1918
Operation(al) Order(s)	1st Bn R Dublin Fusiliers. Minor Operation Order R.I.	29/08/1918	29/08/1918
Miscellaneous	Strength 15.8.18. 42 Offs. 904 of Ranks.	15/08/1918	15/08/1918
Heading	1st Royal Dublin Fusiliers September 1918.		
Heading	War Diary of 1st Bn. Royal Dublin Fus for Month of September 1918. Volume 42.		
War Diary	Near Station of Strazeele (Jobbery Crossing)	01/09/1918	01/09/1918
War Diary	Outtersteene.	02/09/1918	02/09/1918
War Diary	Lacreche & Ploegsteert	03/09/1918	03/09/1918
War Diary	Ploegsteert	04/09/1918	05/09/1918
War Diary	Bailleul	06/09/1918	10/09/1918
War Diary	Hazebrouck	11/09/1918	19/09/1918

War Diary	Brake Camp A.30.c Sheet 28.	20/09/1918	25/09/1918
War Diary	Brake Camp	26/09/1918	30/09/1918
Miscellaneous	Strength 31.8.18. 44 Offs. 872 O/Rs.	31/08/1918	31/08/1918
Miscellaneous	1st Bn. Royal Dublin Fusiliers. Appendix A	04/09/1918	04/09/1918
Operation(al) Order(s)	1st Bn R. Dublin Fusiliers. Operation Order No. 12	04/09/1918	04/09/1918
Miscellaneous	1st Bn. Royal Dublin Fusiliers.	04/09/1918	04/09/1918
Operation(al) Order(s)	1st Bn. Royal Dublin Fusiliers. Operation Order No. 13	19/08/1918	19/08/1918
Miscellaneous	Administrative Instruction No. 13	22/09/1918	22/09/1918
Miscellaneous	C.R.E. 29th Div. No. 45/17/11/1.	22/09/1918	22/09/1918
Operation(al) Order(s)	86th Infantry Brigade Administrative Order No. 42.	22/09/1918	22/09/1918
Operation(al) Order(s)	1st Bn R. Dublin Fusiliers Operation Order No. 11	22/09/1918	22/09/1918
Operation(al) Order(s)	86th Infantry Brigade Administrative Order No. 41	22/09/1918	22/09/1918
Miscellaneous	A.D.M.S. 29th Division No. SR. 11/194.	28/09/1918	28/09/1918
Miscellaneous	1st Bn. Royal Dublin Fusiliers. Administrative Instructions.	23/09/1918	23/09/1918
Miscellaneous	86th Infantry Brigade Operation Instructions No. 3	24/09/1918	24/09/1918
Miscellaneous	86th Infantry Brigade Operation Instructions No. 4.	24/09/1918	24/09/1918
Miscellaneous	86th Infantry Brigade Operation Instructions No. 5.	24/09/1918	24/09/1918
Miscellaneous	86th Infantry Brigade Operation Instruction No. 6.	24/09/1918	24/09/1918
Operation(al) Order(s)	86th Infantry Brigade Administrative Order No. 44.	25/09/1918	25/09/1918
Miscellaneous	Administrative Instruction No. 14	25/09/1918	25/09/1918
Miscellaneous	1st Bn. Royal Dublin Fusiliers. General Instructions.	25/09/1918	25/09/1918
Miscellaneous	Addendum No 1 to 86th Inf. Brigade Operation Instructions No.3	26/09/1918	26/09/1918
Miscellaneous	86th Infantry Brigade Operation Instructions No. 7.	26/09/1918	26/09/1918
Miscellaneous	Amendments To Administrative Instruction No. 13	26/09/1918	26/09/1918
Miscellaneous	1st Battalion Lancashire Fusiliers. Operation Instructions No.1	24/09/1918	24/09/1918
Miscellaneous	86th Infantry Brigade Operation Instructions No. 9	26/09/1918	26/09/1918
Operation(al) Order(s)	2nd Bn. Royal Fusiliers. Operation Order No. 70	26/09/1918	26/09/1918
Operation(al) Order(s)	2nd. Bn. Royal Fusiliers. Addendum No. 1. to Operation Order No. 70.	26/09/1918	26/09/1918
Miscellaneous	Amendments To Administrative Instruction No. 14	26/09/1918	26/09/1918
Miscellaneous	Amendments To Administrative Instruction No. 14	25/09/1918	25/09/1918
Operation(al) Order(s)	1st Bn. Royal Dublin Fusiliers. Operation Order No. 14	26/09/1918	26/09/1918
Miscellaneous	Administrative Instruction No. 15	26/09/1918	26/09/1918
Miscellaneous	1st Battalion Lancashire Fusiliers. Operation Instructions No. 2	26/09/1918	26/09/1918
Operation(al) Order(s)	2nd Bn. Royal Fusiliers. Addendum No. 2 to Operation Order No. 70.	27/09/1918	27/09/1918
Operation(al) Order(s)	1st Battn. Royal Dublin Fusiliers. Operation Order No. 15	27/09/1918	27/09/1918
Miscellaneous	Narrative.		
Miscellaneous	September 29.		
Miscellaneous	Strength 14.9.18. 48 Offs. 983 of Rs.	14/09/1918	14/09/1918
Heading	War Diary Of 1st Bn. Royal Dublin Fusiliers For Month Of October, 1918. Volume 43		
War Diary	Zuidhoek K.19.a (Sheet 28)	01/10/1918	02/10/1918
War Diary	Ypres.	03/10/1918	05/10/1918
War Diary	Ledeghem	06/10/1918	09/10/1918
War Diary	Becelaire J.12.d.77	10/10/1918	10/10/1918
War Diary	Ypres	11/10/1918	13/10/1918
War Diary	Ledeghem	14/10/1918	15/10/1918
War Diary	Heule a11.c.53 (Sheet 29)	16/10/1918	16/10/1918
War Diary	Heule	17/10/1918	21/10/1918
War Diary	Steenbrugge 29/1.25. Central	22/10/1918	22/10/1918

War Diary	Cuerne	23/10/1918	25/10/1918
War Diary	Roncq	26/10/1918	26/10/1918
War Diary	Bondues 36/E 17.C	27/10/1918	31/10/1918
Miscellaneous	1st Bn. Royal Dublin Fusiliers. Relief Order. No. L.5.	18/10/1918	18/10/1918
Operation(al) Order(s)	1st Bn. Royal Dublin Fusiliers. Operation Order No. 16.	13/10/1918	13/10/1918
Operation(al) Order(s)	1st Bn. Royal Dublin Fusiliers. Operation Order. No. L.6.	19/10/1918	19/10/1918
Operation(al) Order(s)	1st Bn. Royal Dublin Fusiliers. Operation Order No. L.7.	21/10/1918	21/10/1918
Miscellaneous	1st Bn. Royal Dublin Fusiliers. Administrative Order.	12/10/1918	12/10/1918
Miscellaneous	1st Bn. Royal Dublin Fusiliers.	28/09/1918	28/09/1918
Miscellaneous	1st Bn. Royal Dublin Fusiliers.	14/10/1918	14/10/1918
Miscellaneous	1st Bn. Royal Dublin Fusiliers.	21/10/1918	21/10/1918
Miscellaneous	1st Battn. The Royal Dublin Fusiliers.	00/10/1918	00/10/1918
Heading	War Diary of 1st Battalion Royal Dublin Fusiliers For Month Of November 1918. Vol 32		
Heading	War Diary of 1st Royal Dublin Fusiliers for month of November 1918 Volume 44		
War Diary	Bondues 36/E.17.C	01/11/1918	08/11/1918
War Diary	Luigne 29/S.23.d.5.6	09/11/1918	09/11/1918
War Diary	(Near) Ruddervoorde T.6.a.22	10/11/1918	10/11/1918
War Diary	Saint. Genois. 29/n.16.a	11/11/1918	11/11/1918
War Diary	Pottes 29/n 30.d.8.8.	12/11/1918	12/11/1918
War Diary	near Bawreux 37/E.17.C.0.8	13/11/1918	13/11/1918
War Diary	Flobecq 30/T.27	14/11/1918	17/11/1918
War Diary	Fouleng. 38/P.17.a & D	18/11/1918	20/11/1918
War Diary	Rebecq-Rognon	21/11/1918	22/11/1918
War Diary	Lillois-Witterzee	23/11/1918	23/11/1918
War Diary	Court St Etienne	24/11/1918	24/11/1918
War Diary	Wilhain St Paul.	25/11/1918	26/11/1918
War Diary	Eghezee	27/11/1918	27/11/1918
War Diary	Moha	28/11/1918	28/11/1918
War Diary	Warzee	29/11/1918	29/11/1918
War Diary	Aywaille	30/11/1918	30/11/1918
Miscellaneous	1st Bn. Royal Dublin Fusiliers. Move Order No. 3	07/11/1918	07/11/1918
Miscellaneous	On Strength	31/10/1918	31/10/1918
Heading	1st Battn Royal Dublin Fusiliers War Diary for December 1918 Vol 33		
Heading	War Diary of 1st Bn. Royal Dublin Fusiliers for Month of December 1918 Volume 45		
War Diary	Basse-Desnie	01/12/1918	03/12/1918
War Diary	Ster	04/12/1918	04/12/1918
War Diary	Weywertz	05/12/1918	05/12/1918
War Diary	Simmerath	06/12/1918	06/12/1918
War Diary	Embken	07/12/1918	07/12/1918
War Diary	Lechenich	08/12/1918	08/12/1918
War Diary	Cologne (Sulz Subarks of)	09/12/1918	09/12/1918
War Diary	SWL1. Subark of Cologne	10/12/1918	12/12/1918
War Diary	Bensberg	13/12/1918	20/12/1918
War Diary	Berg-Gladbach	21/12/1918	28/12/1918
War Diary	Kurten	29/12/1918	31/12/1918
Miscellaneous	On Strength	30/11/1918	30/11/1918
Heading	1st Battalion Royal Dublin Fusiliers. War Diary For January 1919 Vol 34		
Heading	War Diary of 1st Royal Dublin Fusiliers. for Month of January 1919 Volume 46		

War Diary	Kurten	01/01/1919	01/01/1919
War Diary	Germany	02/01/1919	13/01/1919
War Diary	Berg-Gladbach	14/01/1919	31/01/1919
Miscellaneous	On Strength	31/12/1918	31/12/1918
Heading	War Diary of 1st Bn Royal Dublin Fusiliers for Month of February Volume 47		
War Diary	Berg-Gladbach (Germany)	01/02/1919	11/02/1919
War Diary	Berg-Gladbach	12/02/1919	16/02/1919
War Diary	Batt H.Q. Kurten (Maps 2 Lt 2K)	17/02/1919	22/02/1919
War Diary	Kurten Batt HQt	22/02/1919	28/02/1919
Miscellaneous	On Strength	31/01/1919	31/01/1919
Heading	April Intelligence Summary of the 1st Royal Dublin Fusiliers. Volume 49		
War Diary	Mulheim.	01/04/1919	05/04/1919
War Diary	Lequesnoy	06/04/1919	30/04/1919
Heading	War Diary of the 1st Bn Royal Dublin Fusiliers for the month of May 1919 Volume 50		
War Diary	Le Quesnoy	01/05/1919	31/05/1919

WO95/2301/2
1 Battalion Royal Dublin Fusiliers
1918 May - 1919 May.

SOUTHERN (LATE 29TH) DIVN
86TH INFY BDE

1ST BN ROY. DUBLIN FUS.
JAN - ~~DEC 1919~~
1919 JAN - 1919 MAY

29 DIV
86 BDE

1 BN R. DUBLIN FUS

1918 MAY

1919 MAY

FROM 16 DIVISION 48 BDE

WO 259

25 X
17 sheets

War Diary

1st Royal Dublin Fusiliers.

May 1918

Joined 86 Bde from 16 Div
26/4/18

Army Form C. 2118.

1st Royal Dublin Fusiliers.

WAR DIARY
or
INTELLIGENCE SUMMARY.
(Erase heading not required.)

Instructions regarding War Diaries and Intelligence Summaries are contained in F. S. Regs., Part II. and the Staff Manual respectively. Title pages will be prepared in manuscript.

Place	Date	Hour	Summary of Events and Information May 1918.	Remarks and references to Appendices
Batt H.Q.				
PAPOTE.	1.		Battalion move to front line & relieve 2nd Bn Royal Fusiliers in Right Sub sector (vide	Batt.
B.22.a Sheet 36.A.			operation order No 26 attached) Eastern fringe of the BOIS D'AVAL Forest of NIEPPE - from	Strength. 37. 992
			line being a series of outposts - Relief complete by 10.30 p.m.	
Batt H.Q. E.19.C. Sheet 36.A.	2		"Y" Company relieve "C" Company 1st Lancashire Fus in Right Support (Vide Junction order No 27 attached). Fighting patrols at night in hope of getting identifications.	37. 993
—"—	3		Line subjected to heavy bursts of artillery fire. Patrols go out as before. Draft 11 Officers & 2/Lieuts P.G.GURET, H.McALLEN, J.W.KIRWAN, C.KIRWAN, M.A.CONDRON, T.A.COONEY, R.J.McGOWAN, W.MARTIN, F.G.ROSS, P.H.LENNON, R.C.H.CANDLISH	
			and 138 ORs join - 1 OR wounded. Patrols as before.	48. 1127.
—"—	4		Lt. G.P.N.THOMPSON and his servant killed 4 ORs wounded - Hostile artillery very active. - 1 OR wounded. Lt M.S.HARTERY M.C. T.O.R. to 86th Trench	
			Mortar Battery. Patrols at night as before.	46. 1120
—"—	5		Line a form heavily shelled at dawn & dusk.	—
—"—	6		2/Lt. R.S.BOLES dangerously wounded Remainder his Officers on being admitted to C.C.S. Line shelled intermittently - 4 ORs wounded, 10 & gas.	45. 1117.
—"—	7		Nothing unusual happened Batt. H.Q. in western fringe of wood near T	

WAR DIARY or INTELLIGENCE SUMMARY

Army Form C. 2118.

1st Royal Dublin Fusiliers

for month of May 1918.

Place	Date	Hour	Summary of Events and Information	Remarks and references to Appendices
Batt. H.Q. E.19.c	7.	continued	LA MOTTE village reasonably shelled – 20 ORs killed 6 ORs wounded	45–1107.
	8.		Nothing unusual to report. Intels as before. 2 ORs wounded. 5 ORs evacuated	
–do–		Draft 34 ORs.		45–1136
–do–	9.	2/Lt. ST JOHN. 9. E IRVINE arriving wounded – 1 OR killed 12 wounded – Batt. relieved by 2nd Royal Fus. (Operation order No 2 8 attached) relief completed by 12 Midnight – Batt. move to Brigade reserve PAPOTE area – many thousand gas shells over back area during night – nil casualties.		
PAPOTE D.22.a.S4	10.		Batt. provide working parties in forward area also guards on numerous bridges in LA MOTTE area. Capt A.S. DELANEY. MM WRy companies, Lake Ore Command of system known as "LA MOTTE – MARQUETTE Defences" – at night reserve area open heavily gas shelled. 11 ORs wounded 2 ORs killed, 1 OR appears	44–1112
–do–	11.		nissus working parties. At midnight enemy heavily shelled Reserve area. Specially in vicinity of LE TIRAN CLAIS and PAPOTE with gas shells also noted over 4000. Brief Rig stained our numerous Company Hills causing following casualties 6 killed, 11 wounded + 231 gassed. Since 4 whom have since died – all usual precautions were taken but	

Army Form C. 2118.

WAR DIARY
or
INTELLIGENCE SUMMARY.

(Erase heading not required.)

1st Royal Dublin Fusiliers

Instructions regarding War Diaries and Intelligence Summaries are contained in F. S. Regs., Part II. and the Staff Manual respectively. Title pages will be prepared in manuscript.

Place	Date	Hour	Summary of Events and Information	Remarks and references to Appendices
PAPOTE			May 1918	
Dr. R. S.W.	11		Continued owing to the nature of gas shells employed (yellow "mustard") many men were severely blistered throughout the body. Mencre [men?] every 15 about hits or billets where men were crowded together and asleep a certain amount permanent confusion in its dark often killed were responsible for a number of the Casualties	
			draft to OR's + 1 OR from hospital join	44. 875
—	12		Immediate notes given by Corn. Off. for men to be screened from affected areas. M.G. Batt. Keefe evacuated in Ironwar S.W. of PAPOTE – Kraft Lieut M.F. MONTGOMERY	882
			2/Lt CLEAR + 9 OR's join – 2 OR's killed by shell fire	46 –
—	13		Working parties training	
—	14		do. Capt G.W.B TARLETON M.C. + draft 19 OR's join 1 OR from hospital	47. 902
—	15		Enemy early hour MARQUETTE area shelling gas shelled 39 men being gassed. 11 OR's wounded – draft 15 OR's join –	47. 867
Batt HQ			Batt relieve 2nd Royal Fusiliers in line (vide operation order No 29 attached) relief complete 12 midnight	
E.15.C.2	16 – 19		Nothing unusual to report. Same patrols at night – weather fine. 2/Lt J. ALEXANDER from D.R.M. join in Corps Rest Camp. 9 OR's + 2 OR killed + 9 OR wounded 8 OR. evacuated	48. 956

WAR DIARY or INTELLIGENCE SUMMARY

Army Form C. 2118.

1st Royal Dublin Fusiliers

For Month of MAY 1918.

Place	Date	Hour	Summary of Events and Information	Remarks and references to Appendices
Batt. H.Q. E.19.c	19th		86th Infantry Bde relieved by 87th Inf Bde in Right Brigade Sector. 86th Inf Bde going into Divisional Reserve – Battalion relieved by 2nd Bn LEINSTER Regt (vide operation order No 30 attached) relief complete by Midnight – Battalion move to Hutments by Cross Roads GRAND HAZARD on main HAZEBROUCK – MORBECQUE Road. 4 ORs from A Coy, 2 ORs from B Coy, 9 ORs wounded & 43 ORs wounded or unwounded "gas". There is total of men ORs who previously reported who developes symptoms of gas at different periods after gas attacks.	48.8.10
Batt. H.Q. GRAND HAZARD D.14.d.	20th		Capt G.W.B. TARLETON M.C. takes over duties of adjutant from Capt E. BAILEY M.C. – Batt provide working parties to forward area - Remainder employed cleaning panniers. Divisional Band play in Camp 5:30pm – 7pm.	48.8.10
" "	21		Training & Baths. Camp shelled at intervals by long range High Velocity gun. 1 OR killed 3 wounded. Camp continued - unsafe for Troops - Battalion then fell accommodated in bivouacs placed under hedgerows in neighbouring fields. Draft joins 130 ORs. 8 ORs wounded.	48.8.12
" "	22		Working parties & cleaning, weather very fine & forenoon warm	
" "	23-26		as above. Capt W.H. STITT, Lieuts A. HAMMOND, A.E. SETH-SMITH, R.H. BURNS, join own	

1st Bn Royal Dublin Fusiliers

WAR DIARY
or
INTELLIGENCE SUMMARY.
(Erase heading not required.)

Army Form C. 2118.

Place	Date	Hour	Summary of Events and Information	Remarks and references to Appendices
Batt H.Q GRAND HAMAGE			for month of May 1918	
		Continued	Strength of Battalion although employed elsewhere incorporated 15 ORs invalided	
			6 ORs permanently attached 86th T.M. Battery. Reprised from hospital 13 ORs – Drafts	
			at Corps Reinforcement camps but when on Batt Strength when they arrive there 37 ORs	44. 838.
- " -	27.		Training etc in morning - Battalion relieve 1st K.O.S. Borders & 1st BORDER Regt.	
			in Support sector of 9th Division left sector. relief operation order no 31 attached.	
			Drafts 17 ORs & 1 OR from Hospital join, 3 ORs invalided 1 OR struck off Strength	44. 852.
			as a Deserter.	
- " -	28.		Quiet day. Slight evacuation of gas shelling at PETIT SEC BOIS - june	
			water. 1 OR to Base inspt, 1 OR from Hospital. Draft 22 ORs join	44. 874.
- " -	29		Quiet day. Capt C.H. EALY posted in own Stand off Strength	43. 874.
- " -	30		Midly enemy x Corps positio. dearly shelled 7 ORs wounded. 15 ORs evacuated	
			Draft 1 officer 2/Lt S. OWENS. 83 ORs at Corps Depot, 18 ORs departed from base taken on strength	
			20 ORs from hospital	44. 955
- " -			Hostile artillery more active - Vicinity of Batt H.Q. heavily shelled. 4 ORs wounded.	
			Capt: A.L. MATTHEWS M.C. invalided to Enghand, 2 ORs at Corps Depot taken on Strength	43. 953

Tribution
for Lt Col.
Captain & Adjutant,
1st Bn. Royal Dublin Fusiliers.

Secret. 1st Bn Royal Dublin Fusiliers. Copy No 10.

Operation Orders No [illegible]

[illegible] May 1918.

Reference Sheet 36A. N.E. 1/20000 & LA MOTTE Special Sheet.

1. The 1st Bn Royal Dublin Fusiliers will relieve the 2nd Bn Royal Fusiliers in [illegible] sub sector this [illegible] day of May 1918.

2. Details of Relief as follows:-

(a) "Y" Coy 1st R. Dublin Fusiliers relieves "X" Coy 2nd Royal Fusiliers in Left Support
"Z" " " " "W" " " " Right "
Above companies will move off at 2 p.m. and carry out relief in daylight.

(b) "W" Coy 1st R. Dublin Fusiliers relieves "Z" Coy 2nd Royal Fusiliers in [illegible] Left Front
"X" " " " "Y" " " " Right "
Above companies move off at 6 p.m. and carry out relief by night.

(c) Guides ~~to meet "Y" and "Z" Coys will be up [illegible]~~ 1 per Platoon, 1 per Coy & H.Q. Coy to meet "Y" and "Z" Coys will be up at Huts E.19.c.9.1. at 2.45 pm
Guides 1 per Platoon, 1 per Coy & H.Q. Coy to meet "W" & "X" Coys will be up at Huts E.19.c.9.1. at 7.30 pm

3. Advance parties consisting of 1 Officer, 1 N.C.O. 1 Signaller & 1 Runner per Coy & H.Q. Coy will proceed in advance and take over all Trench Stores &c..

4. The Lewis Guns under 2Lt. [illegible] J.G. [illegible] will be relieved during the afternoon by Lewis Guns of 2nd Royal Fusiliers, and on relief will proceed to small Red Brick [illegible] [illegible] of Support Coy [illegible] Royal Fusiliers.

5. Transport Officer will arrange for the following:-
(a) 1 Limber and Maltese Cart - Headquarters Coy - 2. p.m.
(b) 1 " "Y" & "Z" at 1-30 pm.
(c) 1 " W & X " 5. 0. p.m.
(d) Maltese Cart - Aid Post - 2 p.m.
(e) To collect all Officers Kits etc. and convey same to Q.M. Stores.

6. Quartermaster will arrange for the following.
(a) Early delivery of Rations
(b) Cookers to be brought to E.19.c.9.1. where further orders will be given.

7. O.C. Coys will arrange to hand over present billets to incoming Unit in a clean and sanitary condition and obtaining the usual certificate.
All Trench Stores Maps Intelligence Reports, notes, and works proposed and in hand will be taken over from outgoing Battalion.
[illegible] in duplicate will be in Orderly Room by 12 noon 2/5/18.

8. Completion of relief will be notified to Battalion H.Q. by the code word "BACKAGAIN" with surname of Coy Commander.

9. Acknowledge.

[illegible] Captain & Adjutant.
1st Bn Royal Dublin Fusiliers

Copies to No 1. H.Q. [illegible] Infy Bde.
" 2. O.C. 2nd Royal Fusiliers
" 3. Commanding Officer.
" 4. O.C. "W" Coy
" 5. " "X" "
" 6. " "Y" "
" 7. " "Z" "
" 8. [illegible]
" 9. Quartermaster.
" 10. [illegible]
" 11. [illegible]
" 12. [illegible]
" 13. [illegible]

Secret

Operation Order No 27.

Copy No 10.

1st Bn. Royal Dublin Fusiliers

Reference Sheet 36b. N.E. 1/20,000 & LA MOTTE 1/20,000

1. Relief.

   (a) Y Coy 1st Battn. Royal Dublin Fusiliers in Right Support will relieve "C" Coy. the Left Front line coy. of the 1st Battn Lancashire Fusrs. this night.

   (b) Relief to be carried out under inter-company arrangements, and will take place before 8.30 pm.

   (c) On completion of relief, Y Coy. 1st Bn Royal Dublin Fusrs will be distributed as follows:-

   3 Platoons with 4 Lewis Guns in Front Line
   1 Platoon in close support.

2. Completion of relief to be notified to Battalion Hd Qrs by code word TAKEAFALL.

Acknowledge.

C. Riley.
Captain & Adjutant
1st Bn. Royal Dublin Fusrs

2nd May 1918.

1st Bn Royal Dublin Fusiliers
Operation Order No. 29.   11th May 1918.

Reference Map 36A. N.E.

1. The 1st Royal Dublin Fusiliers will relieve the 2nd Royal Fusiliers in the Left Subsector of the Riche Brionne Sector on the night of the 10th/11th May 1918.

2. Details of Relief as follows:—

   X   1st Royal Dublin Fusiliers will relieve   W Coy 2nd Royal Fus.   Right Front
   W   "   "   X   "   "   "   Left   "
   Y   "   "   Z   "   "   "   Support
   Z   "   "   Y   "   "   "   Strong Point E.20 Central

3. Guides:— 1 per platoon & Coy H.Q. for front line Coys will leave Huts E.19.c.9.1. 8 p.m.
            Support Coys   3 p.m.

4. LA MOTTE DEFENCES.
   The 2nd Royal Fusiliers will arrange for relief of the undermentioned in LA MOTTE DEFENCES as early as possible:—
   "W" Coy 1st Royal Dublin Fusiliers PTE MARQUETTE }
   "Y"   "   "   LA MOTTE   } LA MOTTE DEFENCES.
   4 Lewis Guns & teams on the BOUZRE RIVER.
   1 N.C.O. and 9 men on Bridge at D.30.a.5.4
     N.C.O.   6   "   do. (from) D.30.c.95.65
   1 N.C.O.   6   "   "   D.18.c.7.87 } BRIDGE GUARDS
   1 N.C.O.   6   "   "   D.18.c.7.52 }
   1 N.C.O.   9   "   "   D.24.a.0.3

   On relief Lewis Gun teams and Bridge Guards will rendezvous at Huts E.19.c.9.1 where respective Coys will pick them up.
   O.C. LA MOTTE DEFENCES will arrange to hand over and on completion of relief notify Battalion Headquarters.

5. Advance Parties:— 1 Officer, 1 N.C.O. 1 Signaller and 1 Runner per Coy & H.Q. Coy will proceed in advance and take over all Trench Stores etc.

6. Transport Officer will arrange for the following:—
   (a) "X" Coy 5 p.m.
       "W" "   6 p.m.
       "Y" "   7.30 p.m.
       "Z" "   8 p.m.
   (b) Ration lorry to collect "Y" limber H.Q. at 9 p.m.
   (c) To collect all Officers Kits etc, and carry same to Quartermaster's Stores.
   (d) Removal of Cookers to their original positions at E.25.a.9.8.

7. Quartermaster for distribution of rations as before.

8. O.C. Coys will arrange to hand over all Bivouacs and Billets in a clean & sanitary condition, obtaining Certificate and rendering same to Orderly Room in usual manner.

9. All Bivouacs, Trench Stores, Maps, Intelligence Patrol notes, Work in hand and proposals will be taken over and handed over. Lists of Bivouacs, Trench Stores etc taken over and handed over will be forwarded to Battalion Headquarters by 10. a.m. 11th May.

10. Completion of relief will be notified to Battalion Headquarters by the Codeword "ATTAGEN" with surname of Coy Commander.

11. Acknowledge.

                                              C. Sadley
                                              Captain & Adjutant
                                              1st Royal Dublin Fusiliers.

Copies to:
   Maj. Genl. J.J. Robert D.
   O.C. 1st Royal Fusiliers
   Transport Officer
   Transport Officer
   Quartermaster
   Captain W.K. Delany
   Orderly Room
   War Diary
   Spare

Secret   1st Bn Royal Dublin Fusiliers.   Appx 14

Operation Orders No 31.

Reference Sheet 36ᵃ N.E. 1/20,000   26th May 1918.

1. The 86th Infantry Brigade will relieve the 94th Infantry Brigade in the left sector of the Lawrence Front on the night of 27/28th May 1918.

2. The 1st Royal Dublin Fusiliers will relieve the 1st King's Own Scottish Borderers and 1st Border Regiment in the Support Sector, as follows:-

  "W" Coy. 1st Royal Dublin Fusiliers will relieve No 1. Coy. 1st Border Regiment in the Reserve Line as far as E.14.b.0.0. with half Coy. and will garrison the remainder of the Reserve line as far south as the Southern Brigade Boundary (E.13.d.0.3) with a nucleus garrison of half Coy.

  "X" Coy. 1st Royal Dublin Fusiliers will relieve No 2. Coy. 1st Border Regiment in the left of the Reserve line.

  "Y" Coy. 1st Royal Dublin Fusiliers will relieve 3 Platoons No 1. Coy. 1st King's Own Scottish Borderers in E.9.c. and one platoon in MOLEGHEM Fm. E.10.c.

  "Z" Coy. 1st Royal Dublin Fusiliers will relieve 3 platoons only of No 2 Coy. 1st King's Own Scottish Borderers in Pt SEC Bns Defences and will take over the support line south of the Road to E.15.b.o.o.

3. Advanced parties of 1 Officer, 1 N.C.O., 1 Signaller & 1 Runner per Coy and Headquarter Coy will leave camp at 4 p.m. and proceed to take the stores etc. in their respective Areas. These parties should move at 200 yards distance.

4. The Battalion Lewis Gun Officer will arrange for 2 Lewis Guns and teams of "X" Coy. and 2 Lewis Guns and teams from "W" Coy. to be attached to "Z" Coy and "Y" Coy respectively to strengthen the defences of the sectors to be taken over by the latter two Coys.

5. Coys will leave Camp in the following order Y. Z. Headquarters, X. W. Leading Coy to move at 8 p.m. 100 yards distance to be maintained between platoons.

6. Route. Infantry Track to D.15.b.5.0. – D.10.c.5.3. – D.17.d.0.0. to E.8.c.5.0.

7. Guides will be met as follows:-

  "W" and "X" Coys – 1 guide per platoon and 1 for Coy H.Qs at junction of track and road E.8.c.3.5.

  "Y" & "Z" Coy (incl } 1 guide per platoon, 1 for Coy H.Qs and 1 for Battalion H.Qs at the Shrine by the Battalion H.Qrs } Cross Roads E.8.c.5.0.

8. Officers Spare Kits, etc. will be dumped ready for loading at 4 p.m. on the road at D.14.b.6.7.

9. Transport Officer will arrange for the following:-
  (1) Limbers conveying Lewis Guns, Boxes, etc. to move by road and to meet Coys on the road at D.8.d.7.7 at 9.30 p.m.
  (2) 1 Limber & Mess Cart to report at Battalion H.Q. at 6 p.m.
  (3) Maltese Cart at the Regimental Aid Post at 6 p.m.
  (4) The collection and conveyance to Quartermaster's Stores of Officers Kits, etc., Blankets, Cookers.

10. (a). All Tents, bivouacs, shelters, will be handed over to the incoming Unit, and certificates rendered to Orderly Room that the Coy lines have been handed over in a clean and sanitary condition.
  (b). All maps, Aeroplane photographs, notes on works, S.A.A. Grenades and Trench Stores will be taken over from 1st Border Regiment and 1st King's Own Scottish Borderers.
  (c). Lists showing (a). and (b). and receipts will be rendered to Orderly Room not later than 7 a.m. May 28th.

11. Completion of Relief will be notified by wiring the Codeword "POPPY" with surname of Coy Commander.

12. Battalion H.Q. will close in present locality at 6 p.m. and open at E.7.b.7.7 on arrival.

13. Acknowledge.

                         EWS Tackton
                         Captain & Adjutant,
                         1st Bn Royal Dublin Fusiliers.

Copies to:-
1. "W" Coy.
2. "X" "
3. "Y" "
4. "Z" "
5. Transport Officer
6. Quartermaster
7. Lewis Gun Officer
8. Signals Officer.
9. H.Q. 86th Infantry Brigade.
10. O.C. 1st Border Regiment.
11. " 1st King's Own Scottish Bord.
12. File.
13. War Diary.

Secret

1st Bn. Royal Dublin Fusiliers

Addendum No 1 to Operation Order No 31.

1. The following Guards supplied by the 1st Border Regt and 1st K.O.S.B's will be relieved by Coy's as under:-

No.	Locality	Strength	Found by	Coy to relieve	Time of relief
1.	House at E.8.c.5.5 Brigade S.a.a.rc	L/Cpl and 3 O.R's	1st Border Regt	"W" Coy	a.b.y
2.	House at E.13.d.15	L/Cpl and 3 O.R's	1st K.O.S.B.	"X" Coy	3.0 p.m.

Guard No 2 should report to Major OLDFIELD, 455 Field Coy. R.E. and will be a permanent Guard, relieved from 29th inst by R.E.

Men selected for this Guard should be those deserving of a rest.

2. The Regimental Aid Post will be established at E.8.c.8.6.

J.W.B. Tarleton
Captain & Adjutant
1st Bn Royal Dublin Fusiliers

26th May 1918.

Secret.

1st Bn Royal Dublin Fus.

Amendment No 1 to Operation Order No 31

1. Addendum No 1, para 1. is cancelled, and the following substituted:-

   (a) The party of 1 Officer + 20 O.R. found by 1st Royal Dublin Fus. at Hazebrouck will be relieved by 1st K.O.S.B's at 12 noon to-day + will rejoin unit.

   (b) O.C. "X" Coy will detail 4 O.R's to report to N.C.O. i/c R.E. Dump at D.2.d.5.6 at 9.0 a.m. 28th inst. This party will be permanent and no change will be made in its personnel without reference to Battn H.Q. It will act as a loading party, and be accommodated + rationed by R.E.

   (c) O.C. "Y" Coy will arrange to take over the Dump at E.10.a.4.7 (wire + pickets). List of material in Dump should be included in list of Trench Stores rendered to Battn H.Q. on 28th inst.

   (d) "Z" Coy will take over a Dump of 250 Reserve Iron Rations at E.9.a.5.5. (Coy H.Q.) + will include these rations in list of Trench Stores taken over.

   (e) 2nd Lieut B.G. Fisher M.C. i/c Headquarters Coy advance party will take over + post a guard over all Trench Stores, S.A.A. + other ammunition (less 250 reserve Rations + Stokes Gun Ammunition) at E.7.d.7.9, Hd Qrs. 1st Border Regt.

2. O's C. Coys will re-distribute Ground Flares taken over, if necessary, on the scale of 10 per platoon + 20 per Coy H.Q., + render the usual certificate on the 28th as to the condition of Flares. Any deficiencies should be noted + any surplus maintained at Coy H.Q. until further instructions regarding their distribution are issued.

27 May 1916

Captain + Adjutant
1st Bn Royal Dublin Fus.

Secret.   1st Bn Royal Dublin Fusiliers.   Appx No 10.
                       Operation Order No 32.
                                                              31st May 1918
Reference Map 36ᵃ N.E (Edition 7ᵃ) 1/20000

1. The 1st Royal Dublin Fusiliers will relieve the 2nd Royal Fusiliers on the night 31st M/
1st June 1918 in that part of the Front line and immediate support between the existing
NORTH Brigade Boundary and the road (inclusive to 1st Royal Dublin Fusiliers) at E.23.a.
30.48.   Upon completion of relief the inter-Battalion Boundary will be from
E.23.a.30.48 (road inclusive) to E.15.a.88.48. to E.14.b.05.75.

2. (a). 1 Platoon "X" Coy will relieve No 12 Platoon "Y" Coy in MOLEBHEIN FM. under
arrangements between O.C. "X" and O.C. Y Coy.
        No 12 Platoon "Y" Coy to return to the Support line E.9.d. upon relief.
   (b). 1 Platoon "X" Coy will relieve 1 Platoon 2nd Royal Fusiliers around MERE FM.
   (c). 2 Platoons "X" Coy will relieve 2 Platoons "Z" Coy, 2nd Royal Fusiliers in the Front line
        from the North Brigade Boundary to E.16.a.8.4.
        Guides for (b) and Coy H.Q. will be met at 10.30 p.m. at E.16.a.8.4. (Z Coy 2nd
        Royal Fusiliers H.Q.)

3. 1 Platoon of "Y" Coy will relieve 1 Platoon of "Z" Coy 2nd Royal Fusiliers in the Front line
between E.16.d.8.4 and E.17.c.0.0.   Guide for this Platoon will be with Guides
for 2.(c).   1 Platoon of "Y" Coy will take up a position in E.16.a.& c. under
instructions to be issued personally by Commanding Officer. Remaining Platoon of "Y" Coy
will remain in present support line.   O.C. "Y" Coy will establish his H.Q. at
E.16.a.8.4. with O.C. Z Coy   relieved from MOLEBHEIN FM.

4. 1 Platoon "Z" Coy will relieve 1 Platoon "Y" Coy 2nd Royal Fusiliers in the Front line between
E.23.a.30.48. (road inclusive) to E.17.c.0.0.   1 Guide for this Platoon and
Guide for Coy H.Q. will be at SANITAS CORNER (E.15.a.8.9) at 10.15 p.m.
1 Platoon "Z" Coy will take up a position in immediate support in E.16.d. under instructions
issued personally by Commanding Officer. Remaining 2 Platoons "Z" Coy will take over the
vacated positions of "Y" Coy in Support line.
O.C. "Z" Coy will establish his H.Q. at E.22.a.8.5.8. with O.C. Y Coy 2nd Royal Fusiliers.

5. "W" Coy with 4 Lewis Guns less 1 Platoon will relieve "Z" Coy in the PETIT SEC BOIS
Defences under arrangements between O.C. "Z" and O.C. "W" Coy.
1 Platoon of "W" Coy will remain in the Reserve line between E.14.b.05.75 and road
(inclusive) / E.8.d.8.7.

6. All Picks and Shovels will be dumped at present Coy H.Q. and a guard placed over
them (unfits if possible).

7. Guard mentioned in para. 6. will also be responsible for handing over to any relieving Unit
all Lists of Trench Stores etc. in vacated areas.

8. Completion of Relief will be notified by the codeword "PANSY."

9. Lists of all Trench Stores taken over from 2nd Royal Fusiliers will be forwarded to Battn H.Q.
by 9 a.m on 1st June 1918.

10. Battalion H.Q. will remain in the present locality.

11. Medical Aid Post will remain in present location. Cases to be evacuated along the
track E.9.c.7.1. — E.14.b.7.2. — E.8.c.5.5.

12. Acknowledge.

                                                    Jnob Saulton
                                                    Captain & Adjutant.
                                                    1st Bn Royal Dublin Fusiliers

Copies to:- No 1. O.C. "W" Coy   No 8. O.C. 2nd Royal Fusiliers.
            " 2. " "X" "   " 9. H.Q. 50th Inf. Bde.
            " 3. " "Y" "   " 10. 1st R. Dublin Fus. (Rear)
            " 4. " "Z" "   " 11. File.
            " 5. Signals Officer   " 12. War Diary
            " 6. Transport Officer
            " 7. Orderly Room

26 +
42 sheets

War Diary

1st Bn Royal Dublin Fusiliers
for
Month of
June 1918.
Volume 39.

Army Form C. 2118.

1st Royal Welsh Fusiliers

WAR DIARY
or
INTELLIGENCE SUMMARY.
(Erase heading not required.)

Instructions regarding War Diaries and Intelligence Summaries are contained in F. S. Regs., Part II. and the Staff Manual respectively. Title pages will be prepared in manuscript.

Place	Date	Hour	Summary of Events and Information June 1918	Remarks and references to Appendices
PETIT SEC BOIS E.7.b.9.7	1.		At about noon Battalion relieved 2nd Royal Fusiliers on the left subsection of No. 86½ Brigade front. To allow of all three companies who were warned for probable minor operation to reconnoitre the ground Relief the area opposite them. X was delayed till 2 Companies Y & Z should go in on one platoon front. X Company have 3 platoons in the line, upon relief the Battalion was distributed as under: on platoon on platoon Z Coy in front line Right from E.23.a.3.4. (road inclusive) to E.23.a.2.9. one platoon Y Coy in front line Centre from E.23.a.2.9. — E.16.d.9.2. Each of these Coys have 1 platoon in immediate support. Three platoons X Coy in line Left from E.16.d.9.2 to North Brigade boundary E.11.c.3.1 remaining platoon X Coy in MOLECHEIN Fm E.10.c. in support – 2 platoons each of Y & Z Coys in support line E.9.b. W.Coy in PETIT SEC BOIS. Relief was completed by 3 a.m. Other Units – Batt. H.Q. E.7.b.9.7. No previous warning of the operation to advance our line to line May pass spicetz - front line top by one & front aeroplane photos sharp air T Sperne points taken - original warning of the operation to advance our line to line 1 H.Q. BECQUE postponed to early morning of 3rd instant – advance of Groups of ammunition RE Material formed. W Coy & 2 Platoons 1 LANC.Fus	43. T.S. 3

1st Royal Dublin Fusiliers

WAR DIARY
or
INTELLIGENCE SUMMARY.
(Erase heading not required.)

Army Form C. 2118.

Place	Date	Hour	Summary of Events and Information	Remarks and references to Appendices
			June 1918	
	1	continued	Supplying carrying parties.	
Batt H.Q E.17.b.9.7 Sheet 36A.	2.		Quiet day - Enemy artillery not active by night and barrage on enemy front by night - Att. operation orders Nos 33 & 34 received - Batt. operation orders Nos 33 & 34 issued. (see attached) The general scheme of operations being as follows - The 2 Royal Fusiliers to attack Maple Lng F'm E.23.c. 7. The 1 S.R. Dub Fus to capture line to line 1. 1st RDF to consolidate on the western bank between E.23.a.8.4 & E.17.c.6.4 - on the night 3/4th June 1918 proposals to be established along the remaining line of the RECQUE on this objective front i.e. E.17 c.6.4 to E.17 a.2.3. Zero hour to be 1 am morning 3rd instant. attack to be supported by artillery Trench Mortars & M.G. barrages to assemble the necessary troops in the line a slight readjustment has to take place which was completed by 11pm. — The 2 platoons each of Y Coys in support & 2 reserve lay in front line. W. Coy moved out of PETIT SEC Bois defences to occupy line vacated by above 4 platoons. Fresh front line manned by W Coy take up positions behind assembly trench	

1st Royal Welsh Fusiliers

Army Form C. 2118.

WAR DIARY
or
INTELLIGENCE SUMMARY.
(Erase heading not required.)

Instructions regarding War Diaries and Intelligence Summaries are contained in F.S. Regs., Part II. and the Staff Manual respectively. Title pages will be prepared in manuscript.

for month of June 1917

Place	Date	Hour	Summary of Events and Information	Remarks and references to Appendices
			2. continued. (Front line) of Y & Z Coys. work orders to occupy it when those Coys left it to form up outside the line at Zero less 15 minutes T to form its permanent garrison. The remaining R.E. stores were delivered to Coys & all battle stores issued by midnight. Hot meals had been brought up for attacking Coys. Gaps in our own wire had been cut – batallion was synchronised at 10.30 pm and at 12 midnight Companies reported everything ready.	
Bn. Q. Eqt.47 Sect 58.A.	3rd	12.45 am	At ZERO less 15 minutes (12.45 am) Y & Z Coys began to form up outside the wire, which they had much difficulty in negotiating owing to its dismantling being great & the number of large fallen trees in no-man's land. At ZERO (1 am) the barrage came down & Coys moved as close as possible under it – On the left Coy (Y) front the artillery had previously made good gaps in the hedges but the Right Coy (Z) had more trouble negotiating hedges & Cotterne – The attack progressed excellently from the start & in spite

WAR DIARY or INTELLIGENCE SUMMARY

Army Form C. 2118.

1st Royal Dublin Fusiliers

Place	Date	Hour	Summary of Events and Information	Remarks and references to Appendices
	June 1918			
	3rd continued		Appendix G. The ground offered cover was not always sufficient owing to post darkness. Companies should have reached their objective at 2.50 a.m. plus 7 minutes allowing for resistance met with from M. guns turning in on objective. Reconnaissance should have to the ["] objective" mopping up necessary. No signal showing objectives had been reached was met sent up by right Coy until 1.25 a.m. The difficulty 1.40 a.m. Companies immediately commenced consolidation of Front on Supports & Distribution Trenches as far as possible in depth. Lewis guns being pushed out to form Company's trench being organised by means of strong patrols. The original front had being used as a line of support. No efforts to affard more depth to the defence. A reconnaissance was immediately carried out. Establish the fact that Companies were firmly in their objectives - 2 Coys were then Spectre throughout not an Y Coys front a gap existed between E.17.c.6.3 & E.17.c.8.2. Though it was no ever from the rear. From the prisoners captured - 22 of whom 4	

WAR DIARY or INTELLIGENCE SUMMARY

Army Form C. 2118.

1st Royal Welch Fusiliers

Place	Date	Hour	Summary of Events and Information	Remarks and references to Appendices
			June 1918	
	3rd	continued	was killed by hostile artillery on way down – machine guns known (?) number of German dead – it was apparent some retaliation had been mounted but had only temporary effect. Major ascended toys convoy. The early morning of the 3rd a machine gun fired from about E.23.a.8.3 harassed the consolidation of the right C/By but was silenced by 2/Lt. Mc Gowan who taking out a party from his Park combed a dug out killing 2 German officers (one apparently a Colonel) nineteen others. The M.G. which he came out near to withdraw when it was discovered that 2/Lt. J.J. GYVES commanding Y Coy had been killed on his objective having gallantly led his Coy to it. 2/Lt. C.K. KIRWAN also of Y Coy was missing – Lieut. MONTGOMRY M.C. commanding Z Company had been wounded earlier in the fight. 2/Lt. E.J. ALEXANDER Y Coy & 2/Lt. ROSS now assumed command of their respective Coys rapidly organising parties and the scheme of consolidation. The enemy barrage is reply apply to ours had been strong – when ours died at	

Army Form C. 2118.

1st Royal Welsh Fusiliers

WAR DIARY
or
INTELLIGENCE SUMMARY.
(Erase heading not required.)

Place	Date	Hour	Summary of Events and Information	Remarks and references to Appendices
	for month of June 1918.			
	3rd continued		down, the enemy, apparently with the idea that our operation had been but a raid, attempted to cross over from the Eastern of the RECQS between trench rail partons. They were met by heavy Lewis gun rifle fire from the Coys on the new line & Stopped. Several were seen behind them. The remainder opposing were quiet - however nothing not willing on new positions through a heavy bombardment was kept up against an old front line about E.23.a.2.7 - 81st Brigade order was received giving instructions that the whole line of the RECQS from the N. Bn. boundary as far South as E.23.a.8.4 had to be secured by means of posts before relief by 18th L.N.L.C.S. Tks. In the case of Z. Coy, the posts remained unchanged as the line of the RECQS was strongly held - in the case of Y Coy it was necessary for the posts previously referred to, to be filled with posts of X. Coy had to establish posts along the remainder of the RECQS from E.17.C.6.17, to E.17.a.2.3. This latter premises little difficulty as on the night of 2/3 June X Coy Lewis Patrols had reached the line	

Army Form C. 2118.

1st Royal Wiltshire Fusiliers

WAR DIARY
or
INTELLIGENCE SUMMARY
(Erase heading not required.)

Summary of Events and Information June 1918

Place	Date	Hour	Summary of Events and Information	Remarks and references to Appendices
	3rd		continued	

mentioned & reported all clear. At dusk the new distribution of posts was commenced & quickly completed. Companies being in position by 10pm. 'X' Coy had no difficulty in reaching the required line & establishing 'Z' Coy continued consolidation, improving communication trenches & flanks. 'Y' Coy however encountered some resistance but ground was eventually taken – it – The distance was due to any enemy post which had been not noticed. Vantage of the gap in 'Y' Coy front, bored the BECQUE established itself in a slit trench. This post with a M.G. made it impossible for 'Y' Coy to establish its post necessary on villa to secure its whole line of its BECQUE Z. Lt.

O.C. Y Coy (afsr Lt. T. ALEXANDER) deciding on a scheme quickly put it into action. It Stokes Mortar was in position at E.17.c.2.2. – There was a decoy to fire a few rounds at the enemy post whilst at the same time a L.G. & Y Coy employed beforehand at E.17.c.7.5. rifle grenades were discharged at it from E.17.c.6.6. – Against this a garrison of 3 weapons the enemy post failed to respond & withdrew over the NE. Our pursuit by Lts. Y Coy & 'D' Coy men who however were unable to capture the garrison on the M.G. –

Army Form C. 2118.

WAR DIARY
or
INTELLIGENCE SUMMARY.
(Erase heading not required.)

1st Royal Welsh Fusiliers

Place	Date	Hour	Summary of Events and Information	Remarks and references to Appendices
			June 1918	
	3rd	Unlimited	The new post was established by 9/4 the gap filled by 11 p.m.	
			Consolidation was continued and at 12 midnight a heavy enemy barrage came down along the entire battalion front — from the weight of the barrage	
			& the simultaneous general of the Hostile artillery 7th Series, it was apparent that this was the prelude to a hostile infantry counter attack. Whilst the barrage on our new posts was comparatively light, practically every movement at Wing heaviest on our old front line redoubts Dunkirk H.Q. at E.22.b.7.9.	
	4th	12.30 a.m.	At 12.30 a.m. the enemy in 2 parties (strong patrols) of 3.0 each advanced against 7 Coy but were easily repulsed with heavy losses. 7	
			rifle fire enemy never gave in dead. At the same time a bombing attack on the newly established post of Y Coy (No 5 post) was beaten off and at least ten Germans bodies were afterwards seen in front of this	
		12.45 a.m.	post. At 12.45 a.m. the enemy barrage died down to reconnaissance of our line showed all posts intact & the companies busily digging in —	
		1.45 a.m.	At 1.15 a.m. the 1st Lancs. Fus. Nothing more work 2 Corps the front had been by our	
		3.15 a.m.	3 front line Coys. Relief was complete by 3.15 a.m. the Battalion	

WAR DIARY or INTELLIGENCE SUMMARY

Army Form C. 2118.

1st Royal Dublin Fusiliers

For month of June 1918

Place	Date	Hour	Summary of Events and Information	Remarks and references to Appendices
	4th		Battalion moved into Brigade Reserve. Companies being distributed as follows:— W Coy E.7, N.5.9. with 2 platoons in L5 Reserve line about E.13.d and E.14.a. X Coy in trenches about E.7.a. Y Coy in trenches D.6.a. Z Coy in trenches D.12.a. Batt. H.Q. D.6.a.9.7. Total strengths: 22 ORs, 10 machine guns. Our casualties 2/Lt. C.K. KIRWAN missing. 2/Lt. J.J. SYKES killed, Lt. M.F. MONTGOMERY, 14.C. wounded. 7 ORs killed, wounded 44 ORs. In Bde Reserve Coys rest temporarily - bdy who have not been engaged in active operations supply working parties of 50 ORs towards party of 10 ORs.	
Batt. H.Q. D.6.a.9.7. (36R sheet)	5th		This week continues - Coys commence training but owing to large working parties to the supplies not much could be done -	
—||—	6th		Working parties 210 ORs by day, 150 ORs by night engaged under R.E. supervision mostly improving Reserve line & instructing troops in its use. A lewis gun range being available Coys make as much use of it as possible	
—||—	7th		At night a patrol of 8 ORs under 2/Lt. P.S. McGOWAN of Z Coy proceeded to R. bank by of N.E. LANES Fm - They leave front line about E.23.a.8.5	

Army Form C. 2118.

1st Royal Dublin Fusiliers

WAR DIARY
or
INTELLIGENCE SUMMARY.
(Erase heading not required.)

Instructions regarding War Diaries and Intelligence Summaries are contained in F. S. Regs., Part II. and the Staff Manual respectively. Title pages will be prepared in manuscript.

Place	Date	Hour	Summary of Events and Information	Remarks and references to Appendices
BATT.HQ Dt.d.9.7	7th	Continued	June 1918. In the proper of reconnoitring Dugouts along western F.Eastern Bank of the BEAUNE about E.23.a.9.2 (which the officers and efficiency engaged in the operation of 3rd inst killing 2 German men. P.Belonging 7. F.) The Brigade were found unoccupied but an enemy machine gun was found in the vicinity strength unkn. Casualties: 2nd Lieut Wale wounded 16 O.Rs wounded 6 O.Rs wounded 7 hrs. died of wounds 1. O.R.	
			2/Lt E.R. COLDWELL instructed VI reinforcement shown off - reinforcements from Base taken on to strength 1 officer 2/Lt E.C. BOURKE 53 O.Rs from Hospital 1 O.R. from corps. support 1 O.R.	40 - 943
— " —	8th		Battn to report quiet day - 5 O.Rs upon from Hospital 5 O.Rs departed - reinforcements from Base taken on strength - 10 R wounded.	40. 952.
— " —	9th		Relieved 1st LANCS. Fus. (Kale operation order No 34 attached) an left sub sector, left Brigade of Div Front. W.Lg on Right held ANKLE Fm + the FACTORY, X Coy in left, Y Coy in Support, Z Lg in PETIT BOIS Defences. Patrols for identification unsuccessful. Regt party from Base taken on Strength.	40. 958.
PETIT SEC BOIS E.7.4.7.	10th		Enemy artillery active on Right Coy front - seven or eight hundred shells of	

A6945   Wt. W1422/M1160   350,000   12/16   D. D. & L.   Forms/C./2118/14.

1st Bn Royal Dublin Fusiliers

WAR DIARY
or
INTELLIGENCE SUMMARY.
(Erase heading not required.)

Army Form C. 2118.

Place	Date	Hour	Summary of Events and Information	Remarks and references to Appendices
	10th	continued	Various calibre trench mortars. 1 man killed & 2 wounded. Patrols good at night unsuccessful in capturing a prisoner. SOS from Bde	40.960
PETIT SEC BOIS	11th		Enemy artillery activity continues - W by By H.Q. heavy bombardment by trench mortars. Companies withdrawn from front line for discharge of gas cylinders in accordance with operation order No 35 attempted but wind proved unfavourable. 60th wounded 90th afterwards	40.963
— " —	12th		Companies again in trenches for gas discharge but wind again unfavourable. Bn relieved by 4th Worcestershire Regt (Quaker Rds No 36 attacked) - on relief Bn move to Brigade Reserve at LE TROCADERO on the HARE BROOK — MORBECQUE ROAD — Accommodation tents & billets. 2/Lt. MARTIN wounded also 6 ORs - Evacuated 4 ORs. 2/Lt R MAGUIRE M.C. reports Batt (wounded return 28/3/18) Lieut C NEILL & 2/Lt W.A. HINDD join from hospital. 1 Officer departure from Base Kalken on strength.	43.954
LE TROCADERO	13th & 14th		Batt. Training etc.	
— " —	15th & 16th		Batt put under Half hours Notice. Enemy attack expected.	
— " —	17th		Relieve 1st K O S Borderers in the Right Sub Sector, Right Brigade Sector in	

1st Royal Dublin Fusiliers

WAR DIARY or **INTELLIGENCE SUMMARY**

Army Form C. 2118.

For month of June 1918.

Place	Date	Hour	Summary of Events and Information	Remarks and references to Appendices
	17th		Continued. Divisional front line operations were No 37 attached] - Y Coy in front line - Z Coy in close support X Coy in Reserve with in LA MOTTE Defences. One man killed by a sniper during relief.	
Batt H.Q.			Lt Col A. Moore D.S.O. resumed command of Bn. Bde during illness of Brigadier.	
TROTTLE Fm	18th		Quiet day = Capt J.W.B. TARLETON M.C. appointed 2/IC 19th Bn. Capt R.	
D.14.a.8.2.			MCGUIRE M.C. takes over duties of Adjutant 15th instant.	
— " —	19th		Batt relieved by 1st K.O.S.Bs & on relief moved to old billets at LE TROCODERO and D.Q.a. = Operation order No 38 attached =	
LE TROCODERO D.9.a	20-22		Training & inspections.	
— " —	23		Divine service for all Denominations - Batt. Bining Competition in the afternoon - Talent set up to standard but plucky fighting.	
— " —	24th		Battalion relieved in Divisional Reserve - Wide operation order No 39 attached - Batt. moved to BLARINGHEM area, accommodation Tents	
			Shelters & billets. Some heavy showers of rain.	
BLARINGHEM	25th		Reorganisation & Training	
R.16.d.7.2. (Sheet 3ga)	26th		do	

1st Royal Dublin Fus.

Army Form C. 2118.

WAR DIARY
or
INTELLIGENCE SUMMARY.
(Erase heading not required.)

Instructions regarding War Diaries and Intelligence Summaries are contained in F.S. Regs., Part II. and the Staff Manual respectively. Title pages will be prepared in manuscript.

for Month of June 1918.

Place	Date	Hour	Summary of Events and Information	Remarks and references to Appendices
BLARINGHEM B.16.b. Sheet 5A PAPOTE	27th 28th		Battalion move to forward area - Rifle operation order No 40 attached. Weather fine throughout. Battalion in position at 11 pm attack by 31st Division 75th Division to serve line of the RECQUE River - ZERO hour 6 am. Attack entirely successful. Battalion in readiness to advance	
D.22.			attack in the event of Enemy forcing our advanced troops to retire beyond our original front line.	
— // —	29th		Situation Quiet. Battalion return to BLARINGHEM area, all in by 8.30 pm (Rifle operation order No 41 attached)	
BLARINGHEM B.16.b	30		Battalion moved afternoon to CAMPAGNE all in rifted down 5.30pm reconnaissance good. Weather fine warm. (Operation order No 42 attached)	
			Since 14/6/18 to 30/6/18 beyances from hospital 19.ORs. Traffic 7.OR. Lieut WR KIDD M.C. joined 15th inst from R.A.F., 2/Lt T.P.DARBY R.I.Regt joined 24th inst. 1/C of E.J A. MELDON joined 27th inst for medical attendant. 1 OR from 25th W Bn. R = Off Strength Killed 1OR, wounded 1OR. Evacuated from Divn area 39.ORs, to base in't 1OR, k86th TM B 5ORs, to 1/5 C, 2/1st WLL CLEAR YIOR. Strength 30/6/18 42 officers 939.ORs	

W.I.Taggmayor
(Commanding) 1st Royal Dublin Fusiliers

Secret.   1st Bn. Royal Dublin Fusiliers.

Operation Order No. 3A.

Reference Map 36th N.E. (1:10,000).

The following moves will take place on the night of [...] /3.

1. The two platoons each of "Y" and "Z" Coys. will leave the Support Line at 10 p.m. and rejoin their companies in the Front Line. O.C. "Y" and "Z" Coys. will arrange to have the necessary guides at these platoons H.Q. by 9.30 p.m. Platoons of "Y" and "Z" Coys. will move from Support Line carrying two sandbags per man, and 50 shovels which have already been issued.

2. Lieut. McAllen and four Lewis Guns and Teams of "W" Coy. will be detailed by O.C. "W" Coy. to move with the two platoons each of "Y" & "Z" Coys. (two each) to the Front Line. O.C. "Y" and "Z" Coys. will arrange for these teams to be met and shown their position behind the front line held by "Y" and "Z" Coys. At Zero less 15 these four Lewis Gun Teams will move - two into each sector of the Front line till recently held by "Y" and "Z" Coys, and will form the garrison of the line.

3. O.C. "W" Coy. will send an advance party to take over the Support Line in E.9.b. from the present garrison of "Y" and "Z" Coys, on the afternoon of the 2nd [...], Remainder of "W" Coy. moving into Support Line from the Railway on the North to E.9.d.0.6. upon relief by 1st Lancs. Fusiliers.

4. One Coy. 1st Lancs. Fusiliers will relieve "X" Coy. in PETIT SEC BOIS Defences and the Reserve Line. Advanced parties from 1st Lancs. Fusiliers will take over early in the evening "X" Coy. to move out upon relief. One guide for platoons of "W" Coy. in PETIT SEC BOIS Defences and one for Coy. H.Q. will be at the [...] Shrine E.8.a.6.5. at 9.30 p.m.

5. List of all Trench Stores taken over and handed over will be forwarded to these H.Q.

6. Reliefs to be complete by 11 p.m.

7. Completion of relief to be notified by the code word "Daisy".

8. The four platoons ("Y" and "Z" Coys.) at present in Support Line will have their dinners by 9 p.m.
   All rations for tonight of "X", "Y", "Z" Coys. (including those platoons lately in Support Lines) will be dumped at [...] Coy. Cookhouse as early as possible. O.C. Coys. should arrange that all men have a hot meal before Zero hour, and that water bottles are carried filled.
   Rations for "W" Coy. will be dumped tonight as last night, i.e. E.9.a.5.5, where "W" Coy. will arrange for a party to meet limbers and carry rations to Coy.
   Rations for Bn. H.Q. will be dumped at present H.Q.

9. ACKNOWLEDGE.

                                        J.W.A. [Sandilin]
                                        Capt. & Adjutant
                                        1st Bn. Royal Dublin Fusiliers.

Copies to:
1. O.C. "W" Coy.   8. 86th Bde H.Q.
2.   " "X" "   9. Transport Officer
3.   " "Y" "   10. [...]
4.   " "Z" "   11. Asst. Adjutant
5. M.G. Officer   12. File
6. Asst. [...]   13. [...]
7. 1st Lancs. Fus.   14.

DISPOSITIONS 1st R.D.F. 3/6/18.

"W" Coy. in Support line (See attached Sketch).

Secret.   1st Bn Royal Dublin Fusiliers.   Copy No. 11.

Operation Order No 53.

Reference Map. 36ᴬ N.E (Edition 7ᵃ)   2nd June 1918.

1. The 1st Bn Royal Dublin Fusiliers in conjunction with 2nd Bn Royal Fusiliers on the right will carry out a minor operation on the morning of the 3rd June at a time Zero to be notified later.

2. **Objective.** The objective of the 1st Royal Dublin Fusiliers will be the line of the BEEK from E.17.c.10y.50 to E.23.a.85.25. (Objective B).
Objective of 2nd Royal Fusiliers — LUB FARM (Objective A).

3. **Method of Assault.** 1st Bn Royal Dublin Fusiliers will attack "B" Objective with two Companies with 10 Lewis Guns — "X" Coy on the right, "Y" Coy on the left, inter-Coy boundary being as shown on attached Map A. (To Coys only). Each will attack on a two platoon front. Platoons moving in section in line preceded by Scouts.
"Y" Coy will detail 1 Platoon to protect the left flank, by moving on the North side of the Hedge with runs at right angles to the "B" edge of the Objective, this Platoon being prepared to co-operate with flanking fire if necessary. "X" Coy will detail 1 Platoon to act similarly on the right flank to the south of the FANTASY FM. Road. In each case flanking Platoons will move in the same formation as the two leading Platoons. Both attacking Coys will detail a Supporting Platoon which will carry material for consolidation and ammunition.
A party of 10 R.E. with 3 Bangalore Torpedoes will be attached to each of the leading Sections of the attacking Coys in order to destroy any obstacles that may be encountered. The Platoon operating on the left flank of "Y" Coy will take one torpedo to destroy the heavily wired gate on the road leading to ANKLE FM ENCLOSURE at E.17.c.4.4. The six approximate places where the use of torpedoes is anticipated are marked on attached Map B. Numbered One to Six. 3 Bridges will be carried by each assaulting Coy.

4. **Assembly.** The two remaining Platoons of each of "Y" and "Z" Coys will rejoin their Coys by 11 p.m. night of 2nd/3rd June, and "Y" and "Z" Coys will then hold the portion of the Front line as shown on attached Map A.
"X" Coy will arrange to close down to his left flank to allow of accommodation being provided for the attacking Coys.
At ZERO less 15 assaulting Coys will leave their trenches and form up outside their wire. O.C. "X" Coy will extend his Coy southwards to his original boundary and the four Lewis Gun sections of "X" Coy will occupy the Front line as local supports to "Y" and "Z" Coys. At Zero Artillery, Trench Mortars, and Machine Guns will open fire, and assaulting Coys will move as close under the barrage as possible.

5. **Gaps.** On the evening of 2nd June, O.C. "Y" and "Z" Coys will ensure that sufficient gaps are cut in our own wire to allow of the exit of the assaulting Platoons.

6. **Action of Artillery.** Details of times and lifts of barrage will be notified later.

7. **Action of Trench Mortars.** One Trench Mortar will move on the left of the rear section of "Z" Coy in the assault and will be prepared to assist in the capture of the objective of both Coys, and later on reaching the objective to deal with enemy Machine Guns and snipers from a position about E.17.c.5.75.
8 Trench Mortars will thicken the barrage conforming to artillery times and lifts.

Action of Machine Guns.
(1) 4 Guns about E.17.a.90.75 from ZERO to Zero plus 4 will cover with continuous fire the WEST bank of the Beek above ANKLE FM and CHIMNEY STACK E.23a. From ZERO plus 4 onwards they will sweep the eastern side of the BEEK in front of the Objective.

(2)

(f) H Guns in E.10.a. will be prepared to open indirect fire on any hostile movement.

9. **Consolidation.** As soon as the Objective has been taken it will be consolidated and every effort made to distribute Platoons in depth, covering parties will Lewis Guns taking up positions on the BEEK and on the flanks, patrols being sent out to gain touch with neighbouring units, and the original front line being used as a line of immediate support to the front line.

10. **Light Signals** (1). The S.O.S. Signal will be RED over RED over RED and will be carried on the scale of 12 per Coy. Flares will be used when called for by aeroplanes, sounding the KLAXON HORN. They will be carried on a scale of 10 per Platoon and 20 per Coy.H.Q. and should be lit in groups of three.

11. **Dress – Issue of Stores.** Coys will assault in Battle Order – haversack on the back – all battle stores will be distributed from Coy Dumps in the front line immediately after dusk. Wire-cutters will be distributed between assaulting and supporting Platoons in the proportion of 2 to 1. Shovels – 50% of the men will carry shovels and 5% Picks, Bill-hooks and Axes – 2 per section. Bombs and Rifle Grenades. Bombs 2 per man – 2 men per platoon to carry Rifle Grenades. Very Pistols 2 per Coy. Platoon Scouts will be equipped as lightly as possible, and will carry Bill hooks. Bridge Carriers should follow Scouts closely.

12. Advanced Battalion H.Q. will be established at E.22.b.60.45.

13. **Communications.** (1). On the Objective being reached a message will immediately be sent back by Runners (2). to Battalion Headquarters, and the signal 1 Green, 1 Green, 1 Green Very Light in rapid succession will be fired.
    (2). Pigeons will be sent forward with the attacking Companies.
    (3). O.C. Signals will arrange for telephone wires to be run out to Coy H.Q. as soon as objective has been taken.

14. No Secret Maps, documents or letters which would supply information to the enemy if captured will be carried by Officers or Other Ranks of the attacking Coy.

15. Advanced Regimental Aid Post will be established at E.15.d.O.5:- Route via E.16.c.8.3 – E.15.d.O.6. The advanced Regimental Aid Post of 2nd Royal Fusiliers will be at E.21.a.8.2.

16. Coys have already established forward dumps in the front line whence assaulting Platoons will be equipped, and where reserves of S.A.A. and R.E. material are being maintained. In addition a forward Battalion Dump has been established at E.15.b.8.8.

17. Watches will be synchronized by an Officer from Battalion H.Q. about 10.30 p.m. on 2nd instant.

18. Acknowledge.

Jno T Sutton
Captain & Adjutant,
1st Bn Royal Dublin Fusiliers.

Copies to No 1 :- O.C. "W" Coy. No 8. H.Q. 86th Infy Bde.
        - 2 -   - "X" -   - 9. 9th Australian Batt.
        - 3 -   - "Y" -   -10. Medical Officer
        - 4 -   - "Z" -   -11. 1st R.D.F. (Rear)
        - 5 Signals Officer   -12. File
        - 6 Intelligence Officer -13.
        - 7 O.C. 2nd Royal Fus. -14. War Diary.

86/9

Minor Enterprise carried out by 1st RDF
on the morning of June 3rd 1918

The attack was carried out by two
companies 1st RDF - Z coy on right
Y coy on left with the object of gaining
the line of the BEEK from E.17 d 75
to E.23 a 75 (road inclusive to 1st RDF)
Previous to Zero hour the remaining platoons
of Y and Z Coys had rejoined their
Coys from the Support line - battle stores
had been issued out and watches
synchronized.
Zero hour was fixed at 1 am and our
Barrage which seemed very heavy
descended promptly.
For the first two or three minutes there
was heavy enemy machine gun fire but
this died down as Coys reached their objectives
and finally ceased.
The enemy artillery barrage came down about

FIFTY SECOND ... BATTLE OF ... JUNE 28th-30th 1915 (contd).

(155th Bde.)

few minutes after our own and was
not extraordinarily heavy and
consisted of 4.2's and 77mm intermingled
with a few 5.9's on the front line and
area immediately behind.

It appeared later in the morning that the
enemy had been shelling the vicinity of
the support line with Sneezy gas which
was carried back in the direction of the
front line by the wind.

At about 1.25am the coloured signal
denoting objective taken was seen on right
coy front and this was confirmed about
1.40am by message from platoon Comdr to
their Coy Comdr which came to Bn HQ by
mistake saying objective had been taken
and consolidation proceeding.

At about 1.40am the coloured signal was
seen on left coy front but no further
message was received confirming this.

A reconnaissance was therefore carried out
and it appeared that the right (?) coy
was on its objective and consolidation

it was found that Fr. had re-occpd them. Retrnd to BROWN HOUSE leaving 2 coys in sppt, who rejnd in the evg.

proceeding but on the left coy front half the objective had been taken. The remaining half coy being about 150 yards behind the objective. This half Company appeared to be without Officers at all and were very weak indeed. The Coy Comdr had apparently been hit (from reports) early in the advance and no further news of him has been obtained. The general line held appears to run as follows from right to left. E23a 95 — in front of ANKLE Fm to E17c 70 thence to E17c 92 with post at E17c 62.
The other side of the ROAD the line ran from E17c 43 to E17c 45.
Consolidation continued rapidly and was not interfered with by the enemy.
The enemy shelling of the original front line continued for some time and the fumes of the smoke from the bursts together with the existing slight mist made observation difficult. The ground forward was

4/1st.   ...trenches.
                                                                th Bde.

7/1st.   ...not being shelled much by the enemy
          up to 5 a.m. and enemy M.Gs occasionally
          fired rapid bursts.

7/26th.   By this period 17 prisoners taken
          and in addition four had been killed

8/26th.   by enemy shell fire whilst they
          were being marched away. Two
          of the bodies being 100x from Bn
          H.Q. One M.G. had been sent down
          by this period and one other was
          seen to be in use against enemy by
          the Lft Coy.
          Our total casualties 2 officers
          1 wounded, 1 wounded & so far missing.
          & 26 ORs wounded. No of
          killed not known.

                        Signed A Moneth Col.
                                 1st RDF
31.1.

Secret.

1st Bn. Royal Dublin Fusiliers
Operation Order No 34.

Reference Map. 36ᴬ N.E (Edition 4ᴬ)   Copy No 10

9th June 1918.

1. The 1st Bn Royal Dublin Fusiliers will relieve the 1st Lancashire Fusiliers in the left sub-sector of the 86th Brigade Front on the night of 9/10th June.
   (a). "W" Coy will relieve "C" Coy 1st Lancashire Fusiliers front line Right.
        "X"   -   -   "A"   -   -   -   -   -   Left.
        "Y" - (less one Platoon) "D" - - - - Support line E.9.b.
        One Platoon "Y" Coy will relieve 1 Platoon "D" Coy 1st Lancashire Fus. in MOLEGHEIN Fm.
        "Z" Coy will relieve "B" Coy 1st Lancashire Fusiliers in Pᵗ SEC BOIS Defences.
   (b). Coys will leave their lines at 10 p.m sharp in the order 'W'. 'X'. 'Y'. 'Z'.
   (c). Guides will be met as follows "W" Coy (5 guides) Shrine E.8.c. H.H.
                                     "X" -   SANITAS CORNER E.15.A.
                                     'Y' & 'Z' Coys (5 guides each) E.y.b. y.y. H.Q 1st Lancashire Fuss.
   (d). Completion of relief will be notified by the code word "GABY." with surname of Coy Commander.

2. Advanced parties of 1 Officer, 1 N.C.O. & 1 Runner & Signaller per Coy & H.Q.Coy will proceed in advance to take over from Coys of 1st Lancashire Fusiliers.
   (a). 1 N.C.O. per Coy will be left behind to hand over all trench stores to incoming Units.
   (b). All aeroplane photos, trench stores, S.A.A. German Machine Guns in use will be taken over from 1st Lancashire Fusiliers and lists of (a) & (b) will be forwarded to Orderly Room by 9 a.m. 10th instant.
   (c). Officers Commanding Coys will ensure that their lines are left in a clean and sanitary condition and obtain certificates to this effect from incoming Unit.

4. Battalion H.Q. will close in present locality at 10 p.m. and open at E.y.b.8.y at 10.15 p.m.

5. Acknowledge.

    E W B Tarleton
    Captain & Adjutant
    1st Bn Royal Dublin Fus.

Copies to No 1. O.C "W" Coy.
           - 2.   -   "X" -
           - 3.   -   "Y" -
           - 4.   -   "Z" -
           - 5.   -   HQ
           - 6.   O.C 1st Lancs Fus.
           - 7.   86th Bde H.Q.
           - 8.   Rear HQ. 1st R.D.F.
           - 9.   File
           - 10. War Diary
           - 11.
           - 12. Spare.

SECRET. 1st R. Dublin Fusiliers.   Copy No. 12

Operation Order No 35.   June 11, 1918.

Reference Map 36A 1/20,000. Edn 7a.

1. Gas Cylinders are installed along the road in E 16 a and c.
   The gas will be discharged on the night of the 11th/12 June, or on the first subsequent night that weather conditions are suitable.

2. The following Code messages will be sent from Bn H.Q. –
   a. DAISY – Weather conditions are right. Discharge of gas will take place tonight. Take action as laid down in 1st R.D.F. Operation Order No. 35.
   b. MARY – Weather conditions unfavourable. Discharge will not take place tonight.
   c. KATE – Weather conditions have become unfavourable. Discharge will not take place tonight. Original line to be reoccupied forthwith.

   Message (a) or (b) will be sent about 8 p.m.; message (c) will only be sent if message (a) has been sent and weather conditions have changed.

   The receipt of any of the messages (a) (b) (c) will be at once acknowledged by wire.

2.

▲. Action to be taken on the Code word 'DAISY' being received:

a. As soon after dusk as possible the local supporting platoon of 'X' Coy. will withdraw and take up a line of posts along the line E 10 c 0.0 – E 10 c Central.

Remaining platoons of 'X' Coy. will withdraw and proceed to E 16 a 0.6, where guides from 'Y' Coy. will show them into the Support Line in E 9 b, which will be evacuated by 'Y' Coy, who will proceed to the Reserve Line in E 8 b and d.

The platoon of 'Y' Coy. in MOLEGHEIN FM. will withdraw behind the ridge N of MOLEGHEIN FM.

b. As soon after dusk as possible, the supporting platoon of 'W' Coy. will withdraw and form a line of posts along the line E 10 c 0.0 to E 16 a 0.0. An Officer from 'Z' Coy. will meet this platoon at E 16 c 0.6, and show it to position.

The remaining platoons of 'W' Coy. will withdraw and will be met by guides from 'Z' Coy. at the Bn Dump E 15 b 1.8, and shown into that part of the Support Line in E 15 a and E 9 d.

c. In all cases platoons will move as soon after dusk as possible a maximum distance of 200 yards between each being maintained as rapidity of withdrawal to the rear is the essence of the operation.

3.

1. Officers Commanding 'W' and 'X' Coys. will be the last of their respective Coys. to cross the line of cylinders, so as to ensure that every man is West of the danger zone.

The message to Advanced Bn. H.Q. re completion of withdrawal will be sent by runner as quickly as possible.

d. Headquarters will be established as follows:—
   'X' Coy at E 9 d 1.4.
   'W' " " E 15 a 9.7.
   Advanced Bn. H.Q." E 15 a 9.8.

4. All messages dealing with these operations will
   a. If sent by wire be contained in a Code word.
   b. If sent by runner be forwarded in duplicate, a copy going by separate runner.

5. Before evacuation of forward area O's C. Coys. ('W' and 'X') will ensure that all ammunition and stores likely to be corroded by gas are covered up with earth.

6. Reoccupation of evacuated area may not take place till 24 hours later, but 'W' and 'X' Coys. will have ready Officers' patrols to proceed forward on receipt of orders to

4

re-occupy posts at ANKLE FM. (W Coy) and on the extreme left of 'X' Coy (E 17 a).

7. A counter-attack may be necessary to retake the evacuated positions. Instructions to this effect, if necessary, will be issued separately.

8. There is to be no reference to this operation on the telephone and every possible step is to be taken to keep it secret.

9. Rations and water will be dumped tonight at the Advanced Coy Dumps. Arrangements for issue will be notified later.

10. ACKNOWLEDGE by wire.

Geo. D. I. Cotton.
Capt. / Adjutant.
1st Bn. R. Dublin. Fusiliers.

SECRET.   1st Bn R. Dublin Fusiliers.   Copy No. 12

Operation Order No 36.

Reference Map 36A NE. 1/20,000.   June 12th, 1918.

1. The 4th Worcester Regt. will relieve the 1st Royal Dublin Fusiliers in the Left sub-sector of the 86th Infy. Bde. Front on the night of 12/13th June.
   'W' Coy, 4th Worcesters, will relieve 'W' Coy, 1st R. Dublin Fusiliers.
   'X', 'Y', 'Z' Coys, 4th Worcesters, will relieve 'X', 'Y', 'Z' Coys, 1st R. Dublin Fusiliers respectively.

2. Guides will be provided as follows:-
   'W' Coy, 5 Guides at 9.45 pm at Shrine E 8 c 5.5
   'X', 'Y', 'Z' Coy, 5 guides each at 9.45 pm, at junction of roads, E 9 c 3.7.
   2/Lt. G. H. Noblett will meet 'X', 'Y', 'Z' Coys' guides at latter place and take charge.
   1 Guide for Bn H.Q. at the Shrine, E 8 c 5.5 at 9.45 pm.

3. All copies of Defence Schemes, Trench Stores, S.A.A., Grenades, Work in progress, Air Photos, Intelligence will be handed over to incoming Unit & lists forwarded to Orderly Room by 10 a.m., June 13th.

4. Completion of relief will be reported by wiring Code word 'RUBY' with surname of Coy. Commander.

5. Upon completion of relief Coys. will move to Camp in the area E D 9 a via the road in E 8 c and d – E 13 a – Track to TIR ANGLAIS-

2

road as far as D 10 c 6.4, where guides will be met to conduct Coys. to camping area.

'W' & 'X' Coys' Lewis gun limbers will be at the Shrine, E 8 c 5.5, at 10.30 p.m. 'Y' and 'Z' Coys' Lewis gun limbers will be at Coys' H.Q. at same hour. O's. Cmdg. 'W' and 'X' Coys. will arrange for their petrol tins and boxes to be brought back to the Lewis Gun limbers.

Transport Officer will arrange for a limber to be at the Battn. Dump, E 15 b 6.8 at 10 p.m. to pick up remaining petrol tins and boxes.

6. Battn. H.Q. will close in present locality upon completion of relief, and open in new area on arrival.

7. ACKNOWLEDGE.

JWA Daulton
Captain & Adjutant,
1st Bn Royal Dublin Fusiliers.

Distribution: Copies 1-5: 'W' 'X' 'Y' 'Z' H.Q. Coys.
6. 1st R Dublin Fusrs (Rear)
7. 4th Worcester Regt.
8. 86th Inf. Brigade.
9. Signal Officer.
10. Lewis Gun Officer.
11. File.
12 & 13. War Diary.

SECRET.   Copy No. 12

1st Bn Royal Dublin Fusiliers.

Operation Order No 37.

17th June, 1918.

1. The 2/Royal Fusiliers will relieve the 2/South Wales Borderers (H.Q. E.14.c.8.0) in the left sub-sector of the 87th Brigade Front, and the 1st Royal Dublin Fusiliers will relieve the 1/K.O.S.B. (H.Q. FETTLE FM. D.24.a.8.2) in the right sub-sector of the 87th Brigade Front tonight June 17/18th.

2. Y Coy, 1st R.D.F., will relieve C Coy, 1/K.O.S.B., in firing line (Coy H.Q. E.27.b.2.2)
   Z Coy, 1st R.D.F., will relieve D Coy, 1/K.O.S.B. in Support Line (Coy H.Q. E.27.c.70.90).
   X Coy, 1st R.D.F., will relieve B Coy, 1/K.O.S.B. in Reserve Line (Coy H.Q. E.25.d.50.60)
   W Coy will relieve A Coy in LAMOTTE DEFENCES (Coy H.Q. D.30.c.00.35).

3. 5 Guides per Coy will meet Y & Z Coys. at the SAWMILL (E.19.d.2.2) and 5 Guides per Coy for W and X Coys at FETTLE FM (D.24.a.8.2).

4. Advance Party of 1 Officer, 1 N.C.O.,

and 1 Signaller per Coy, & 2/Lt Blackwell, 1 N.C.O. & 1 Signaller for Bn H.Q, will proceed to take over, reporting at Bn H.Q., FETTLE Fm., for guides. Advance party to leave at 6.30 p.m. The following will be taken over:—
　　Defence Schemes.
　　List of work done & to be done.
　　Maps & Trench Stores.

5. Coys will march off as follows, by platoons at 200yds distance:—
　　Z Coy.　　　　7.20 p.m.
　　Y "　　　　　8.0 p.m.
　　X "　　　　　8.20 p.m.
　　W "　　　　　8.40 p.m.
　　Bn HQ　　　　 8.50 p.m.

6. Greatcoats will be carried on haversacks as directed.

7. Completion of relief will be notified by sending O.C. Coy's name.

8. Transport Officer will make the following arrangements:—
　　Collect Lewis Guns and 2 boxes No 36 Grenades per Coy, and deliver

3

as follows:-
Y & Z Coys to SAWMILL at E 19 d 2.2.
W & X "   to Railway Crossing at D 30 b
55.30.

Rations and 12 petrol tins of water
per Coy. to be delivered at the same
dumps.

[NOTE. All ranks will be warned
of the danger of drinking or cooking
with water taken from shell holes or
other sources in the Forward area,
as there has been a considerable
amount of sickness from these causes.]

9. ACKNOWLEDGE.

D.H. Mason
Capt. & Adjutant
1st Royal Dublin Fusiliers

Distribution:-
1. OC. W.   7. Q.Mr.
2. " X.   8. 1/K.O.S.B.
3. " Y.   9. 86th Infde. H.Q.
4. " Z.   10. 1st R.D.F. (Rear)
5. Sig Off.   11. File.
6. T.6.   12 & 13 War Diary.

SECRET.   Copy No. 10
            1st Bn Royal Dublin Fusiliers.

                  Operation Order No. 38

                                    19th June, 1918.

1.   The 1st Royal Dublin Fusiliers will
be relieved by the 1st K.O.S.B. in the
Right Battn Sector tonight, 19/20th
June 1918. On being relieved the 1st
Royal Dublin Fusiliers will occupy
camps vacated by 1st K.O.S.B. Coys
will occupy same positions as on
last occasion.

2.   W Coy, 1st Royal Dublin Fusiliers,
will be relieved by D Coy, 1st K.O.S.B.
       X Coy will be relieved by C Coy.
       Y "   "   "   "   "   " A "
       Z "   "   "   "   "   " B "

3.   1 Guide per platoon and 1 per Coy. H.Q.
will assemble as follows:-
       W and X Coys at Bn H.Q. at 8 p.m.
       Z Coys at SAWMILLS at 7.45 p.m.
       Y Coys at SAWMILLS at 9 p.m.
       A qual. N.C.O. to be sent in
charge of Z and Y Coys guides.

4. Advance parties will take over. All copies of Defence Schemes, Notes of work, Also Photographs, S.A.A., grenades, trench stores, etc will be handed over, and receipts taken. Receipts to be sent to Bn HQ by 11 a.m. tomorrow, 20th inst.

5. Lewis Gun limbers for W and X Coys will be at Bn H.Q. and for Y and Z Coys at SAWMILLS.

6. O's C. Coys will take particular care that all camp kettles, water tins, etc are at dump in time.
  W and X Coys. will have theirs at Ration Dump by 7 p.m
  Y and Z Coys will dump theirs at SAWMILLS after being relieved.

7. O. C. LA MOTTE DEFENCES, will obtain a duplicate receipt for Reserve Rations and water handed over; also a receipt stating the number of tins of fresh water handed over.

8. Completion of relief to be notified by sending O. C. Coy's name, followed by time.

9. ACKNOWLEDGE

R.H. Maguire
Captain & Adjutant,
1st Bn Royal Dublin Fusiliers.

DISTRIBUTION.

1. O.C. W Coy   7. Quartermaster
2. " X "   8. 1st K.O.S.B.
3. " Y "   9. 87th Bde H.Q.
4. " Z "   10. 1st R.F. (Res)
5. Signal Officer   11. File
6. Transport Officer 12 &13. War Diary

SECRET   Copy No.

1st Bn R. Dublin Fusiliers Order No 39.

                                    June 24th, 1918.
Reference Map: Sheet 36A.

1. The 86th Infy Bde will be relieved in Divisional Reserve by the 94th Infy. Bde. on June 24th, & B'ns of the Transport will move independently on completion of relief, to billets in the BLARINGHEM Area.

2. 1st Royal Dublin Fusiliers will be relieved today by 12th Royal East Fusiliers. On relief the 1st Royal Dublin Fusiliers will march to camp at B.16.b.7.2 at present occupied by 12th Norfolk Regt. Relief expected about 12.10 p.m. On being relieved Coys will be prepared to move off at once on receipt of orders.

3. All Defence Schemes, duties, Reserve Rations, bivouacs & tents, ground flares, & S.O.S. grenades to be handed over to incoming Unit. Original receipts, signed by Officers of both handing over & receiving

2

Battns. will be forwarded to Bn HQ by 8 p.m tonight, 24th inst.

4. The following distances will be maintained on the march:-
   Between Coys.   100 yards.
   Between Transport & Battn.   100   "
   Between every section of 6 vehicles.   25   "
   Caps will be worn.

5. Billeting party under 2/Lt Blackwell has been sent in advance & will act as guides for the Battn. in new area.

6. The Hazebrouck patrol, under 2/Lt Johnson will be relieved today. 2/Lt Johnson will meet the relief at noon, at the cross roads Q 8 d 7.0. On relief, 2/Lt Johnson will march his party independently to new area, reporting his arrival to Bn H.Q

7. Bn Drums will meet Bn on road at present Brigade H.Q, about 1.30 p.m

8. All other details at present at Transport Lines will be marched independently to new area.

9. Officers' kits to be dumped at Bn HQ by 9.45 a.m. for transport. One Coy will report to Bn HQ at 10 a.m.

10. O's.C. Coys will be responsible that their camps are left in a scrupulously clean & sanitary condition; usual certificates to be obtained.

11. ACKNOWLEDGE.

                 [signature]
                 Capt. & Adjutant,
             1st Bn R. Dublin Fusiliers.

DISTRIBUTION

1. O.C. W Coy.
2. " X "
3. " Y "
4. " Q "
5. T.O. + B.M.
6. 2/Lt Jameson
7. 1st R.D.F. (Rear)
8. 86th I.f. Bde HQ
9. File
10. War Diary
11.

SECRET.   Copy No. 9

1ST. BN.-ROYAL DUBLIN FUSILIERS.

OPERATION ORDER NO. 40.

Refce. Map sheets 36a and 27.   27th June 1918

1.   An Operation to be referred to as "BORDERLAND" will be carried out by the 31st and 5th Divisions on the morning of 28th June.

2.   The 86th Infantry Brigade will move to-day, June 27th, to the Forward area.
        The 1st Lancashire Fusiliers will be disposed as follows:-
        Battalion H.Q.   D.30.d.35.00
        3 Companies in Reserve Line at BOURRE RIVER and vicinity.
        1 Company, in LA MOTTE DEFENCES.

        2nd Royal Fusiliers:-
        Battalion H.Q.   LE TIR ANGLAIS, D.17.a.5.4., the Battalion occupying positions in the SECOND ZONE between points D.18.a.5.0.- D.12.d.2.7. - D.15.d.8.5. - D.11.c.7.5.

        1st Royal Dublin Fusiliers.
        Battalion H.Q.   PAPOTE, D.22.a.3.3., the Battalion occupying positions in the SECOND ZONE between points D.18.a.5.0. - D.23.a.3.3 - D.16.c.8.7. - D.11.c.7.5.

        86th Brigade H.Q.-
        LE TIR ANGLAIS, D.17.a.5.4.

3.   Advance parties of 1 Officer per Coy and 2nd Lieut NOBLETT for Battalion H.Q., will proceed in advance of Battn. These parties to report to Adjutant at 4.30 p.m. The Battn. will not relieve any troops in the SECOND ZONE.

4.   Companies will take into the line a minimum strength of 135.
        The neucleus over and above will remain in their present camps. A nominal roll of the personnel to be left behind will be rendered to Orderly Room by 2.0 p.m.

5.   Officers kits will NOT be taken.
        Packs to be left in Billets under Company arrangements. Great Coats will be carried bandolier-fashion round haversacks. Company Mess boxes will be carried on Company Cookers. Officers' kits to be left in present billets, but rolled ready for removal.
        Lewis Guns and Ammunition will be carried by Transport, to be at Quartermaster's Stores at 2.0 p.m. to-day ready for loading, Battalion Lewis Gun Officer to superintend loading.

6.   Companies will be on Road, facing S.E. at 5.0 p.m., head of column at B.18.b.90.05 in following order,- Battn H.Q., "X", "Y", "Z", "W" Coys.
        100 yds between Companies as far as D.8.d.70.00, when distance will be altered to 100 yds between platoons.
        Platoon will halt for Two hours at 7.0 p.m. on the march to the Forward area.

(Contd)

--- 2 ---

7. Transport Lines will be at the same location as on June 21st, i.e., C.6.b.3.6.

8. Mobile reserves of S.A.A. will be taken to Forward Transport Lines.

9. Rations for consumption on the 29th inst will be delivered at Forward Transport Lines.

10. The Brigade will probably be in the Forward area for FORTY-EIGHT HOURS, and in the event of a heavy German counter attack driving back the 31st Division beyond our original Front Line, the Brigade may be used either for counter-attack or for holding the Reserve Line on the BOURRE RIVER.

11. ACKNOWLEDGE.

(sd) Robt Maguire

Captain & Adjutant
1/Royal Dublin Fusiliers.

Copies to:-
1. Hd.Qrs., 48th Inf. Bde.
2. O.C., Hd.Qrs.Coy.
3. " "W" Coy.
4. " "X" Coy
5. " "Y" Coy
6. " "Z" Coy
7. Quartermaster.
8. Transport Sergeant.
9. War Diary.
10. " "
11. File.
12.

SECRET. Copy No.

1ST. BN. ROYAL DUBLIN FUSILIERS.

Amendment No. 1 to Operation Order No. 40.

27th June 1918

Para 5 is cancelled, and the following substituted:-

5.   Officers' kits will not go forward. Kits to be taken to Q.M.Stores. Packs will not be carried. They will be stacked at Q.M.Stores.

Only two cookers will go Forward: they will remain at Transport Lines, Forward. Camp kettles will be taken forward by Transport. Cooking utensils for Company Officers can be carried with Coy. Camp kettles.

Lewis Guns and ammunition will be carried by transport, and will be at Q.M.Stores at 2.0 p.m. to-day ready for loading. Battn. Lewis Gun Officer to superintend loading. He will make allowance for loading a Stokes Mortar which should move with Battalion.

6.   After "Forward Area", read :-
Quartermaster to arrange for an extra issue of tea to be available at 7.30 p.m.

Captain & Adjutant.
1/Royal Dublin Fusiliers.

Issued to all recipients of Operation Order No. 40.

1st Royal Dublin Fus.
Operation order No 41.

Secret

Ref Sheet 36 A.

1. The 1st R.Dub.Fus will move (situation permitting) the afternoon of June 29th to the Battalion Camps in BLARINGHAM AREA. The Trench Mortar Team at present with Battalion will move with Battalion.

2. Coys will be notified when move will commence. On receipt of orders Coys will move off independently but care will be taken that at least 100 yds distance is maintained between Platoons. After crossing HAZEBROUCK - MORBECQUE ROAD 100 yds between Coys will suffice.

3. Coys will halt on Road short of D 13 a. 6. 2 Battalion will move off from that position at hour to be notified later.

4. One Baggage wagon will be at Dump for W & X Coys & one Baggage Wagon at Dump

1st R. Dublin Fus.

Operation order No 42

Secret

Ref Sheet 36.a & 27.

1) 1st R. Dublin Fus will move this afternoon June 30th to next area in CAMPAGNE

2) The Battalion will move at 3.30 pm. Battalion less Z Coy to be in position at Starting Point B 10. a 50.60 facing N.W in following order HQ. W. X. Y – 100 yds distance between Coys. Z Coy will form line of march at a convenient place near Coy area. DRums at head of Column.

3) Officers kits to be at Q.M Stores by 2.30pm Coy Mess boxes on cookers.

4) Billets to be left scrupulously clean. O.C Coys to render certificates

5) Transport will move independently under

arrangements of Q.M

6) Advance parties of 1 Off + N.C.O party + 2/Lt Fisher + N.C.O from HQ Coy to report to adjutant at 12.45 p.m.
2/Lt Lennon to guide Transport to new area.

7) Steel Helmets & Packs will be carried by Transport. They will be stacked at Q.M Stores at 12.45 pm
Care to be taken that haversacks are neatly strapped on the back.

8) Acknowledge.

30/4/18.

Sgd R Maguire
Capt & Adjt
1st R.Ir.Fus.

for Y & Z Coys – Lewis guns & S.A.A., empty
Petrol Tins & Tools – In addition a limber
will report at Coy Dumps for salvage.
Mess cart & H.Q. Cart will report Batt HQ
at 2 p.m. – Coy officers chargers will meet
Coys at X Roads D.8.d.70-00.
Coys will report "Ready to move" to typist
orderly specially detailed.
Route will be D.8.70.00, D.8.c.0.0
D.3.a.6.3.
Battalion will halt for Teas at
C.10.a.8.9.
S/ acknowledge.

29.6.18

Signed
R. Maguire
Capt & Adjt.
1/R Dub Fus.

WL 27

27 X
7 sheets

War Diary
of
1st Bn Royal Dublin Fusiliers
for
month of
July 1918
Volume 40

1st Bn. Royal Dublin Fusiliers

Army Form C. 2118.

WAR DIARY or INTELLIGENCE SUMMARY.
(Erase heading not required.)

Place	Date	Hour	Summary of Events and Information July 1918.	Remarks and references to Appendices
CHAMPAGNE. Sheet 27.	July 1st		Company Training - Practice for Sports in afternoon	
S 30	2		Battn. for tr. men.	
	3		Ceremonial practice by Bde. for presentation of medals by G.O.C. 2nd Army	
	4		Brigade Parade & presentation of decorations by General Sir Herbert PLUMER G.C.B, G.C.M.G, G.C.V.O, A.D.C. commanding 2nd Army. The following of the Battalion received:- 2/Lt (actg capt) E.S. ALEXANDER D.C.M, & 2/Lt. P.S. McGOWAN both the Military Cross, R.Q.M.S. F.O. COPS, M.S. Henderson Silver Medal, 16123 Pte R. FOSTER M.M. Bar to M.M. — 20080 Cpl J. HAMILL, 27757 M". P. HANLON, 17812 M". P. LENATHEN, 22172 L/cpl S. BATCHELOR, 10099 Cpl A. FINLAY, 27907 Pte G. BRUNTON all the M.M. = In afternoon Battalion beat No 2 Coy Div'n Team 3 goals to 2 in football competition also won 4 weights at Bde Eliminating Boxing competition to put out three to represent Brigade in tank weight at Divn. no Boxing tournament. All Battalions of Bde present.	
	5th		Company Training & lecture by Lt. Campbell on Recuperative Training - all Battalions of Bde. present.	
	6th		Company Training - In a/Cromer Batt. beat 89th field ambulance in football com- petition 1 - 0	

1st Royal Dublin Fusiliers

WAR DIARY or INTELLIGENCE SUMMARY

Army Form C. 2118.

Summary of Events and Information July 1918

Place	Date	Hour	Summary of Events and Information	Remarks and references to Appendices
CAMBRAI SING	7th		Divine Service for all Denominations during morning - In afternoon Battalion Sports - Shoot interesting + some very good performances.	
	8th		Divisional Horse Competition in afternoon. Company Training during morning. Pte Rowen wins Middle Weight cup. At the Boxing, the Pte Rowen runs up in light heavy weight. Lt Col A Moore D.S.O. the Commanding Officer, Coals in exhibition 3 rounds with one of the enemy Gymnastic Staff.	
	9th		Holiday for all ranks of the Battalion. The Divisional Horse Show. The Battalion Shot himself out - company commanders charge of X Company, Horse "Billy" ridden by Lieut E. NEILL) also the "D" Rivers competition. Open to all the Battalions of the Division - great credit being due to Sgt Drummer HALLETT for the fine performance given by the Battalion "DRUMS".	
	10th		Training in morning - Brigade Sports in afternoon. Battalion failed to win Championship. Being 2nd to 89th Field Ambulance 30 points. Battalion 28 points. 2nd Royal Fusiliers 18 points. 1st Lancashire Fus 11 points. R.D.H.Q & T.M. Bty 7 points.	

A8915 Wt. W14422/M1160 350,000 12/16 D.D. & L. Forms/C./2118/14.

1st Bn Royal Dublin Fusiliers

Army Form C. 2118.

WAR DIARY
or
INTELLIGENCE SUMMARY.

(Erase heading not required.)

For Month of July 1918

Place	Date	Hour	Summary of Events and Information	Remarks and references to Appendices
CHAMPAGNE	11th		Training	
-,,-	12th		Wet day - Instruction classes in Billets	
-,,-	13th		Arrangements made for presentation of ARMY & Divisional Parchments for gallantry - afternoon Battalion Scheme. Divine Service & Presentations - In afternoon officers beat Sergeants at football 4 goals - 2.	
-,,-	14th		Training in morning. In afternoon Battalion play a drawn match we & good all neat 2nd Royal Fusiliers in final of Brigade football competition - first series of Brigade Boxing Competition fought. Battalion representatives did well.	
-,,-	15th		Training in the morning. In the afternoon Royal Fusiliers beat Battalion 3 goals to nil in final of football competition - cups presented to winners by G.O.C. Brigade - finals of Boxing Competition - Battalion winning won champion ships of Brigade in work feather, Bantam, Welter & Middle weights who had the only 2 entries in the Heavy weight for which no prize was given	
-,,-	16			

Army Form C. 2118.

1/5 Bn. Royal Scots Fusiliers

WAR DIARY
OR
INTELLIGENCE SUMMARY.
(Erase heading not required.)

July 1918

Place	Date	Hour	Summary of Events and Information	Remarks and references to Appendices
LAMPAGNIE	16		Continued as the recreation grounds of Entries were not received at the luncheon. Boxing challenge cups presented to the Battalion to hold until next competition by Major Brigadier (Brig. Gen. G.R.H. CHEAPE D.S.O. M.C.)	
"	17		Brigade Tactical Scheme – A practice prior to one on larger scale tomorrow at which G.O.C. Division is to be present.	
"	18		Brigade Tactical Scheme. Scheme well carried out. In afternoon visited Band fixing for the men at 4pm and at 6.30pm the Divisional Concert Troupe (36th Division) gave a most excellent entertainment. A Hangar having kindly been placed at the disposal of the Battalion for this purpose by the Balloon Section R.A.F.	
"	19		Battalion Training –	
"	20		Scheme carried out in conjunction with 1 LANCASHIRE FUS.	
"	21		Divine Service for all Denominations. Football in afternoon Sergeants v Officers – former won 2 goals to 1. Orders received about 10pm that Batt. would probably move by March Route in the morning.	

1st The Royal Dublin Fusiliers

Army Form C. 2118.

WAR DIARY
or
INTELLIGENCE SUMMARY.
(Erase heading not required.)

Summary of Events and Information July 1918

Place	Date	Hour	Summary of Events and Information	Remarks and references to Appendices
CAHAGNE	21	continued	at 9 am in a Northerly direction	
"	22		Bath parade at 9.30 am - halt for dinners at 12 midday arrive NOORDPEENE about 2 pm Reconnaissance Billets - good. A trying march owing to the great heat. NOORDPEENE is about 5000 yards due West of CASSEL (Sheet 27 - N.5 a & b). Division passes from XV to X Corps.	
NOORDPEENE	23		Very wet day - Coy & Officers inspections.	
"	24		Training - fine day. Reconnaissance by Officers of forward zones.	
"	25		Training. Company football matches in afternoon.	
"	26		Training. do.	
"	27		Training.	
"	28		Church Services for all Denominations - Rugby football match in afternoon. In the morning Companies in turn shoot on the Range.	
"	29		Training - Weather fine & very warm.	
"	30		Training.	
"	31		Training - In afternoon Battalion play Brigade at Rugby football & are beaten after a good game.	

W.J. Trigger
Lt. Col.
Commanding 1st Royal Dublin Fus

Arrivals

Officers
- 2Lt. J.E. Clarke 2.7.18
- Capt. R.W. Hughes (rtd) 6.7.18
- " O. Trencher (rtd) 7.7.18
- 2Lt. J.P. O'Reilly 12.7.18
- Lieut. J. Barker Savage 22.7.18
- 2Lt. R.W. Owens 25.7.18
- " E.C. Bourke 25.7.18

Total: 7

O/Ranks
- from Hospital — 31
- " Base — 35
- Deserters from Base — 17
- " to I.B. — 2

Total: 85 [88]

Departures

- Lt. W.R. Kidd MC
     Base Unfit 12.7.18
- " W.B. St.G. Cameron
     Invalided 12.7.18
- 2Lt. R.W. Fitzgerald 19.7.18
- Lt.Col. C.C. Grantham
- " J.V. Staples
     Invalided 28.7.18

Total: 4

- To Base Unfit — 14
- Evacuated — 51
- 86 I.B.D. — 7
- Died — 1
- 11th R.I. Res. — 1
- Base for Reposting — 1
- England for Commission — 6
- 2nd Bn R.I.F. — 12
- S.O.S. — 1
- Not arrived from Base — 11

Total: 105

	Offrs.	O/Ranks
Strength 30.6.18	42	939
Arrivals	7	88
	49	1027
Departures	4	105
Strength 1.8.18	45	922

1st Royal Dublin Fusiliers

War Diary

for

August 1918.

Army Form C. 2118.

WAR DIARY
or
INTELLIGENCE SUMMARY.
(Erase heading not required.)

1st Royal Dublin Fusiliers

For Month of

August
1918.

Volume 41.

1st Royal Welsh Fusiliers

Army Form C. 2118.

WAR DIARY
or
INTELLIGENCE SUMMARY.
(Erase heading not required.)

Place	Date	Hour	Summary of Events and Information	Remarks and references to Appendices
			August 1917	
NOORDPEENE	1		Very warm day. Batt. did no training. At 7.15 pm Batt. moved by march route to HAZEBROUCK - on the march Bombs dropped very close to Batt. 2 men of X Coy slightly wounded. accommodation Tents & shelters. Batt. H.Q. V.22.c. Sheet 27. on arrangement to one Division will relieve 1st AUSTRALIAN Division in night of 2/3rd inst. Batt. moving into Reserve. Division have not passed back to XV Corps to be taken up	
HAZEBROUCK	2		Day very wet. Officers in morning reconnoitre Batt. positions forward area. Batt. moved up at 8pm to position in Brigade in Reserve area vide operation order No 2 attached. Details Q.14 Stores Transport remain about HAZEBROUCK V.22.c. Sheet 27.	
BATT. H.Q. W.20.d.6.9. Sheet 27	3		Batt. in support - Day very wet. CAPT. F. TREACHER M.C. 0/c "X" Coy appointed Staff. capt. 116 Brigade. 2/Lt BRONSON Marsh of Attingth of this Battalion.	
"	4		Showery morning. Some shelling on firing & support line. 86 hf hostile relieve 134 Inf. Bde 40th Div in Right Bde sector of the Divisional front. Batt. relieve 23rd Welsh Regt in front line vide Operation order No 3 attached relief completed by 12.30 am.	

1st Royal Dublin Fusiliers

Army Form C. 2118.

WAR DIARY
or
INTELLIGENCE SUMMARY.
(Erase heading not required.)

AUGUST 1918.

Place	Date	Hour	Summary of Events and Information	Remarks and references to Appendices
Bn H.Q E.10.b.8.9 sht 36A.	5		Dull day inclined to rain. at night Z Coy under command of 2/Lt A.H. WEIR put forward their line installing posts, Y Coy also sent out Patrols.	
— " —	6	in morning	A Patrol of Z Coy under 2/Lt SPOTTISWOODE sent an enemy post taking a machine gun. At 3 p.m. the enemy during afternoon a sharp patrol of Y Coy under command of the Coy comdr Capt B.D. HUGHES M.C. with a Lewis Gun, go out to ELLERY COPSE. They encounter a strong enemy force and are subjected to heavy M.G. & trench mortar fire. Casualties CAPT. HUGHES killed, C.S.M. KAVANAGH wounded (since died from wounds) 2 O.R.s wounded 1 O.R. surrendered missing, 1 O.R. missing. In Capt HUGHES' death the Batt. lose a very gallant officer universally popular.	
— " —	7		W Coy & X Coy relieve Y & Z Coys respectively. With operation order No 8 attached. During daylight' scouts patrol 500 yards forward, at night fighting patrols go out. Casualties inflicted on enemy but no identification secured. Heavy hostile artillery fire on forward areas causing casualties.	
— " —	8 & 9		Patrols etc as before — no change — Heavy enemy artillery fire — Enemy artillery very alert but inclined to retire into	

1st Royal Dublin Fusiliers

WAR DIARY
or
INTELLIGENCE SUMMARY.

Army Form C. 2118.

(Erase heading not required.)

Place	Date	Hour	Summary of Events and Information	Remarks and references to Appendices
Batt HQ	August 1918			
VITZ	10th		Working parties to dept. Batt. relieved by 1st LANCASHIRE Fus, relief complete	
		12.45 am (11th)	Moved into Batt. Reserve - Billets vacated by 2nd Royal	
			Fus who moved into Support, Sheet 27. V.12 c & d - Ville Quesnoi Mr	
			No 5 attached accommodation reserved - Farm Houses Barns.	
Batt HQ VITZ	11th		Baths, cleaning, reorganization	
Study	12th 13th	7.13	Training, Lectures by Officers etc	
	14th		do – at night demonstration of night patrolling by officers + NCOs	
			Capt E.J. ALEXANDER MC DCM meant of Y by.	
	15th		Training in the evening. Officers then attd lecture by Lt DIAMOND	
			TROUPE (Divisional Concert Party)	
	16th		Batt moved to support trenches from 2nd Royal Fus, who relieve 1st	
			LAN. Fus in front line Vile Quesnoi etc No 6 attached – 250 men	
			engaged in R.E. working parties	
Batt HQ VILLERS	17th		250 men engaged on working parties under R.E. Hostile Shell fire cause	
CURFEW HOUSE			casualties among a "carrying party" from W by 9, 10R killed, 40R wounded.	
	18th		Working Parties supplied. Enemy Barrage on our left by 87th Brigade on the	

1st Batt Royal Dublin Fusiliers

WAR DIARY
or
INTELLIGENCE SUMMARY.
(Erase heading not required.)

Army Form C. 2118.

Summary of Events and Information — AUGUST 1918.

Place	Date	Hour	Summary of Events and Information	Remarks and references to Appendices
CURFEW H.Q.	18th		Continued: 9th Division on the left. ZERO Hour 11.a.m. Must encompass attack. OUTTERSTEENE Ridge village captured with many prisoners —	
			At night W.by very very Stokes mortar shells to forward positions —	
—"—	19th		Quiet day. At 5.0.p.m 2nd Royal Ffs attack under a very good barrage. All objectives (arived over 100 prisoners 18 machine guns & etc.) engaged in carrying ammunition rations etc forward to captured positions — No casualties — W.by were found to relieve Reserve Coy of the 2nd R. Fus also on their wind forward to stricken their line.	
—"—	20th		Quiet day. Carrying & working parties. W.by relieved by a Coy of R.Fus Regina move back to support position at BORRE Village [W. 19.— sheet 7]	
—"—	21st		On relief by 1st LAN. Fus: in support area Batt relieve 2nd Roy al Fus in the forward area (newly won ground) Relief completion without No 7 attached.	
B4H.Q HRS STAZEELE Rly STATION	22nd		At dawn Y.by leave our advance line under Bde instructions to establish touch with the enemy — Touch established about two yards in advance of our line. Casualties 1 OR killed 2 wounded. Patrols out by day & by night.	
	23		At dawn Z Coy push forward 2 Platoons establish touch with the enemy	

Army Form C. 2118.

17th Royal Fusiliers

WAR DIARY
or
INTELLIGENCE SUMMARY.
(Erase heading not required.)

Instructions regarding War Diaries and Intelligence
Summaries are contained in F. S. Regs., Part II.
and the Staff Manual respectively. Title pages
will be prepared in manuscript.

Place	Date	Hour	Summary of Events and Information	Remarks and references to Appendices
Batt. H.Q. near STAZEELE STATION	Aug. 1918			
	23rd		Continued at the same front as yesterday. Heavy hostile artillery barrage on Batt. area during the day. Patrols out during night. Hostile Trench Rept. with enemy. Change of dispositions – no operation or attack. No. 8 attacked.	
F.H.B. Sect. 36.A	24th		2/Lt. G.G. HOLMES that his Platoon (W.loy.) to reconnoitre to "Scuppers" an enemy party by daylight - unable to secure identification, but many enemy killed. Our casualties 2 O.Rs wounded. Hostile Coy. relief took operation in No. 4 attacked.	
	25th		Quiet day. Two patrols out during night 25/26. Attempted to establish touch with the enemy.	
	26th		Enemy early morning front system heavily shelled by hostile artillery. At night 2/Lt HOLMES with a patrol of 7W. loy. go out to DESPOT fm. to reconnoitre my fairside wire & interpretation. When about to rush the post they were observed by the enemy & party 1 Warrant double rummed in an attempt to cut them off. Our patrol engaged the enemy & withdrew to our lines.	
	27th		Batt. relieved by 1st LAN. Fus. & move to Support Batt. area wire operations on No. 10 attacked. Batt. H.Qrs about 200 x. W. of STAZEELE Ry. Station	
Amm. H.Q. E.H.C.S.2 sheet 36A	28th		Batt. Rest return info -	
	29th		3 Officers & 160 O.Rs Engaged on R.E. working parties. X. Coy. have Batt. relief change Icandentting at Batt. Transport lines in East HAZEBROUCK.	

1st Batt Royal Dublin Fus

WAR DIARY or INTELLIGENCE SUMMARY

Army Form C. 2118.

Summary of Events and Information — August 1918

Place	Date	Hour	Summary of Events and Information	Remarks and references to Appendices
Bn. H.Q. E.4.c.5.3. Sheet 36A	30th		At dawn raid by Y. Coy on DESPOT FM. Lieut. J CASSIDY M.C. (i/c Party) 2/Lt. M. F. O'DONNELL & 2/Lt. R. H. LENNON 1st R.I. attached. The Farm & surrounding Buildings found unoccupied. 2/Lt. LENNON 1st R.I.R. wounded by getting too close to our Barrage. Body of German Officer (dead for about 24 hours) found, identification normal. Enemy withdrawal apparently on this front. Many fires at night in this line, whole divisional line being actively engaged in keeping no man's advanced daily. Patrols blank. Rean Change further than touch — Half of W by & half 4 Y by. New Baths Clean Canteen open all day for the men & Divine play at Transport Lines. Battn. Canteen open all day for the men & Divine play for them in afternoon. Report their Companies about 8 p.m. Battn. Still in old support area which to was well behind line on account of enemy withdrawal. Weather fine. X Coy & Y Coy move into Z line. Half Y & half Z coy Bn. R.E.s engaged on various patrols under R.E.s.	
	31st		300 O.R.s engaged on Working Parties. Very wet night. Have baths etc at Transport huts. Attached operation orders Nos 2-10. Warning order dated 11/8/18. Rear order R.I. also Batt. Strength showing Variation.	

Otto Moor
Lt Col
Commanding 1st Royal Dublin Fusiliers

SECRET.

1ST BATTN. ROYAL DUBLIN FUSILIERS.
****

WARNING --- ORDER. *Map Ref. Sheet 27.*

The 29th Division will relieve the 1/Australian Division on 1st, 2nd, and 3rd of August in the STRAZEELE Sector.

On the night of 2/3rd August the 86th Infantry Brigade, plus 1/Lancashire Fusiliers, will relieve the 2nd Australian Infantry Brigade in the Front and Support Lines.

The 86th Infantry Brigade will move to the Support Brigade Area, the 1st Royal Dublin Fusiliers moving into the ROUGE CROIX Switch and Reserve Line, and the 2nd Royal Fusiliers into the "B" and "C" Lines.

86th Brigade Headquarters and 86th T. M. Battery will move to W.21.c.1.6.

The 1st Royal Dublin Fusiliers will not relieve any troops in the ROUGE CROIX SWITCH and Reserve Line.

O.C., Coys will be prepared to reconnoitre and select positions for their Coys in the Support area on the morning of the 2nd.

Further details regarding move on the 2/3rd August will be notified later.

Robt Maguire.
Captain & Adjutant.
1st Royal Dublin Fusiliers.

1st August 1918.

Copies issued to:-
O.C., Hd Qrs Coy.
" "W" Coy.
" "X" Coy.
" "Y" Coy.
" "Z" Coy.
Quartermaster.
Transport Officer.
Regtl.Sergt.Major.

SECRET.   Copy No: 11

1st Battn Royal Dublin Fusiliers Operation Order No. 2

1. **INTENTION.**
    The 1st Royal Dublin Fusiliers will move into Support Area to-night 2/3rd August 1918.

2. **ADVANCED PARTIES.**
    Advanced parties of 2nd Lieut FISHER and 1 N.C.O. for Battn. Hd. Qrs; 1 Officer per Coy and 1 N.C.O. and 1 guide per platoon to move off at 7 p.m.

    Guides will meet Platoons as follows:-

    "W" and "X" Coys at STELLA CROSS, W.16.d.10.40.
    "Y" Coy at W.16.c.05.10 where road meets RESERVE LINE.
    "Z" Coy at Battalion Headquarters, W.20.b.6.9.

    Guides to be at Rendezvous by 9.30 p.m.

3. **TIME.**   Battn will move as follows:- Headquarters, 8.0 p.m "W" Coy, 8.30 p.m. and remaining Coys at 15 minute intervals in following order:- "X", "Y", "Z".

4. **ROUTE.**   HAZEBROUCK-BORRE Road as far as V.24.b.9.3. - thence to CONGO CROSS, W.13.c.9.3., and by most direct route to position,

5. **DISTANCE.**   100 yards between platoons.

6. **TRANSPORT ARRANGEMENTS.**
    Coy Limbers will move in rear of Coys.
    Cookers and Water Carts will not move with Battn.

7. **RATIONS.**   Rations for to-morrow will be carried on the men.
    Ration Limbers will be met by Coy Guides at 9.30 p.m. as follows:-
    "W" and "X" Coys at STELLA CROSS. "Y" Coy at W.16.c.05.10., and "Z" Coy at Battn. Hd.Qrs.
    15 Petrol tins of water will be taken on Coy Limbers to-night. Future arrangements will be detailed later

8. **DRESS.**   Full Marching Order.

9. **COMPLETION OF MOVE.**

    O.C., Coys will report by runner when in position.

                                                    Captain and Adjutant.
2nd August 1918.   1st Royal Dublin Fusiliers.

Copies issued to:-
    No. 1. 86th Inf.Bde.   7. Transport Officer.
        2. O.C., Hd.Qrs.Coy   8. Quartermaster.
        3. "   "W" Coy   9. Regtl.Sergt.Major.
        4. "   "X" Coy   10. War Diary.
        5. "   "Y" Coy   11. "   "
        6. "   "Z" Coy   12. File.

SECRET.   Copy No 10.

1st Bn. Royal Dublin Fusiliers.

Operation Order No 3.

4th August, 1918.

1. **INTENTION.** The 86th Infy. Bde. will relieve the 121st Infy. Bde. in the Right Bde. Sector of the Divisional Front, on the night of 4/5th August, 1918.
    1st B. Dublin Fus. will relieve the 23rd Cheshire Regt. in the Front Line (Battn. H.Q. E 10 b 8.9).

2. **ADVANCE PARTIES.** 2/Lt. Fisher, 1 N.C.O, 1 Signaller, & 1 Runner from Battn H.Q., & 1 Officer, 1 N.C.O, 1 Gas N.C.O, 1 Signaller, & 1 Runner from each Coy. will report to Bn. H.Q., 23rd Cheshire Regt, as follows:—
    Bn. H.Q. Party at 8.30 p.m.
    X, Y, Z Coys' Parties at 9.0 p.m.
    Advance party from W Coy. will report direct to Coy. H.Q. (TIFLIS HOUSE) at 8.30 p.m.

3. **DETAIL OF RELIEF.**
    Z Coy. will relieve A Coy. Right Front

2

Left

Y Coy. will relieve D Coy. Front
X Coy.   "   "   B Coy. Mid Support.
W Coy.   "   "   C Coy. Rear Support

The platoon post at E.11.d.65.3?
will be manned by the 31st Division.
O.C. Z Coy. will arrange to have an
inter-locking post at this point.
As only 2 platoon posts will be taken
over by Z Coy., O.C. Coy. will arrange to
reconnoitre positions for remaining 2
platoons in close support.

5 Guides per Coy. will be
at rendezvous, E.11.a.40.95 at following
times:– For Z Coy., 10 p.m. Y Coy. 10.30
& X Coy. at 11 p.m. For W Coy. guides will
be at W.29.c.40.15 at 11 p.m.

4. ROUTE STRAZEELE – Road due S.
as far as Railway Crossing, E.11.a.40.95,
where guides will rendezvous.

5. HOUR OF MOVE & DISTANCE Coys. will
march off:–

    Z Coy.   8.45 p.m.
    Y Coy.   9.15 "
    X Coy.   9.45 "
    W Coy. 10.15 "
    Bn H.Q. 10.00 p.m.

100 yards between platoons.

3

6. **TO BE TAKEN OVER.** Defence Schemes, Maps, Air Photos, Intelligence, Programmes of Work, A.A. Defences, etc.

7. **TRANSPORT ARRANGEMENTS.** All Stores & kits not for line will be dumped by 7.30 p.m., ready for removal, at following points:— Y & Z. Coys. at W 16 a 05.10, where trench meets road; and W & X Coys. at a point 50 yards W. of STELLA CROSS.

Lewis Gun limbers to report to Coys. at same positions by 8.0 p.m. Lewis gun limbers will move with Coys. as far as E 11 a 40.95.

8. **RATIONS.** Rations for tomorrow will be issued to Coys. before marching off. Tea for Battn. to be delivered to Ration Dump (E 5 c 4.3) in Food Containers.

W. Coy's will be delivered to TIFLIS HOUSE (E 4 b 85.90).

Rations will be delivered in future to these Ration Dumps at 10/p 10 tins of water per Coy & 4 for Battn H.Q. to be delivered nightly.

4

9. <u>DRESS</u>. Full Marching Order.

10. <u>PATROLS</u>. Instructions issued separately.

11. <u>RELIEF COMPLETE</u>. To be notified by O.C. Coy's name and time.

12. ACKNOWLEDGE.

       Robt Macquire
       Capt. & Adjutant,
       1st R. Dublin Fusiliers.

Copies to :-

1. 86th Inf. Bde. 7. Transport Officer.
2. OC HQ Coy.   8. Quartermaster.
3. OC W Coy.   9. R.S.M.
4. OC X Coy.   10. War Diary.
5. OC Y Coy.   11.   "   "
6. OC Z Coy.   12. File.

SECRET.   Copy No. 9

               1st Bn Royal Dublin Fusiliers

                    Operation Order No 11

                                        7th August, 1915.

1. INTENTION
      W Coy 1st RDF will relieve Y Coy
   2nd Royal Fusiliers
      X Coy will relieve Z Coy in Right
   Sub Section on 7th August

2. TIME & DISTANCE
      W Coy will march 15 minutes between platoons
      X Coy; to march platoons at 15 [pace]

3. ADVANCE PARTIES
      Advance party [?] W & X Coys
   composed of 1 NCO & 1 [?] of [?], 1 [?]
   [?] of 1 [?], [?] [?] of
   [?] & [?] to [?] Coys to act as
   [?] [?]
      [?] [?] [?] W & X Coys
   of 1 Officer & 1 Coy 1 NCO & 4 [?] [?]
   with [?] [?] of a Coy [?] [?] 1½
   at [?]

Strength 31.7.18   45 Offrs.,   932 O/Ranks

Offrs   O/Ranks

Increase	Decrease	Increase	Decrease	
Nil	Capt. F. Treacher M.C. To 116 Inf. Bde. 4.7.18		To Base unfit	10
	Capt. B.D. Hughes M.C. Killed in Action 6.7.18	Nil	Killed in Action	2
			Wounded	6
			W'ded Missing	1
			Missing	1
			Evacuated	1
	2			21

Strength 7.8.18   43 Offrs.   911 O/Ranks.

SECRET   Copy No. 10

<u>1st Bn Royal Dublin Fusiliers.</u>

<u>Operation Order No 5.</u>

9th August, 1918.

1. <u>INTENTION</u>. The 2nd Royal Fusiliers will relieve the 1st Lancs. Fusiliers in the Support Battalion lines on the evening of the 10th August

    1st Lancs. Fusiliers, upon relief, will move forward and relieve the 1st Royal Dublin Fusiliers.
    D Coy. 1st L.F. will relieve X Coy. 1st R.D.F. Right Front
    B   "   "   "   "   W "   "   "   Left Front Position
    A   "   "   "   "   Z "   "   "   Mid Support
    C   "   "   "   "   Y "   "   "   Support Position (2 Lines)

2. <u>ADVANCE PARTIES</u>. Advance parties of 1st Lancs Fusiliers from B & D. Coys. will report at PARADISE INN at 3 p.m. Advance parties from H.Q & A & C. Coys. will report to the respective H.Q in the course of the afternoon

3. <u>TRENCH STORES, ETC</u>. All maps, aeroplane photographs, work tables, S.A.A., Intelligence, trench stores, etc. to be handed over.

2

Receipts for same to reach H.Q. by 9.0 a.m., 11th inst.

4. GUIDES. 1 guide for Coy. H.Q. & 2 guides per platoon (1 per Lewis gun Section) from W & X Coys. will rendezvous at E 5 c 4.2 at 10.0 p.m.

1 guide per Coy. H.Q. & 1 guide per platoon from Z Coy. will rendezvous at the same time & place. Guides to have chits stating party which they are to guide. 2/Lt ROSS will assemble guides & report to these H.Q. when East Coy. has passed.

O.C. Y Coy. will arrange with O.C. C. Coy., 1st Lancs. Fusiliers, reference details of Coys. in relief.

5. TRANSPORT ARRANGEMENTS. Coys will collect Food Containers, Water Tins, etc. & deliver same to Ration Dump; 1 man per Coy. to be left in charge until loaded on transport. Lewis gun limbers will not arrive at Ration Dump until 11.30 p.m.

6. PATROLS. Instructions reference patrols during relief will be issued later. Patrol leaders from 1st Lancs

3

Forbes will report with advance parties.
2./Lts CONDRON & BURNS will be responsible
that all information and detail helpful
to patrols is handed over to these leaders.

7. RELIEF COMPLETE. Completion of
relief will be notified by the code
word "FAT", followed by O.C.'s name.

8. ACKNOWLEDGE.

[On completion of relief Co.
will move off independently to billets
in Reserve Area. Route, location &
point where guides will be met will
be notified later.]

Robt Mayne
Capt & Adjutant,
1st Bn R. Dublin Fusiliers.

DISTRIBUTION.
1. 56th Inf Bde.   7. Quartermaster
2. O.C. W Coy.   8. 1st James Fusrs
3. "   X "   9. R.S.M.
4. "   Y "   10. Wn. Diary
5. "   Z "   11. "   "
6. Inns. Short Offrs.   12. File.

SECRET   1st Bn R. Dublin Fusiliers.
Addendum to Operation Order No 5.

10th August, 1918.

1. On relief Coys. will move off independently & march to billets in Reserve Area, V 24 c & d.
ROUTE: STRAZEELE - PRADELLES - BORRE to cross-roads at V 24 b 95.25, where billet guides will be met.
200 yards between platoons.

2. Reference para 5. Lewis gun limbers for Y Coy will report to Y Coy's Ration Dump at 10.30, & not as stated.

3. Capt. DELANEY, who has already been instructed to take over billets from 2nd Royal Fusiliers, will arrange to post billet guides at V 24 b 95.25. Y Coy. should reach this point about 12 o'clock.

Robt Maguire
Capt. & Adjutant
1st Bn R. Dublin Fusiliers.

Issued to Capt. DELANEY & all recipients of O.O. No. 5.

4. GUIDES. O.C. Y Coy. will detail 1 good N.C.O. per platoon to act as Guides to W Coy. Guides from each platoon S. of Railway will reconnoitre by daylight route from platoon posts to PARADISE INN.

Guides from platoon on left of Railway will guide relieving platoon along path N. of Railway. On no account will they platoon go along Railway track.

Guides for X Coy will be arranged between O's C. X & Z Coys.

Guides for Y & Z Coys. will be provided as stated in para. 3. Rendezvous for Y Coy guide - PARADISE INN.

5. PATROLS. Y & Z Coys. will provide covering patrols till relief complete.

6. ~~DRESS~~ AMMUNITION. Lewis guns will be carried to new positions. S.A.A. in magazines will be handed over.

7. RATIONS. Coys. will deliver all empty water Tins & food Containers to Ration Dumps after dusk, & leave 1 man in charge. Y & Z Coys. will detail 1 N.C.O. & 10 O.Rs., who will go to Ration Dumps & await limbers. They will carry food Containers & day rations for W & X Coys. to the respective Coy. H.Q.

3.

W & X Coys will arrange to take up water Tins on relief. No ...
Y & Z Coys will draw rations from dump when relieved.

8. COMPLETION OF RELIEF will be notified by O.C. Coys name & time.

9. ACKNOWLEDGE

Capt. & Adjutant
1/4th R. Berks ...

Copies to :-

1. Bn. Hd ... Rep.
2. Hq. W Coy
3.   " X   "
4.   " Y   "
5.   " Z   "
6. 2/4 R. B. W.F.
7. 4th ... Regt.
8. War Diary
✓9. "   "
10. File

SECRET.   1st BN. ROYAL DUBLIN FUSILIERS.   Copy No.

                 OPERATION ORDER NO. 6

                                              15th August 1918.

1. INTENTION. The 1st Royal Dublin Fusiliers will relieve the
   2nd Royal Fusiliers in the Support Battalion area on the
   evening of the 16th August.

2. ADVANCE PARTIES. Advance party of 2/Lt FISHER, 1 Gas N.C.O.
   and 1 Signaller, and 1 Runner from H.Q., and an Officer,
   Gas N.C.O. and Runner per Coy will report to take over in the
   course of the afternoon.

3. GUIDES. Where necessary, Guides will be arranged for
   between O's.C., Coys direct.

4. HOUR OF RELIEF. "W" Coy will relieve at 9.0 p.m. Remainder
   of Coys at 9.30 p.m.   Coys will march off as follows:-
   "W" Coy, 8.15; "Z" Coy, 8.15; "X" Coy, 8.30; "Y" Coy, 8.45.

5. DEXTAILS OF RELIEF.
      "W" Coy, 1st R.D.F. will relieve "W" Coy, 2nd R.F., Hd.Qrs
                                                    W.19.d.2.8.
      "X" Coy   "   "   " "X" Coy, 2nd R.F., Hd.Qrs
                                                    E.3.c.15.99
      "Y" Coy   "   "   " "Y" Coy, 2nd R.F., Hd.Qrs
                                                    W.28.b.1.2.
      "Z" Coy   "   "   " "Z" Coy, 2nd R.D., Hd.Qrs
                                                    E.4.c.8.8.

6. ROUTE. "W" Coy, by most direct route. Remainder of Coys by
   cross-country tracks.

7. DISTANCE. 300 yds distance between platoons. (NOTE: If enemy
   balloons are up, or visibility is very good, platoons will move
   by sections or by two's and three's.

8. STORES TO BE TAKEN OVER. All maps, aeroplane photographs, work
   policy, S.A.A., Intelligence, trench stores, etc., will be
   taken over.

9. TRANSPORT ARRANGEMENTS. Lewis gun limbers, rations, and water
   will move with Coys. "W" Coy's cooker will move with Coy.
   All kits and stores not moving forward will be packed ready
   for removal by 7.30 p.m.

10. RATIONS. Rations wil be delivered to Coy H.Q., nightly at
    10 p.m. In the case of "W" and "X" Coys and Headquarters,
    water cart will visit daily. For remainder of Coys water will
    be delivered nightly in Petrol tins. Travelling cooker for
    "W" Coy will go forward. Remainder of Coys to use camp kettles.

11. MEDICAL Arrangements.
            Regimental Aid Post will be at Battalion Headquarters
    CURFEW HOUSE. Sick Parade at 10.0 a.m. daily

12. DRESS.   Full Marching Order.

                          (Contd)

OPERATION ORDER No. 6 (Contd)

---

13. **WORKING PARTIES.** R.E. working parties will be detailed from Battalion Headquarters.

14. **RELIEF COMPLETE.** To be notified by O.C., Coy's name and time of relief complete.

15. **ACKNOWLEDGE.**

Robt Mangin

Captain & Adjutant.
1st Royal Dublin Fusiliers.

Copies issued to:-
  No. 1. 86th Infy. Bde.
    2. O.C., "W" Coy
    3. O.C., "X" Coy
    4. O.C., "Y" Coy
    5. O.C., "Z" Coy
    6. Transport Officer.
    7. Quartermaster.
    8. 2nd Royal Fusiliers.
    9. R. S. M.
    10. War Diary.
    11 do
    12. File.

Strength 7.8.18. 43 Offrs. 911 O/Ranks

Officers

Increase
2/Lt J. Cassedy M.C.
 Joined 9.8.18
Capt G.B.L. Webb
 " 9.8.18

_____
 2

Decrease
2/Lt W.H. Pierce
 SOS 7.8.18
 " J.W. Kirwen
 SOS 9.8.18
 " D.W. Harris
 To RAF 14.8.18

_____
 3

O/Ranks

Increase
From Base   21
 " Hospl   2

_____
 23

Decrease
Killed in Action   5
Wounded   11
Evacuated   4
To 2.R.W.F.   6
SOS   4

_____
 30

Strength 15/8/18. 42 Offrs. 904 O/Ranks

SECRET.   Copy No. 10

1st R. Dublin Fusiliers.
Operation Order No 7.
                    21st August, 1918.

1. **INTENTION.** 1st Lancs. Fus. will relieve 1st R. Dublin Fus. in the Support Battn. Area this evening 21st Aug.

  1st RDF, on relief, will move forward & relieve 2nd Royal Fus. in the Front Battn. Area.

2. **ADVANCE PARTIES.** O's C. Coy. will reconnoitre new positions this morning. In addition, advance parties of 2/Lt. BLACKWELL, Gas NCO., & Signallers from H.Q., & an Officer, N.C.O. & Runner per Coy. will proceed to take over in the course of the afternoon. Care will be taken to use all available cover in going forward.

3. **DETAILS OF RELIEF.**
  W. Coy. 1st RDF relieve X Coy. 2nd R.F. Left Front, on line F 14 a 40.30 to F 8 c 60.60 approximately.
  X Coy. 1st RDF. relieve Z Coy. 2nd RF. with 2 platoons on line F 14 c 40.40 (road inclusive) to F 14 a 40.30; 1 platoon on VIEUX BERQUIN — OUTTERSTEENE ROAD, about F 13 6 1.4;

2

and 1 platoon about LYNDE FM.
Y Coy. 1stRDF. will relieve Y Coy. 2ndRF.
in STRAZEELE STATION DEFENCES.
Z Coy. 1stRDF. will relieve W Coy. 2ndRF.
in Northern portion of "Z" LINE.

4. HOUR OF RELIEF.
W Coy. will leave billets in BORRE at
8.30 p.m., moving by platoons at 300 yds distance
X Coy. will move from present position
at 9 p.m.; platoons at 300 yards distance.
Y Coy. will move off at 9.30 p.m.
O.C. Z Coy. 1stRDF. will arrange to
take over from O.C. W. Coy., 2ndRF. this evening

5. GUIDES. 1 Guide per platoon & 1 for Coy HQ
for W Coy will meet Coy. at E 5 c 4.0.
1 Guide for each of the Front
platoons of X Coy. will be at same rendezvous.
No other Guides will be supplied.

6. STORES. All maps, aeroplane photos, wire
policy, S.AA., Intelligence French stores, etc., will
be taken over on relief.

7. TRANSPORT ARRANGEMENTS. Limbers &
G.S. Wagon will report to W & X Coys. &
H.Q. in the course of the afternoon, to take
back kits, salvage, etc. not for Line.

3

Lewis gun limbers for W Coy. will report to billets in BORRE at 8.0 p.m., & will move with Coy. as far as Battn. Ration Dump, STRAZEELE STATION.

Transport Officer will arrange for W Coy's cooker to be taken forward tonight for use by Z Coy.

8. RATIONS. Rations for Z Coy. to be delivered to new Coy. Ration Dump near TIFLIS HOUSE.

Rations for Y Coy. to be delivered to Ration Dump, E 5 c 4.0, at 11.0 p.m.

Dry rations for W & X Coys. to be delivered by 7.0 p.m. this evening. Hot food in containers for these two Coys. to be delivered to Battn. Ration Dump, E 5 c 4.0, at 10.30 p.m.

9. PATROLS. Battalion Scouts will report to 2/Lt. BLACKWELL at Battn HQ. at 7 p.m., & will relieve patrol scouts of 2nd R.F. as soon as W & X Coys. have got into their new positions. Patrols will remain out till dawn, when they will be relieved by Coy. patrols.

10. RELIEF COMPLETE. Completion of relief by 1st Lancs Fus. will be

4

reported by Code-word "GRASS".
   Completion of relief of 2nd R.F. will be reported by O.C. Coys name & hour of relief.

11. <u>ACKNOWLEDGE</u>

Robt Maguire
Capt. & Adjutant,
1st R. Dublin Fusiliers.

DISTRIBUTION.

1. 86th. Inf. Bde.
2. O.C. W. Coy.
3. "   X "
4. "   Y "
5. "   Z "
6. Transport Offr & QrMr.
7. 2nd Royal Fusiliers.
8. 2/Lt. BLACKWELL.
9. R.S.M.
10. War Diary.
11.   -do-
12. File.

SECRET.   Copy No. 8
To the R. Dublin Fusiliers.

Operation Order No. 8.
                          23rd Aug, 1918

1. Z. Coy., 1st RDF, will relieve Y Coy. in STRAZEELE STATION DEFENCES today, 23rd inst., at a time to be arranged between O's.C. Coys. concerned.

2. O.C. Z. Coy. will leave a detachment to hand over to a Coy. of 1st Lancs. Fus. in "Z" LINE. Time to be notified later.

3. O.C. Y Coy., on relief by Z Coy., will move to positions as follows:—
   1 platoon LESAGE FM, F 13 b central.
   1 platoon F 8 c 1.4.
   The other 2 platoons in depth at LYNDE FM, F 13 a 7.5 and F 7 c 8.8.

4. Time should be arranged so that the whole move may be completed before dark.

5. The move forward must be in small parties, moving at different times.

6. A representative of Coys. concerned will call at Battn. H.Q. before 4.0 p.m.

                                    R H Mayin
                                    Capt. & Adjutant,
                                    1st R Dublin Fusiliers.
Copies to:—
1. 86th Infy. Bde.   6. Transport Off.   8 & 9. War Diary
2-5. O's. C. Coys.   7. Quartermaster.   10. File.

SECRET   Copy No. 7
1st Bn. R. Dublin Fusiliers.

Operation Order No 9
                          24th Aug, 1918.

1. There will be an inter-Coy relief tonight, 24th August. Y Coy will relieve W Coy & Z Coy will relieve X Coy. On relief W & X Coys will take up positions occupied by their relieving Coys.

2. Details of relief to be arranged between O's C Coys concerned.

3. Y Coy will side forward to relieve the advance platoon of W Coy in daylight if suitable movement forward possible.

4. Z Coy will side forward to relieve the advance platoon of X Coy in daylight if movement possible. Sgt forward in one all parties at different times to obtain practice.

5. Battn Scouts under 2/Lt Rockwell to take up covering positions until relief of both front Coys is complete.

6. RATIONS. 1 Officer & 25 O.R. will take ration party up to Y Coy. This party will be found from platoon of W Coy relieved

2

Early Party to be at dump by 7.30 pm.
W Coy will also arrange to draw
their own rations.

The relieved pl—toon of X Coy
under an Officer will carry rations for Z Coy.

X Coy's rations will be dumped
under C.Q.M. Sgt. till available carriers
have been relieved by Z Coy.

7. Trench Stores to be handed over and
receipts given. These to reach H.Q. by
morning returns.

8. Attention of O.C. Coys is again called to
the necessity of rendering returns to time.
It is also pointed out that unless food
containers and the like are returned
nightly it will be impossible to keep the supply
of hot food & water up to present quantity.

9. ACKNOWLEDGE.

Robt Maguire
Capt. & Adjutant,
1/8th R. D. Fusiliers.

Copies to:—
1. 86th Inf. Bde.   6. Quartermaster
2-5. O.C. Coys.   7/8 War Diary.
            9. File

SECRET.   Copy No 8

1st Bn R. Dublin Fusiliers.

Operation Order No 10.
                                    27th Aug. 1918.

1. INTENTION. The 1st Lancs. Fus. will relieve the
1st R. Dublin Fus. in present Front Line Bn. Ctn.
Area tonight, 27/28th Aug.

2. ADVANCE PARTIES. Advance parties from 1st
Lancs. Fus. will report in course of the afternoon.

3. DETAIL OF RELIEF.
    A Coy, 1st L.F. will relieve Z Coy, 1st R.D.F. Right Front.
    C "   "   "   "   "   Y "   "   "   Left Front.
    B "   "   "   "   "   W "   "   "   Support
    D "   "   "   "   "   X "   "   "   Reserve.

4. GUIDES. 1 Guide for Coy H.Q. & 1 per platoon to
rendezvous at STRAZEELE STATION, under Lt. BLACKWELL at:
        X Coy.   7.20 pm.
        W, Y, Z Coys. 8.0 pm.
Guides to have shits stating party to be guided

5. STORES. All maps, aeroplane photos, work policy,
Intelligence, Trench Stores, etc. will be handed over.
Receipts (in duplicate) to reach these H.Q. by 8. a.m. 28th

6. RELIEF COMPLETE. Completion of relief to
be notified by O.C. Coys, name & time of relief

2

7. DISTRIBUTION ON RELIEF. On relief, Coys of the
1/R.D.F. will move to Support Battn. Area.
    Battn HQ   E 4 c 5.2.
    W Coy to 'Z' LINE from E 4 b 5.0 to E 5 b 30.75.
    X Coy to RESERVE LINE in W 27 c and E 3 a.
    Y Coy to SWITCH TRENCH from W 27 b 5.6 to W 28 c 8.7
    Z Coy to 'Z' LINE from Southern boundary to E 4 b 5.0.

8. ADVANCE PARTIES & GUIDES. Advance parties of
2/Lt FISHER & N.C.O. from H.Q., & 1 Officer, N.C.O. & 4 O.R.
per Coy, will proceed to take over in course of the afternoon.
    These parties will act as guides to their Coys on
relief. They will meet Coys at STRAZEELE STATION.

9. STORES ETC. Stores etc to be taken over and copy
of receipts to reach these H.Q. by 8 a.m. tomorrow.

10. TRANSPORT ARRANGEMENTS. Limbers will be at
STRAZEELE STATION at 11 pm to take back empty
Food Containers, Water Tins, Camp Kettles, etc.
Lewis gun limbers will not be required. Cookers
will be brought up for all Coys. An Officer from
Rear HQ will reconnoitre positions for them and for
Ration Dump, and will inform Transport Officer
of their locations. Water in tins to be brought up
for all Coys & HQ. Rations to be delivered
~~to Ration Dumps~~ to Coy H.Q. or vicinity

11. RATIONS. Q.M. will arrange for a hot meal

being ready for Coys on relief. Rations to be
delivered daily to Coy. Ration Dumps.

12. MEDICAL ARRANGEMENTS. Sick Parade will
be at 10.0 a.m. daily.

13. RELIEF COMPLETE. Coys will notify HQ on
arrival at new positions.

14. REPORTS. Daily Reports required while in Support.
 SHELLING: 7.30 am
 GAS. 10.0 am
 WORK. 10.0 am

15. GENERAL. O.C. Coys will ensure that all empty
tins & Food Containers are taken to Battn.
Dump tonight and handed over to Guard.

16. ACKNOWLEDGE.

                       Capt & Adjutant
                       1st R. Dublin Fusiliers.

DISTRIBUTION.

1. 86th Infy Bde.   7. 1st Lancs Fus.
2-5. Bn. C. Coys.   8 & 9. War Diary
6. Transport Officer & QM.   10. File

SECRET   Copy No. 1

16th Bn R Dublin Fusiliers.
Minor Operation Order No. 1.
                                          29th Aug. 1918.
(Map Ref: Sheet 36A N.E.)

1. INTENTION   The enemy is reported
occupying posts in the vicinity of DESPOT
FARM in strength.

2. INTENTION   It is intended to raid
DESPOT FARM & buildings, with the object
of securing an identity, & destroying the enemy.

3. METHOD OF ATTACK   Two platoons of
y Coy. will proceed as follows:-
One platoon via DROUANA in a North of
direction East of the DESPOT FARM – TROIS
TILLEULS Road to a position of readiness
South of DESPOT FARM, and be in position
at ZERO minus 5.

One platoon will leave the line at about
the THREE FARMS and will proceed to a
position of readiness West of DESPOT
FARM, to be in position by ZERO minus 5.

At ZERO a box barrage of 18 pdrs.
will be put down on the line F.15.b.5.8
– F.16.a.0.9, and the line F.16.a.0.9 –
F.16.a.3.4.

This barrage will remain till ZERO

plus 5. It will then lift 100 yards till ZERO plus 10.

At ZERO a bombardment of 4.5" Howitzers will engage the farm buildings and the road and hedgerows from F15 b 8.0 to F 16 a 0.5.

The bombardment will stop at ZERO plus 1½ when it will engage buildings and main road through TROIS TILLEULS.

At ZERO plus 1½ the Southern platoon will rush the road and farm buildings at F 15 b 8.3 and F 16 a 00.35.

At ZERO plus 1½ the Western platoon will attack the hedgerow about point F 15 b 65.40 and building at F 15 b 85.50.

Each platoon will send a rifle section or more of men ready to mop up the farm buildings and surroundings.

The whole raiding party will return to our lines via the THREE FARMS by ZERO plus 10. The Officers will be the last to leave the Farm.

4 DRESS Men will be as light as possible. Rifle, bayonet, 50 rounds in bandolier & one bomb per man. Bombs only to be used for clearing cellars or buildings. No papers or identification will be

carried by the party.

5. **REPORTING STATION.** A reporting station will be established at the level crossing, STRAZEELE STATION. Every Officer, N.C.O. & man will report to Lt. BLACKWELL on returning.

All Officers & N.C.Os will report to 2/Lt FISHER at Batt. H.Q. on returning.

6. **PRISONERS ETC.** Details of methods of policing & conduct of prisoners will be given verbally.

7. **SYNCHRONISATION.** Watches will be synchronised according to verbal instructions.

8. O.C. Raiding Party — 2/Lt CASSIDY, M.C.

9. **ZERO HOUR** will be at 4.45 a.m. Aug 29/18.

C. Fisher
2/Lt
a/Adjt 15th R.D.F.

Copies to:-
1. 86th Inf. Bde.
2. 64th Bde. RFA
3. 1st Lancs Fus.
4. 2nd Royal Fus.
5. O.C. Y Coy.
6 & 7 War Diary
8. File.

Strength 15.8.18: 42 Offrs. 904 O/Ranks

Officers

Increase
- Lt. J.G. DeB Danne — Joined 15.8.18
- 2Lt. A. Scott — Joined 17.8.18
- Lt. M. Layton — Joined 26.8.18
- " C.J. O'Carroll — Joined 26.8.18
- 2Lt. E.E.H. Hawkey — Joined 26.8.18

Total: 5

Decrease
- 2Lt. J.E. Johnston — To M.G.C. Grantham 17.8.18
- Capt. E.J. Alexander M.C. DCM — Wounded (Gas) 24.8.18
- 2Lt. P.H. Lennon — Wounded 29.8.18

Total: 3

O/Ranks

Increase
- From Base 139

Total: 139

Decrease
- To I.M.B. — 1
- Evac. — 38
- S.o.S. — 6
- Wounded — 17
- Killed — 4
- Wounded (Gas) — 12

Total: 71

Strength 31.8.18, 44 Offrs, 972 O/Ranks

1st Royal Dublin
Fusiliers

September 1918.

WAR DIARY
of
1st Bn Royal Dublin Fus
for month of
SEPTEMBER 1918.
Volume 42.

1st Royal Dublin Fusiliers

Army Form C. 2118.

WAR DIARY
or
INTELLIGENCE SUMMARY.
(Erase heading not required.)

Instructions regarding War Diaries and Intelligence Summaries are contained in F. S. Regs., Part II. and the Staff Manual respectively. Title pages will be prepared in manuscript.

Place	Date	Hour	Summary of Events and Information SEPTEMBER 1918	Remarks and references to Appendices
Man Station STRAZEELE	1.		Quiet day without further incident. Details not available before Leave Parks at Thenzoor Hines.	
(JORBERT CROSSING) OUTTERSTEENE	2.		Batt. move to OUTTERSTEENE area vide operation order No 11 attached. Transport hived from H.Q. move forward to CURFEW H.Q. Sheet 36A. E.2. d.7.6. General retirement of enemy in this front. 87.T.88. Relieved in the line & take over.	
LA CRECHE	3.		Batt. move to LA CRECHE with 1st line Transport and an outpost 3/4 mile moves up into position for attack on PLOEGSTEERT VILLAGE vide Operation order No 12 attached. During fwd forward 2 Coys suffer casualties from enemy gas shelling of avenues of approaches by enemy. Forward Transport lives at LA CRECHE.	
PLOEGSTEERT			approaches by enemy. Forward Transport lives (2nd line). Then H.Q.S located at OUTTERSTEENE.	
PLOEGSTEERT	4.		Assault by the Batt. of PLOEGSTEERT village. Carried through with the greatest dash & gallantry. Severe casualties suffered from machine Gun fire when in rear of "Peaceful Penetration" garrison laid down an Jumping off tapes. VIDE "APPENDIX A" attached. Casualties 1 officer. HEUT. M.3. M. NULTY killed; 2/Lt. S. OWENS Missing; 4/Lt. T. M. DARBY (R. Irish Regt attached) Wounded, also 2/Lt. F. A Looney Wounded, 2 3.OR's killed, 89 ORs wounded, 14 Missing.	
	5.		Batt. relieved in the early morning by 2nd Royal Irish being to some extent in the Flanders X by (under command 1 Sport. C. H. NOBLETT) was not relieved - on completion of relief Batt move to BAILLEUL & be accommodated in Tents & Bivouacs heavily marched beside what was the old SWINDON CAMP.	

D. D. & L., London, E.C.
(A10266) Wt W5300/P713 750,000 2/15 Sch. 82 Forms/C2118/16

Army Form C. 2118.

1st Royal Dublin Fusiliers

WAR DIARY
or
INTELLIGENCE SUMMARY.
(Erase heading not required.)

Instructions regarding War Diaries and Intelligence Summaries are contained in F. S. Regs., Part II. and the Staff Manual respectively. Title pages will be prepared in manuscript.

SEPTEMBER 1918 -

Place	Date	Hour	Summary of Events and Information	Remarks and references to Appendices
BAILLEUL	6th		Inspections of Billets etc. At night area of camps shelled by H.V. guns. 2 O.R's killed, 1 O.R. wounded. Very disturbed night for all ranks.	
	7th		Camp moved about 700 yards in a southerly direction so as to avoid further shelling. Weather very bad, heavy rain, rifle unsuitable for pitching a Camp.	
	8th	9 & 10	Weather continues very bad, mud and water deep everywhere. A.O. in Coy. Weather & inspections where in progress.	
HAZEBROUCK	11th		Battn. moves by March Route to HAZEBROUCK. The Army Commander General SIR HERBERT C.O. PLUMER G.C.B. G.C.M.G. G.C.V.O. A.D.C. takes the Salute of the Brigade (86th Infantry) as it marches through STAZEELE. Officers have accommodation in Elementat houses in the Town, most of which have been damaged by shell fire. Weather still fine.	
"	12th		Cleaning up & inspections. Zoy boys change then Billets, am being carried out, Kirmp the men at first allotted to them, thought not the right spirit. Training - Lecture at 2 p.m. by G.O.C. Bde to officers Subject "operations"	
"	13th		TANKS with Infantry. Day fine but threatening rain.	
"	14th		Training Baths. Showery day.	
"	15th		Fine day. Church Service for all Denominations -	

Army Form C. 2118.

1st Royal Dublin Fusiliers

WAR DIARY
or
INTELLIGENCE SUMMARY.
(Erase heading not required.)

Instructions regarding War Diaries and Intelligence Summaries are contained in F. S. Regs., Part II. and the Staff Manual respectively. Title pages will be prepared in manuscript.

Place	Date	Hour	Summary of Events and Information September 1918	Remarks and references to Appendices
HAZEBROUCK	16.9.17		Training: Individual Training - Company in Attack. Theatres. Day fine	
"	18.		"Battalion in Attack" practice in morning - In afternoon Battalion Bomb competition. Very good sport & keen fighting.	
"	19th		Batt. moved by Train & Transport by Rayne to POPERINGHE area. [A 20.C started 8] spare from XV to II corps. New camp very comfortable. Batt arrived 1.30 a.m., 20th inst - weather fine though over cast. Wide of junction over No.13 about]	
BRAKE Camp A.30.C Sheet 28.	20th		Showery day. Batt engaged in cleaning up camp. Conference re Training. Coys for instruction under Company commanders. Batt win most fights.	
"	21st		Showery day. 9 am: Lewis Gun competition in afternoon. Staff Ride for Officers M.C.Os. Impromptu Brigade Bomb Competition. Platoon commanders attended to	
"	22nd		Church Service for all Denominations - but instructed at Bde. H.Q. true winds - attended Conference - Company at 7 p.m. finishing area Comdy Officer & Company Coys leader day ice-munkey - Enemy planes over town	
"	23rd		Showery day - Promote forward area. Enemy planes in the neighbourhood. Commanding Reconnoitre forward area. Some Bombs dropped in area in angles.	
"	24th		Fine day.	
"	25		Fine day - Commanding Officer lectures to all Ranks on "Battalion in attack". Divisional Commander inspected DE.CAYLEY C.M.G. visits Battalion.	

Army Form C. 2118.

WAR DIARY
or
INTELLIGENCE SUMMARY.
(Erase heading not required.)

1st Royal Dublin Fusiliers Summary of Events and Information For Month of SEPTEMBER 1918

Place	Date	Hour	Summary of Events and Information	Remarks and references to Appendices
BRAKE CAMP	26th		Battalion in rear of pending operations practise Attack. Enemy drops some shells in vicinity of camp.	
	27th		Commdg Officer holds conference with Coy leaders at 10.30 A.m. Batt. move as per Operation order No 15 to forward zone for ATTACK. Kild 265th Inf. Administrative Operation order No 14 - General Instructions dated 23rd inst. all attached. Rear Party H.Qrs details move to instruction dated 23rd inst. all attached. Major W.T. Rigg (2nd in comd) in orders from Bde takes command of Bde Pack Train - Heavy bombardment on whole front. Transport lines. Major W.T. Rigg (2nd in comd) in orders from Bde takes Weather fine though unsettled.	
	28th		Attack opened at 5.30 a.m. - Most successful. Dry but - Rain during night. Battalion not great deal Carry all objectives allotted to us.	
	29th		Rear Batt. H.Qrs move to SHRAPNEL CROSSING near the Asylum at YPRES. Rain continues intermittently during day & night. Attack continued - Still raining. Ground on which we fought advanced rendered very difficult owing to the deep mud.	
	30th		Attack continued - Still raining. Ground on which we fought advanced rendered very difficult owing to the deep mud. Casualties at present known 1st Lt. W. BLACKWELL Battalion Intelligence Officer and 4/Lt. J. NOLAN M.C. D.C.M. died of wounds. No 9364 C.S.M. P. DELANEY D.C.M, M.M. (W. Coy) KILLED, Capt. G.H. NOBLETT M.C. & 2/Lt. D.P. WAGNER. M.C. Wounded.	

Army Form C. 2118.

1st Royal Dublin Fusiliers

WAR DIARY
or
INTELLIGENCE SUMMARY.
(Erase heading not required.)

Instructions regarding War Diaries and Intelligence Summaries are contained in F.S. Regs., Part II. and the Staff Manual respectively. Title pages will be prepared in manuscript.

Place	Date	Hour	Summary of Events and Information	Remarks and references to Appendices
	For Month of September 1918 —			

Owing to the continuation of Active Operations - "Narrative of these operations up to end of this month has not been written, but will be attached to October WAR DIARY —

ATTACHED to this Month

Operation orders No 11 — 15.

Administrative Instructions for operations commencing 28th Sept 18
       "   "   do.

General Intentions " " do.

C. M. Berts-J Hahn. Capt:
Commanding 1st Bn. The Royal Dublin Fusiliers

On Strength   Strength 31/8/18. 44 Offrs 872 O/Rs.   Off Strength

| Officers | O/Ranks | | Officers | O/Ranks |

Lieut D.J. Wagner M.C.   From Hospl 3   2Lt R.H. Burns   Evacuated 7
  Joined 1.9.18   " Base   8   To Base Depot 1.9.18   Killed in A. 26
  " H. Blake   " Gdr H.W. Smiers   Wounded   90
    Joined 1.9.18   To England 3.9.18   Missing   17
  " G. Lord   Lt A.J. McNulty
    Joined 5.9.18   Killed in Action 4.9.18 To Base   1
  2Lt C.J.F. Coveney   " J. Owens
    Joined 5.9.18   Missing
                                                       2Lt T.H. Deeley
                                                       Wounded
                                                       " T.A. Cooney
                                                       Wounded

                Strength 7/9/18. 42 Offrs 842 O/Rs.

Capt J.F.J. Carroll   From Base 150   Lt Col J.A. Weldon   Evacuated 11
Lieut R.E. Light   " Hospl   10   To Base (B.O. Ohs) 8.9.18 To F.M.B. 7
2Lt T.A.H. Chadwick   " t.S. Ball 1
  " R.A. Semmens
  " W.A. Stewart
  " H.N. Hamilton
    Joined 10.9.18
Capt K. Ryan   Strength 14/9/18. 48 Offrs 983 O/Rs.
    Joined 13.9.18

Appendix A

1st BN. ROYAL DUBLIN FUSILIERS.

REPORT ON MINOR OPERATION CARRIED OUT ON 4/5th SEPTEMBER, 1918.

The Battalion was at LA CRECHE on 3rd September, when orders were received at 5.0 p.m. to move to ROMARIN CAMP to take part in an attack, in conjunction with other Units, on the Divisional Front between HILL 63 and PLOEGSTEERT, inclusive, the Battalion's main objective being the capture of PLOEGSTEERT village.

At LA CRECHE, on 3rd September, 1918, orders were received to attack as above. Battalion was ordered to move to the place of assembly at 6.15 p.m. (ROMARIN CAMP).

At 6.0 p.m. the Battalion Commander and his four Company Commanders reconnoitred the position of assembly in the forward area as thoroughly as possible. The hour of starting the Battalion was postponed, to allow of this reconnaisance, to 7.15 p.m. For purposes of concealment the hour of marching off was postponed to 9.15 p.m.

Battalion was in position at ROMARIN CAMP at 11.15 p.m., sustaining seven casualties from shell fire on the march.

Brigade orders required the Battalion to be in position at the jumping-off line (T 30 c 7.0 running North to T 30 a 30.99) at 6.0 a.m., 4th September. The Battalion therefore took up a position in the old trenches at ROMARIN CAMP at 11.15 p.m., as follows:-

    Two Companies in front, i.e. "W" Company on right, with left flank resting on main PLOEGSTEERT ROAD, in touch with "X" Company on left, with right flank on road.
    One Company in Support, "Y" Company, in a position on NEUVE EGLISE ROAD, South of PLOEGSTEERT ROAD, to act as supports and right flank guard.
    One Company in reserve, "Z" Company, on NEUVE EGLISE ROAD, North of PLOEGSTEERT ROAD.
    Battalion Headquarters at B 4 a 7.3.
    1st Lancs. Fusiliers on left flank, and 31st Division on right flank.

At 3.0 a.m., 4th September, "W" and "X" Companies moved forward, closely supported by "Y" Company. The attack progressed with difficulty to T 29 c 7.3, finding very strong opposition en route. Some casualties occurred, and it was apparent from personal reconnaisance that the ground to the front was strongly held, and thick with enemy Machine Guns. At about 4.0 a.m., having received further casualties, the task of reaching the jumping-off point by 6.0 a.m. appeared to be impracticable without Artillery assistance.

The situation was reported, and it was suggested that a barrage be put down to assist, but this could not be done, and the Battalion was ordered to proceed on its original instructions.

The Battalion therefore, with great difficulty and a great number of casualties, advanced to a line T 30 c 4.0 - T 29 b 60.99 by 9.0 a.m., when it was again reported that the enemy was too strong for further advance and our casualties very heavy.

The 1st Lancashire Fusiliers were reported to have reached their starting-point, and to be advancing under a barrage.

Prior to this a bombardment was ordered on PLOEGSTEERT from 8.0 a.m. to 8.30 a.m., and a further effort was made by the 1st Royal Dublin Fusiliers without material advantage, the barrage on the village having little effect on the immediate front and right flank.

(Contd.)

Minor Operation Report (2)

The O.C., 1st Royal Dublin Fusiliers, then ordered his Battalion to remain in their positions until Artillery assistance could be obtained.

A conference with the Brigadier resulted in orders being issued for the Battalion to again attack, under a creeping barrage, at 3.0 p.m., barrage to come down and rest for 5 minutes on big farm in T 30 c., then lift 100 yards every 3 minutes to PLOEGSTEERT, to remain on PLOEGSTEERT village for 15 minutes and then lift.

At 10.0 a.m. on the 4th. "W" and "Y" Companies had been amalgamated owing to heavy casualties, "Z" Company was held in readiness to move forward in Support, and "Y" Company, 2nd Royal Fusiliers, to move up to Reserve.

At 3.0 p.m. the attack commenced, and was carried out with complete success, and at this time the Battalion was in touch with the 31st Division on the right.

The troops of the 31st Division did not advance with the 1st Royal Dublin Fusiliers, with the exception of a small party on the extreme left flank of the 31st Division (1st Royal Dublin Fusiliers were in touch with this party at final objective).

At 3.0 p.m. the 1st Lancashire Fusiliers were in touch with our left flank, but apparently were unable to advance with us.

All objectives were taken by 4.10 p.m., and a line established at about the narrow guage railway running North and South through U 25 b & d.

Between 3.0 p.m. and the taking of the final objective the Battalion suffered only 17 casualties. The bulk of the total casualties were caused prior to 3.0 p.m.

OUR ARTILLERY.
Our Artillery barrage was exceptionally good, and has been praised by all ranks.

ENEMY ARTILLERY.
Enemy Artillery of all calibres was very heavy. Many air-bursting and other T.Ms. Gas shells were freely used.

ENEMY MACHINE GUNS.
Very heavy Machine Gun fire from front, and later from both flanks, when flank troops were unable to advance.

ENEMY CASUALTIES.
1st Royal Dublin Fusiliers captured about 170 prisoners, including 6 Officers; about 20 of these were killed.

Number of enemy killed during the advance estimated at 100 (very rough calculation).

Enemy wounded unknown.

Some Machine Gunners taken prisoners were wearing Red Cross brassards.

ENEMY AIRCRAFT.
Three low-flying aeroplanes bombed our advancing troops in the early morning of the 4th September.

(Contd.)

Minor Operation Report. (3)

CAPTURES.

Four Field Guns (two vouched for), all located in PLOEGSTEERT VILLAGE.

Seven Trench Mortars were actually seen, but there must be many more.

Many Machine Guns were captured.

ENEMY'S PRESENT POSITION.

Between 100 to 200 yards in front of our line, and on both flanks.

Guns and Transport were clearly heard retiring during the night; light railway also working.

Much commotion and talking took place in enemy's front line during the night.

OUR POSITION.

As shown on disposition map sent Brigade last night. It is enfiladed from both flanks by Machine Gun and T.M. fire.

CLEARING WOUNDED.

The clearing of casualties was admirably carried out by the 89th Field Ambulance.

(sd) Athelstan MOORE,
Lieut.Colonel,
Commanding 1st Royal Dublin Fusiliers.

5th September, 1918.

SECRET   Copy No.

            1st Bn R. Dublin Fusiliers.
               Operation Order No 12
                                    4th Septr, 1918.

1. The Battn will attack PLOEGSTEERT this
afternoon the 4th inst as follows:-
   X Coy on Left of Road with Right resting on Road.
Y & W Coys amalgamated, on Right of Road, with
Left resting on Road.
   Z Coy in Support on either side of Road.
   1 Coy Royal Fus. in Reserve at Battn HQ
2. The attack will be made under a creeping
barrage which will start on FARM in
T.30.c. remain for 5 minutes, move
100 yards in heat [?] minutes after, and
rest on PLOEGSTEERT for 15 minutes.

3. ZERO HOUR will be 3 o'clock today, 4th inst.
4. The Brigade on our Right is attacking
under barrage at the same hour.
5. Report situation immediately objective
is taken.
6. ACKNOWLEDGE
                                   H.J. Holmes

                                   Capt. & Act. Adjutant
Issued at 1.35 pm   1st Bn R. Dublin Fusiliers.

1st BN. ROYAL DUBLIN FUSILIERS.

REPORT ON MINOR OPERATION CARRIED OUT ON 4/5th
SEPTEMBER, 1918.

The Battalion was at LA CRECHE on 3rd September, when orders were received at 5.0 p.m. to move to ROMARIN CAMP to take part in an attack, in conjunction with other Units, on the Divisional Front between HILL 63 and PLOEGSTEERT, inclusive, the Battalion's main objective being the capture of PLOEGSTEERT village.

At LA CRECHE, on 3rd September, 1918, orders were received to attack as above. Battalion was ordered to move to the place of assembly at 5.15 p.m. (ROMARIN CAMP).

At 6.0 p.m. the Battalion Commander and his four Company Commanders reconnoitred the position of assembly in the forward area as thoroughly as possible. The hour of starting the Battalion was postponed, to allow of this reconnaissance, to 7.15 p.m. For purposes of concealment the hour of marching off was postponed to 9.15 p.m.

Battalion was in position at ROMARIN CAMP at 11.15 p.m., sustaining seven casualties from shell fire on the march.

Brigade orders required the Battalion to be in position at the jumping-off line (T 30 c 7.0 running North to T 30 a 30.99) at 3.0 a.m., 4th September. The Battalion therefore took up a position in the old trenches at ROMARIN CAMP at 11.15 p.m., as follows:-

    Two Companies in front, i.e. "W" Company on right,
        with left flank resting on main PLOEGSTEERT ROAD,
        in touch with "X" Company on left, with right
        flank on road.
    One Company in Support, "Y" Company, in a position
        on NEUVE EGLISE ROAD, South of PLOEGSTEERT ROAD,
        to act as supports and right flank guard.
    One Company in reserve, "Z" Company, on NEUVE
        EGLISE ROAD, North of PLOEGSTEERT ROAD.
    Battalion Headquarters at B 4 a 7.3.
    1st Lancs. Fusiliers on left flank, and 31st Division
        on right flank.

At 3.0 a.m., 4th September, "W" and "X" Companies moved forward, closely supported by "Y" Company. The attack progressed with difficulty to T 29 c 7.3, finding very strong opposition en route. Some casualties occurred, and it was apparent from personal reconnaissance that the ground to the front was strongly held, and thick with enemy machine guns. At about 4.0 a.m., having received further casualties, the task of reaching the jumping-off point by 5.0 a.m. appeared to be impracticable without artillery assistance.

The situation was reported, and it was suggested that a barrage be put down to assist, but this could not be done, and the Battalion was ordered to proceed on its original instructions.

The Battalion therefore, with great difficulty and a great number of casualties, advanced to a line T 30 c 4.0 - T 29 d 30.3 by 9.0 a.m., when it was again reported that the enemy was too strong for further advance and our casualties very heavy.

The 1st Lancashire Fusiliers were reported to have reached their starting-point, and to be advancing under a barrage.

Prior to this a bombardment was ordered on PLOEGSTEERT from 8.0 a.m. to 8.30 a.m., and a further effort was made by the 1st Royal Dublin Fusiliers without material advantage, the barrage on the village having little effect on the immediate front and right flank.

(Contd.)

Minor Operation Report (2)

The O.C., 1st Royal Dublin Fusiliers, then ordered his Battalion to remain in their positions until Artillery assistance could be obtained.

A conference with the Brigadier resulted in orders being issued for the Battalion to again attack, under a creeping barrage, at 3.0 p.m., barrage to come down and rest for 5 minutes on big farm in T 30 c., then lift 100 yards every 3 minutes to PLOEGSTEERT, to remain on PLOEGSTEERT village for 15 minutes and then lift.

At 12.0 p.m. on the 4th, "W" and "Y" Companies had been amalgamated owing to heavy casualties, "Z" Company was held in readiness to move forward in Support, and "Y" Company, 2nd Royal Fusiliers, to move up to Reserve.

At 3.0 p.m. the attack commenced, and was carried out with complete success, and at this time the Battalion was in touch with the 31st Division on the right.

The troops of the 31st Division did not advance with the 1st Royal Dublin Fusiliers, with the exception of a small party on the extreme left flank of the 31st Division (1st Royal Dublin Fusiliers were in touch with this party at final objective).

At 3.0 p.m. the 1st Lancashire Fusiliers were in touch with our left flank, but apparently were unable to advance with us.

All objectives were taken by 4.10 p.m., and a line established at about the narrow gauge railway running North and South through U 25 b & d.

Between 3.0 p.m. and the taking of the final objective the Battalion suffered only 17 casualties. The bulk of the total casualties were caused prior to 3.0 p.m.

OUR ARTILLERY.
Our Artillery barrage was exceptionally good, and has been praised by all ranks.

ENEMY ARTILLERY.
Enemy Artillery of all calibres was very heavy. Many air-bursting and other T.MM. Gas shells were freely used.

ENEMY MACHINE GUNS.
Very heavy Machine Gun fire from front, and later from both flanks, when flank troops were unable to advance.

ENEMY CASUALTIES.
1st Royal Dublin Fusiliers captured about 170 prisoners, including 6 Officers; about 20 of these were killed.

Number of enemy killed during the advance estimated at 100 (very rough calculation).

Enemy wounded unknown.

Some Machine Gunners taken prisoners were wearing Red Cross brassards.

ENEMY AIRCRAFT.
Three low-flying aeroplanes bombed our advancing troops in the early morning of the 4th September.

(Contd.)

Minor Operation Report. (3)

CAPTURES.

Four Field Guns (two vouched for), all located in PLOEGSTEERT VILLAGE.

Seven Trench Mortars were actually seen, but there must be many more.

Many Machine Guns were captured.

ENEMY'S PRESENT POSITION.

Between 100 to 200 yards in front of our line, and on both flanks.

Guns and Transport were clearly heard retiring during the night; light railway also working.

Much commotion and talking took place in enemy's front line during the night.

OUR POSITION.

As shown on disposition map sent Brigade last night. It is enfiladed from both flanks by Machine Gun and T.M. fire.

CLEARING WOUNDED.

The clearing of casualties was admirably carried out by the 89th Field Ambulance.

(sd) Athelstan MOORE,
Lieut.Colonel,
Commanding 1st Royal Dublin Fusiliers.

5th September, 1918.

SECRET.   Copy No.____

1st Bn. ROYAL DUBLIN FUSILIERS.

OPERATION ORDER NO. 14.

(Ref. Sheet: 27 and 28.)   19.8.1918.

1. **INTENTION.**
   The Battalion will move to the XXX II Corps Area tonight.

2. **ADVANCED PARTIES.**
   The undermentioned, as Advance Party, will report to Capt. DALTRY at 2.0 p.m. today:-

   Headquarters: Sgt. O'BYRNE and 1 Runner.
   Each Coy: 1 Junior N.C.O. and 1 Man.

   Party will proceed by lorry, and report to Staff Captain at XXX XX Camp, A.30.c (Sheet 26) at 4.0 p.m.

3. **STARTING POINT & TIME.**
   The head of the Battalion will pass Cross-roads, V.22.c.2.7 (Just N.W. of Q.M.Stores) at 6.30 p.m.

4. **ORDER OF MARCH.**
   Battn. Headquarters (to include Drums).
   "E" Coy.
   "Y" Coy.
   "X" Coy.
   "W" Coy.

5. **ROUTE.**
   The Battn. will march to HOUDESHEM station, V.2.d.9.0, entrain there, and detrain at POPERINGHE, whence advanced party will guide to billets.

6. **REAR PARTY.**
   The following rear party to clean up and hand over billets will report to 2/Lieut. HOARE at Orderly Room at 4.0 p.m., and subsequently proceed by train at 6.47:-
   Headquarters: Pioneer Sgt. & 1 Pioneer.
   Each Coy: 1 Junior N.C.O. and 1 man.

7. **TRANSPORT.**

   (a) All stores for loading on Transport will be dumped at Q.M. Stores by 5.0 p.m.
   (b) The S.D. Wagon set free by carrying Officers' kits on advanced lorry will be used for:
         Spare Signal Cable.
         Surplus Orderly Room Material.
         Surplus Q.M. Stores.
   (c) Field Kitchens and Mess Cart will report to Transport Officer at 6.30 p.m.
   (d) Transport will move Brigaded. Head of Transport will pass Cross-roads, V.22.c.2.7, in rear of 1/Lancs. Fus. Transport at 8.5 p.m. Distance of 100 yards between Battalion Transports, and 20 yards between every 6 vehicles will be maintained.
   (e) Following personnel will accompany Transport:-
         Transport men and Grooms.
         Sergt. Cook and 5 Battn. Cooks.
         1 Shoemaker and 1 Tailor.
         Water Cart man.
         Headquarters Mess Personnel.

                                                (Contd.)

OPERATION ORDER NO. 15. (Contd.)

7. RATION.

   (a) Tea will be issued today at 5.0 a.m.
   (b) Rations for consumption on the 20th will proceed on Supply wagons with Regimental Transport. These wagons will rejoin B.H.Q. on the 20th.
   (c) Water bottles will be filled by 5.0 a.m.

8. DRESS.

   Full Marching Order.
   Soft caps to be worn.
   Steel helmets to be carried strapped on pack.

10. ACKNOWLEDGE.

                        Major & A/Adjutant,
                        1st Bn.Royal Dublin Fusiliers.

Copies to:-

   O.C. "A" Coy.
   " "B" "
   " "C" "
   " "D" "
   Quartermaster.
   Transport Officer.
   Lewis Gun Officer.
   Signals.
   6th Infy. Brigade.
   Padre.
   R.A.P.
   War Diary.

SECRET

H.Q. 29TH DIVISION INFANTRY BRIGADE
No 5/65
22/9/18

ADMINISTRATIVE INSTRUCTION NO. 13

1. **AMMUNITION.**

    (a) Brigade Dumps are to be formed forthwith. Demands for all requirements being wired to Division "Q" giving location at which it is required that the ammunition should be delivered. The Dumps must be situated in a position close to tramway and accessible from a road by pack animals (if not limber)

    (b) The tramways in operation are those leading through MENIN GATE and up MENIN ROAD and a branch leading south of the SCHOOL and rejoining the MENIN ROAD Tramway south of WHITE CHATEAU at I.10.c.3.4.

    (c) A Divisional Dump will be formed but this will only be a reserve dump and will only be drawn upon should normal means of supply fail E.G., tramway and wheeled or pack transport.

    (d) Location of Dumps are as follows :-

          88th Inf. Bde.- Vicinity of I.9.d.4.5. or I.10.c.3.4.
          87th Inf. Bde.- Vicinity of I.15.b.4.2.
          Divisional Reserve - Vicinity of tramway crossing (I.9.d.2.0.

    (e) The above dumps are to be filled as soon as possible. All stores should be scattered and in buildings if possible and not stored together where visible from the air or ground, as the enemy has observation on the localities of the dumps. No movement must take place by day ~~whatever~~.

2. **SUPPLIES.**

    Rations to be carried on the men will be one complete day (preserved) and one iron ration. The rations for consumption second day will have to be delivered by normal method on pack on first night together with ammunition requirements etc. and water.

3. **WATER**

    (a) 3,000 extra water bottles will be available at D.A.D.O.S. on 22nd instant and can be drawn on demand up to the numbers as below if so desired :-

        Each Brigade(800)   2400
        C.R.E.   100
        1/2 Mon. Regt.   100
        29th Bn. M.G.C.   300
        A.D.M.S.   100

    These will be required to be handed back after they have been finished with.

    (b) Petrol tins as required may be drawn on application to Div. Hd-Qrs. "Q" in addition to those held on charge. Not more than will be sufficient to allow of sufficient to be sent up to the troops with same number in process of filling at transport line should be drawn, i.e., double the number required in one journey to supply the front troops. Great care must be taken that every full tin delivered an empty one is returned.

    P.T.O.

- 2 -

4. Pack transport lines should be moved forward under orders of Brigade Staff and O.C., Formations, as soon as situation permits, to as near as possible to the dumps so that the animals will have as short a journey as possible to perform. Division "Q" must be kept informed of the locations of these pack lines by Rear Hd-Qrs of each formation.

5. C.R.E. is arranging to construct pack tracks forward to follow the advance, maps of which are being issued separately by G.S.

6. Each Brigade must arrange with O.C., Signal Coy. for Rear Brigade Headquarters to be connected by telephone with Division "Q" (Rear Headquarters) at BRAKE CAMP.

7. Section K.E. personnel of each Infantry Brigade will be accommodated in BRAKE CAMP from "Z" day inclusive. The numbers to be accommodated under this heading are to be notified to Division "Q" by Brigades as early as possible so as to allot accommodation. 86th Inf. Bde. will close up into accommodation now occupied in BRAKE CAMP.
88th Inf. Bde. will report at BRAKE CAMP at 9.0 a.m. on "Z" day.
Accommodation will be allotted by Division "Q".
87 Bde. will be brought up from Rec. Camp under Divn. arrangements

8. A.D.M.S. will issue separate instructions regarding Medical Arrangements.

9. Prisoners of War Cage is at WINDWARD HOUSE, H.4.d.2.5. where prisoners will be taken over by Divisional Escort. Should the advance proceed so far as to prohibit distance for marching of escort, arrangements will be made to take them over further forward.

21st September, 1918.

Lieut-Colonel.
A.A. & Q.M.G., 29th Division.

H.Q.
88th INFANTRY BRIGADE
No. 90/90
25/9/18

K731

O.R.E. 29th Div. No. 45/1711/1.

Reference this office 45/1711 dated 19th September, on and after 22nd September, all R.E. stores will be sent forward via ORILLIA DUMP, 28/H.1.b.8.3., where a small reserve will be kept, and <u>not</u> at CULLODEN as before.

M Cook
Lieut. R.E.
for O.R.E. 29th Division.

22/9/18.

To all recipients of 45/1711.

SECRET

86th INFANTRY BRIGADE ADMINISTRATIVE ORDER NO. 42.

Reference 86th Infantry Brigade Instructions No.1.

22nd September 1918.

1. **AMMUNITION.**
Brigade Dump will be formed at I.9.d.5.5.
All demands to be made on Staff Captain.
All stores to be drawn by night.

2. **TRAMWAYS.**
The tramways in operation are those leading through MENIN GATE and up MENIN ROAD and a branch leading south of the SCHOOL and rejoining the MENIN ROAD Tramway south of WHITE CHATEAU at I.10.c.3.4.

3. **SUPPLIES.**
Rations to be carried on the men will be one complete day (preserved) and one iron ration. The rations for consumption second day will have to be delivered by normal method on pack on first night together with ammunition requirements etc and water.

4. **WATER.**
Battalions have now been made up to 200 petrol tins each.

Great care must be taken that for every full tin delivered an empty one is returned.
Water will be delivered with rations by pack animal. There is a reserve supply of 200 tins at Brigade Dump and these will only be drawn upon, should normal means of supply fail. For location of Water Tanks see this Office No. 5/64 of 20-9-18, (39th Div. Administrative Instruction No. 11 dated 19-9-18).

5. Commanding Officers will arrange for the issue of hot tea for the men in the Assembly Positions on morning of "Z" Day. Arrangements are being made for an issue of rum in Assembly Positions.

6. **PACK TRANSPORT.**
Pack Transport Lines will be moved forward under orders from this Office, as the situation permits.

7. **R.E. MATERIAL.**
R.E. Material can be drawn from Brigade Forward Dump. Indents to be submitted to Staff Captain.

8. **TRACKS.**
The C.R.E. is arranging to construct Pack Tracks to follow the advance, maps of which are being issued separately.

9. **REAR HEADQUARTERS.**
Rear Headquarters of Brigade and Battalions, and personnel to be left out under Section XXX, will be accommodated in BRAKE CAMP, from "Z" Day inclusive.

--- 2 ---

10. MEDICAL ARRANGEMENTS.
    Will be issued later.

11. PRISONERS OF WAR.
    Prisoners of War Cage is at WINDWARD HOUSE - H.4.d.2.0. where prisoners will be taken over by Divisional escort.   Should the advance proceed so far as to prohibit distance for marching of escort, arrangements will be made to take them over further forward.

12.   ACKNOWLEDGE.

        Issued at 5-30 p.m.

                                            Captain,
                                        for Staff Captain,
                                    86th Infantry Brigade.

        Copies to:-
            1 - 3 Staff.
            4 2/Royal Fusiliers.
            5 1/Lancs.Fusiliers.
            6 1/R.Dublin Fusiliers.
            7 86th T.M.Battery.
            8 29th Division "G".
            9 29th Division "Q".
            10 87th Inf. Brigade.
            11 Diary.
            12 File.

SECRET.   Copy No 8

1st Bn R Dublin Fusiliers

Operation Order No 11

2nd Septr, 1918.

1. INTENTION. The Battn will move into the OUTTERSTEENE Area today.

2. RECONNAISSANCE B & C Coys will reconnoitre areas allotted to them last night.

3. ADVANCE PARTIES 2/Lt HOLMES and advance parties of 1 NCO & 6 OR per Coy. to report to Battn HQ at 10.30 am for orders re drawing of tents & bivouacs. B & C Coys will show NCOs i/c advance parties where Coys & bivouacs are to be dumped. Advance parties will be at F 9 a 1.5.

4. HOUR OF MOVE
   W Coy will move at 1.30 pm
   X "   "   "   " 1.35 pm
   Y "   "   "   " 1.35 pm
   Z "   "   "   " 1.40 pm
   Bn HQ "   "   "   " 1.45 pm

   300 yards distance to be kept between Coys.

5. ROUTE: W 30 c 5.0 – Cross Roads in Fia – MERRIS – F 8 c 25.10 to positions.

6. TRANSPORT ARRANGEMENTS. Officers' chargers 9.0 a.m. Limbers will bring up Coys' packs, returning to Transport for another load & reporting to Coys again at 7 pm.

7. MOVE COMPLETE will be notified to Battn. H.Q.

8. BATTN. H.Q. will close at 1.45 pm & open at F 9 a 9.9 on arrival.

9. ACKNOWLEDGE

C. Inglis
2/Lt & a/Adjutant,
1st Bn R. Dublin Fus.

Copies to :-

1. 86th Inf Brigade
2–5. Os. C. Coys
6. Transport Officer & Q.Mr.
7. 2/Lt HOLMES
8 & 9. WAR DIARY
10. FILE

SECRET   Copy No..6...

86th INFANTRY BRIGADE ADMINISTRATIVE ORDER No. 41

Issued with 86th Inf.Bde Order 265.   22nd September 1918.
Ref.map sheet 28 N.W.4.
    1/10,000.

1. **ENTRAINING ARRANGEMENTS.**

    Brigade Headquarters, 2 Coys and Headquarters of 1/Lancs. Fusiliers will entrain at 8 p.m. tonight at HAGLE TRIANGLE (G.6.a.) detraining at ST PIERRE (I.14.a.). Troops to be at entraining point at 7-30 p.m.
    The remaining two Coys 1/Lancs.Fusiliers will entrain on 23rd instant at an hour to be notified later.

    Brigade Headquarters will open on arrival at I.14.b.1.8.
                                            (RAMPARTS)

2. **RATIONS.**

    For 23rd will be taken on train this evening under Battalion arrangements. Rations for 24th will go forward by train carrying remaining two Coys of 1/Lancs.Fusiliers tomorrow evening under Battalion arrangements.

3. **UNLOADING PARTY.**

    O.C. 2/Royal Fusiliers will detail 1 Officer and 30 other ranks to report to Staff Captain at I.8.central (MENIN GATE) at 9 p.m. tonight.

4. **DUMP GUARDS.**

    O.C. 2/Royal Fusiliers will detail 1 N.C.O. and 3 men to report to Staff Captain at I.8.central at 9 p.m. tonight for duty as Dump Guard. They will be rationed for 23rd and arrangements will be made by Unit for subsequent rationing.

5. **TRANSPORT LINES AND Q.M.STORES.**

    Will remain at present locations until further orders.

6.   A C K N O W L E D G E.

        Issued at 2 p.m.
                                                    Captain,
                                            for Staff Captain,
                                             86th Inf. Brigade.

    Copies to:-
            All Recipients of 86th Inf.
            Brigade Order No. 265.

SECRET 1/Roy Dublin Fus.

A.D.M.S., 29th Division No.SA.11/194.

**HEADQUARTERS
86th
INFANTRY BRIGADE
No. 42/176
Date 28/9/18**

**A.D.M.S.,
29th DIVISION.
No. ....
Date ....**

To Regimental Medical Officers.

(Through Os.C.Units.)

---

1. The following Medical Arrangements are forwarded for your information and guidance.

2. DISPOSITIONS.

REGIMENTAL AID POSTS.	St.JACQUES - 28/I.8.d.1.5. St.PIERRE - 28/I.14.b.2.8.
ADVANCED DRESSING STATION.	PRISON, YPRES, -28/I.7.b.2.2.
CORPS WALKING WOUNDED STATION.	TAVISTOCK HOUSE -28/H.1.b.7.1.
EMBUSSING POINT FOR WALKING WOUNDED.	28/I.7.c.6.7.
MAIN DRESSING STATION. and GAS CENTRE.	HOP FACTORY, - 28/H.8.a.6.9.
DIVISIONAL REST STATION.	BOWLBY CAMP - 27/E.6.d.central.
CASUALTY CLEARING STATIONS.	No.3 Aust.C.C.S. No.36 C.C.S.

It is proposed to form the following posts which will be established as soon as the Military situation permits:-

CAR LOADING POSTS.	I.17.a.9.7. and I.17.c.4.4.
BEARER RELAY POSTS.	(I.18.a.4.5. (J.13.a.1.5.(Eastern edge of large crater.) (I.23.b.6.8. (Yeomanry Post) (I.24.b.2.4. (Cross Roads.) (J.13.d.6.9. (Clapham Junction)

3. It is suggested that Regimental Stretcher Bearers should carry 24 Stretchers instead of 15. This would enable more stretcher cases to be carried back by "persons" returning to back areas.

Extra stretchers, blankets etc. can be obtained from the MAIN DRESSING STATION,(HOP FACTORY,H.8.a.6.9.), the ADVANCED DRESSING STATION (PRISON,YPRES,I.7.b.2.2.),or, during operations, at Forward Advanced Dressing Station when established at WHITE CHATEAU,I.10.c.1.4.

Should Regimental Medical Officers consider it necessary, on account of the rapidity of moving forward, to leave wounded, after being dressed, on the ground where they were wounded, the Rifle of the soldier should be stuck in the ground with a piece of bandage tied on to the butt-end, so as to mark the location of the casualty.

After the wounded soldier is removed the rifle will be placed on the ground by the bearers removing the casualty.

Every effort should be made,however, to place wounded on stretchers and cover them with one or two blankets and dump them at one of the proposed Bearer Relay Posts, where they will be looked for and evacuated in the normal way.

23rd September 1918.

Colonel,
A.D.M.S.,29th Division.

S E C R E T.　　　　　　　　　　　　　　　　　　　　　　Copy No. _____
　　　　　　　1st BN. ROYAL DUBLIN FUSILIERS.

　　　　　　　ADMINISTRATIVE INSTRUCTIONS.

　　　　　　　　　　　　　　　　　　　　　23rd September, 1918.

(Reference Sheets 28 N.W.4,
　　　　　　　　28 N.E.3.)

1. AMMUNITION.

　　(a)　Brigade Dump is being formed at I.O.d.5.5. (Sheet
　　　　 N.W.4). Stores will be drawn at night. R.E. material
　　　　 is also available here.
　　(b)　Each Rifleman will carry 150 rounds.
　　　　 Each Rifle Grenadier will carry 75 rounds.
　　(c)　No hand Mills Bombs will be carried.
　　(d)　The scale of Rifle Grenades will be 5 per Grenadier.

2. SUPPLIES.

　　(a)　Every man will carry 1 complete preserved ration and
　　　　 1 Iron Ration.
　　　　 Rations for "Z" and 1 day will be delivered on "Z"
　　　　 night by Pack Transport.
　　(b)　Water bottles will be filled previous to moving to
　　　　 assembly position, and will on no account be touched till
　　　　 after ZERO hour. Water is certain to be a difficulty,
　　　　 and this order is to be enforced under any circumstances.
　　(c)　Hot tea and rum will be issued on arrival in assembly
　　　　 position.
　　(d)　The subsequent supply of water will be by petrol tins.
　　　　 These are scarce, and must not be lost. The Q.M. will
　　　　 only give full petrol tins in exchange for empty ones
　　　　 after the first issue. Units who lose petrol tins will
　　　　 go short of water.

3. TRANSPORT.

　　(a)　The Battalion Pack Train (32 animals) is under the
　　　　 command of Lieut. HAWTREY, who will be assisted by the
　　　　 Transport Sergt. This Pack Train will deliver nightly
　　　　 rations, ammunition, etc. The location of its lines
　　　　 will be moved forward under orders of Brigade Headquarters.
　　(b)　The remainder of the Transport will remain under the
　　　　 orders of the Transport Officer.
　　(c)　Two tramways for forward supplies exist. One runs
　　　　 through MENIN GATE and down MENIN ROAD, the other through
　　　　 MENIN GATE branching South of ECOLE and rejoining MENIN
　　　　 ROAD at the WHITE HOUSE.
　　(d)　C.R.E. will construct and mark Pack tracks in rear of
　　　　 Advance. Maps will be issued shewing these when available.

4. BATTLE STORES.

　　　　 The distribution of YUKON PACKS and normal Battle Stores
　　will be laid down in Operation Orders.

5. PRISONERS OF WAR.

　　(a)　Each Coy. will detail a Section to be prepared to
　　　　 escort prisoners.
　　(b)　Prisoners of War Cage is at WINDWARD HOUSE, H.2.d.2.0.
　　　　 (Sheet N.W.4)

　　　　　　　　　　　　　(Contd.)

ADMINISTRATIVE INSTRUCTIONS. (2)

6. REAR ORGANIZATION.

   (a) Personnel left out will remain at BRAKE CAMP under command of Lieut. TIGHE.
   (b) Rear Headquarters and Q.M. Stores will remain at BRAKE CAMP until ordered to move by Rear Brigade Headquarters.
   (c) Spare kits, equipment, and stores must be clearly labelled by Coys. and Platoons. Each C.Q.M.S. will arrange to take a complete inventory, duplicate of which will be handed to Q.M. Should the Q.M. Stores be moved, only those articles shewn on the inventory will be taken forward and accounted for.
   Each Coy. will be given a hut in which to store articles, which will be in charge of Coy. Storeman.

                                        Major & A/Adjutant.

Copies to:-

   1. O.C. "W" Coy.
   2. "   "X" "
   3. "   "Y" "
   4. "   "Z" "
   5. Quartermaster.
   6. Transport Officer.
   7. Assistant Adjutant.
   8. Lieut. HAWTREY.
   9. Lieut. TIGHE.
   10. File.

SECRET

Copy No...6...

86th INFANTRY BRIGADE OPERATION INSTRUCTIONS No. 3.

Ref. Special Operation Map "B" 1/10,000.   24th September 1918.

1. 86th Infantry Brigade Instructions Nos 1 & 2 are cancelled and the following substituted:-

2. On a date and at a Zero hour to be notified later, the 29th Division will attack the enemy in conjunction with the 9th Division on the Left and the 35th Division on the Right. The day on which the attack is to be made will be known as "Z" Day and the day previous to the attack as "Y" Day.

3. The 29th Division will attack on a two Brigade frontage - 87th Inf. Brigade on the Right and 86th Inf. Brigade on the Left. Boundaries and objectives are shown on Map "B" which has been issued to Units.

4. The 86th and 87th Inf. Brigades will attack under an intense Field Artillery Barrage up to the BLACK LINE, which will be the Final Field Artillery Line. Details of this barrage will be issued separately. The attack will then be pushed forward to the GREEN LINE supported by the Corps Heavy Artillery. Upon the capture of these objectives, the 88th Inf. Brigade will advance through the 86th and 87th Inf. Brigades and continue the attack, with the view of eventually establishing a line on the high ground at GHELUVELT and KRUISEECKE.
   It is essential, however, that the high ground, GLENCORSE WOOD - STIRLING CASTLE, be captured, and if necessary, the whole strength of the Division will be employed to do this.

5. The Infantry Plan of Attack will be as follows:-

(a) The 1st Lancs.Fusiliers, and the 2nd S.W.B. of the 87th Inf. Brigade will attack up to the RED LINE.

(b) The 1st R.Dublin Fusiliers and the 1st Border Regt (87th Inf. Brigade) will pass through this line and attack up to the BLACK LINE (being supported if necessary) by the 2nd Royal Fusiliers and the 1/K.O.S.B. (87th Inf. Brigade), and will make good the ground up to the GREEN LINE.

6. At Zero:-

(a) The 1st Lancs.Fusiliers will attack and capture the RED LINE.

(b) The 1st Royal Dublin Fusiliers will move forward close behind the 1st Lancs.Fusiliers. After crossing the BLUE LINE, they will keep 500 yards behind the 1st Lancs.Fusiliers, and passing through them on the RED LINE, will attack the BLACK and GREEN LINES.

(c) When the 1/R.Dublin Fusiliers have passed through the RED LINE, the Left Support Company of the 1st Lancs.Fusiliers will come under orders of C.O., 1/R.Dublin Fusiliers and will follow in rear of the Left Support Coy of the 1st R.Dublin Fusiliers, forming a flanking party for protection of Left Flank. This Coy. of the 1st Lancs.Fusiliers may be used to assist in taking the GREEN LINE.

(d) If hostile resistance is easily over-come, the 2nd Royal Fusiliers will be used to exploit the success and capture POLDERHOEK SPUR and CAMERON HOUSE co-operating with the 1/K.O.S.B. on Right who will capture TOWER HAMLETS and VELDHOEK.

/7.

--- 2 ---

7. For the purpose of this operation, "A" Coy, 29th Bn M.G.Corps, will be attached to 86th Inf. Brigade and will be disposed as follows

    1 Section with 1st Lancs.Fusiliers.
    2 Sections with 1st R.Dublin Fusiliers.
    1 Section with 2/Royal Fusiliers.

Only two guns per section will go forward with Battalions. The remaining guns will follow on pack mules.

Machine Guns should follow in rear of Flank Support Coys of attacking Battalions.

Date on which Machine Gunners will report to Battalions will be notified later.

8. 86th T.M.Battery will be disposed as follows:-

1st Lancs.Fusiliers and 1st R.Dublin Fusiliers will each have two trench mortars with double teams, carrying 20 shells per mortar.

Date on which these mortars will report to Battalions will be notified later.

9. Instructions as to:-

    (a) Approach March.
    (b) Assembly.
    (c) Artillery.
    (d) Communications.
    (e) Contact Aeroplanes.

will be issued later.

10. A C K N O W L E D G E.

Issued at _____

                        Captain,
                        Brigade Major,
                        86th Infantry Brigade.

Copies to:-

1 - 3. Staff.
4. 2/Royal Fusiliers.
5. 1/Lancs.Fusiliers.
6. 1/R.Dublin Fusiliers.
7. 86th T.M.Battery.
8. 'A' Coy. 29th Bn. M.G.Corps.
9. 87th Inf. Brigade.
10. 9th Division "G".
11. 29th Division "G".
12. 88th Inf. Brigade.
13. No. 7 Squadron R.A.F.
14. 29th Div. Artillery.
15. Diary.
16. File.

S E C R E T
****
Copy No. 6

86th INFANTRY BRIGADE OPERATION INSTRUCTIONS No. 4.

24th September 1918.

Reference 86th Infantry Brigade Operation Instructions No. 3 dated 24th September 1918.

1. The attached trace "A" shows:-

    Tracks to be opened up for pack transport.

2. The attached trace "B" shows:-

    The extension of boundaries and objectives on 29th Division Front.

3. A C K N O W L E D G E.

G. Cudden
Captain,
Brigade Major,
86th Inf. Brigade.

Copies to:-
1 - 3 Staff.
4 2/Royal Fusiliers.
5 1/Lancs. Fusiliers.
6 1/R. Dublin Fusiliers.
7 86th T.M. Battery.
8 "A" Co. 29th Bn. M.G. Corps.
9 Diary.
10 File.

SECRET   Copy No. 6

86th INFANTRY BRIGADE OPERATION INSTRUCTIONS No. 5.

24th Sept 1918.

COMMUNICATIONS

1. **Telephone and Telegraph.**

   Two lines are being allotted by Division on the buried route from I.14.b.1.9. to I.16.a.5.8. which point will be the Brigade Forward Exchange. From this point, a Cable laying party will follow the H.Q. 1/Lancs.Fus., laying as they advance. The 1/Lancs.Fus. will instal a 4 plus 3 Buzzer Board upon reaching their objective and put the line to Brigade on their Exchange. The Cable laying party will then attach themselves to the 1st Royal Dublin Fusiliers and will lay a line from the 1/Lancs.Fus H.Q. to the 1/R.Dublin Fus. H.Q. upon reaching their objective the 1/R.Dub.Fus will place this line on their Buzzer Board. The Cable laying party will then attach themselves to the H.Q. 2/Royal Fus. and lay from 1/R.Dub.Fus H.Q. to 2/Royal Fus. H.Q. If possible, a second line will be laid from the Brigade Exchange, I.16.a.5.8. to the 1/R.Dub.Fus. H.Q.

2. **Visual.**

   The main Divisional Visual Station will be established at I.16.b.5.8. Visual Stations will also be established at:-
   - (a) I.16.b.0.4.
   - (b) J.7.c.6.8.
   - (c) J.14.c.1.7.

3. **Wireless.**

   One Trench Set will be allotted to Brigade for working back to Division. A Loop Set will be disposed as follows:-
   The Rear portion will move with the H.Q. 1/Lancs.Fus. The forward portion will move with the H.Q. 1/R.Dub.Fus. and work back to Rear Portion with the 1/Lancs.Fus. who should transmit to Brigade any messages received by the Loop Set. The 2/Royal Fus. on passing through will pick up the forward portion of the Loop Set and take it on with them.

4. **Pigeons.**

   20 pairs with assault baskets containing message forms are allotted to Brigade and will be disposed of as follows:-
   6 pairs to 1/Lancs.Fus., 7 pairs to 1/R.Dub.Fus., & 7 pairs to 2/Royal Fus.

5. **Message Dogs.**

   Three message dogs are allotted to 1/R.Dub.Fus. and two to 2/Royal Fus.

6. **Runners.**

   One platoon (less one section) Yorks Cyclist Regt will be attached to 86th Inf. Bde and will be used on the Runner route, manning Relay Posts which will be established at (a) HOOGE about I.18.b.1.6. (b) CLAPHAM JUNCTION J.13.b.5.0. (c) GLENCORSE WOOD about J.14.b.0.8.
   N.B. Before Zero hour <u>only</u> Fullerphones will be used. <u>No speaking</u> is allowed, and no wireless sets will be used.

7. ACKNOWLEDGE.

   Issued at _____

                                                  Captain,
                                                  Brigade Major,
                                                  86th Inf. Brigade.

Copies to:-

   All Recipients of 86th Inf. Bde Operation Instructions No. 3.

S E C R E T. Copy. No. 6

90TH INFANTRY BRIGADE OPERATION INSTRUCTION NO. 6.

September 24th, 1918.

1. CONTACT AEROPLANES FOR MARKING POSITIONS OF INFANTRY.

(a) The attacking troops will carry RED FLARES, American Cloth on Box Respirators, and Vigilant periscopes for the purpose of signalling to Contact Aeroplanes.
(b) These, and every other means of signalling their position, will be used by the attacking troops at :-

Zero plus 2 hours 15 minutes.
and at
Zero plus 4 hours.
and at such other times as called for by the contact aeroplane.
(c) Contact aeroplanes will call for Signals from the attacking troops by sounding the Klaxon Horn and dropping WHITE Lights.

(d) Contact aeroplanes will be marked with two BLACK RECTANGULAR FLAGS (2 foot by 1 foot 3 inches) attached to and projecting from the lower plane on each side of the fusilage. Each contact plane will also have a TRAILING STREAMER.
All troops will be warned how to recognise contact aeroplanes.

2. COUNTER ATTACK AEROPLANE

A counter attack aeroplane will be in the air on II Corps Front from Zero plus one hour onwards for the purpose of giving warning of an impending hostile attack.
On perceiving hostile Infantry moving to the Attack the counter attack aeroplane will call for annihilating artillery fire by wireless and will also signal the fact that a hostile attack is impending by dropping a RED SMOKE PARACHUTE VERY LIGHT.

3. DROPPING OF AMMUNITION FROM AEROPLANES.

(a) Arrangements have been made with the R.A.F. to drop ammunition from aeroplanes, if required.
(b) Two kinds of ammunition will be dropped :-
(a) bundle packed S.A.A.
(b) M.G. Ammunition packed in belts (4 belts per box).
The ammunition prepared for dropping will be in the proportion of two of bundle packed ammunition to one of M.G. Ammunition in belts.
(c) Infantry will signal that ammunition is wanted as follows:-

 = Machine Gun Post requiring M.G. Ammunition.

 = Bundle packed ammunition required.

Each signal will be made up of strips of white cloth 12ft. by 1ft. and in each case attention will be called to the signal by the firing of a WHITE FLARE from the ground. Two strips per Battalion and one per Machine Gun Coy. will be carried. The Brigade Signalling Officer will make arrangements for supplying them.

/ d. The aeroplanes.

(d) The aeroplanes will be ready to drop ammunition from ZERO plus two hours onwards and will continue to do so as long as the ground signals are displayed.

Once the signals are removed no more ammunition will be sent by aeroplanes unless a report is received from a contact machine that more is required.

(e) It is probable that each ammunition dropping aeroplane will be able to drop about two boxes of ammunition per hour and possibly at the outside three machines can be made available for the purpose on the Divisional Front.

It will not be practicable with these aeroplanes to continue dropping ammunition for a longer period than about 4 hours and during the day it is calculated that the maximum number of boxes which can be dropped will be 9 boxes of M.G. Ammunition and 16 boxes of bundle packed ammunition.

(f) It is of very great importance, therefore, that ammunition should not be called for except when really required. Platoon and Company Commanders will make every effort to collect enemy rifles, machine guns and ammunition and bring them into use against the enemy.

(g) As many parachutes as practicable must be recovered and returned to Division.

4. ACKNOWLEDGE.

Issued at _____

P. Cudolon.
Captain,
Brigade Major,
86th Infantry Brigade.

Copies to:-

All recipients of 86th Inf. Bde.
Operation Instructions No. 3.

SECRET.   Copy No. 6

88TH INFANTRY BRIGADE ADMINISTRATIVE ORDER NO. 44.

                                           Sept. 26th, 1918.

1. PACK TRANSPORT TRAIN.

   With reference to 29th Div. Administrative Order No. 14 dated 26th instant, (issued under 88th Inf. Brigade No. A/66 of 26th instant), para 2 (b), each Unit should draw 8 shelters from the Area Commandant, DIATI BUCKET, forthwith; Copies of taking over receipts being forwarded to this office.

2. MEDICAL ARRANGEMENTS.

   (a) Stretcher Bearers. (Reference 29th Div. Administrative Order dated 25th Sept, para 5).
       O.C., 1/Royal Dublin Fusiliers, will detail the N.C.O. and 46 men earmarked under this office No. 40/149 dated 23rd instant to report at the PRISON, YPRES, at 6.0 p.m. on "Y" day.

   (b) Dispositions.

       Regimental Aid Posts.   { St.JACQUES - 28/I.8.d.1.5.
                                          { St.PIERRE - 28/I.14.b.2.8.

       Advanced Dressing Station.   - Prison, YPRES - 28/I.7.b.2.2.

       Corps Walking Wounded Station.   - TAVISTOCK HOUSE -
                                            28/H.8.b.7.1.

       Embussing Point for Walking   - 28/I.7.c.6.7.
         Wounded.

       Main Dressing Station and   - HOP FACTORY - 28/H.8.a.6.9.
         Gas Centre.

       Divisional Rest Station.   - DOWLEY CAMP -
                                            27/E.6.d.central.

       Casualty Clearing Stations.   - No. 3. Aust. C.C.S.
                                            No. 36. C.C.S.

   (c) O.C., 88/Field Ambulance, will arrange to establish a Forward Advanced Dressing Station at WHITE CHATEAU, (28/I.10.c.1.4.), when conditions permit. The following posts will also be established, as soon as the Military situation allows:-

       Car Loading Posts.   - I.17.a.9.7. and I.17.c.4.4.

                                          { I.18.a.4.6.
                                          { J.13.a.1.3. (Eastern edge
                                          {   of large crater.
       Bearer Relay Posts.   { I.23.b.6.8. (Yeomanry Post).
                                          { I.24.b.2.4. (Cross Roads).
                                          { J.13.d.6.9. (Clapham
                                          {   Junction).

   (d) O.C., 88/Field Ambulance, will arrange to form a Forward Dump of Stretchers, Blankets, Splints &c. at the SCHOOL, I.9.c.5.8. Also wheeled Stretcher Carriers which will be pushed forward in the hope of finding suitable roads on which to work them.

                                           / 3. Blankets.

-2-

3. BLANKETS AND P.OKS.

Further particulars will be issued later as to the storage of these.

4. RATIONS.

Arrangements are being made by these Headquarters for the issue on "Y" day of Rum, Solidified Alcohol, and sterilizing tablets.

5. ACKNOWLEDGE.

C. Brockington Brown.
Captain,
Staff Captain,
86th Infantry Brigade.

Issued at _____

Copies to:-

1 - 3 Staff.
    7 2/Royal Fusiliers.
    5 1/Lancs.Fusiliers.
    6 1/R.Dublin Fusiliers.
    7 86th T..Battery.
    8 "A" Coy. 29th In..G.Corps.
    9 88th Inf. Brigade.
10 87th Inf. Brigade.
11 29th Division "A".
12 Diary.
13 File.

SECRET   29th DIVISION

ADMINISTRATIVE INSTRUCTION NO. 14 29/9/16

1. (a) Troops will be carrying "Z" days rations and an iron ration on them. Rations for consumption "Z"+1 day and succeeding days will be delivered by Divisional Train to Quartermaster's Stores in rear transport lines on day before consumption as follows :-

    86th Inf. Bde.   in Brake Camp Area (as at present)
    87th Inf. Bde.   Folly Camp G.3.d.7.4. Standings G.4.c.1.1.
    88th Inf. Bde.   28/A.21.a.6.4. (as at present)
    29th Bn. M.G.C.   ORILLIA Camp H.2.a.6.9.
    455th Fd. Co. R.E. 27/H.2.d.7.3. (as at present)
    497th Fd. Co. R.E. 27/A.29.d.7.3.   -do-
    510th Fd. Co. R.E. 27/A.29.c.5.5.
    1/2 Bn. Mon. Regt. 27/A.30.c.9.7.

    (b) On arrival of train wagons, the rations will be sorted and arranged as required by Units' Quartermasters as expeditiously as possible.
    The Train Wagons will wait, and as many as are required will convey the rations to the Unit Pack lines.
    Units will be responsible that there is a man at their Transport Lines who can guide the train wagons to the Pack lines.

    (c) After delivering rations to the transport lines it will be impossible for the Div. Train to accept any further responsibility for delivery except as regards use of G.S. wagon. The above mentioned guide must load the wagons correctly and by roads passable for wheeled. It is up to Battalions to see to this.

    (d) Water will be sent up in petrol tins under Brigade and formation arrangements. Sufficient extra tins have been allotted to admit of normal supply to all forward troops. It must be thoroughly understood that petrol tins must be strictly conserved.

    (e) Machine Gun Companies will be administered as regards supplies ammunition and transport by their own battalion. It is however suggested that the supply pack transport should move and be grouped with the Brigade pack train to which affiliated, to facilitate communication. Fighting portion of pack has to move according to course of operations.

2. **PACK TRANSPORT TRAIN.**

    (a) The Pack Transport Train of Brigades and Units will be moved under the orders of the Brigades or Units concerned, but it is of the utmost importance that Division "Q" should be informed at once of the location of the Pack Transport Lines, and advised of all movements.
    It is suggested that they should be moved to vicinity of Brigade Dumps as soon as situation permits and until this is feasible, to locality in squares H.11 and 12.

    (b) The following shelters will be issued for the use of Pack Train personnel.
    These shelters will be drawn from the Area Commandant, Dir Bucket (sheet 27/A.30.c.9.9.) any time after 24th instant, and taken on charge of Units.
    They will be carried forward on the pack animals, and moved whenever and where ever the Pack Train may go.

P.T.O.

2.(b) (cont).

    Scale of issue

        each Brigade Pack Train   24 shelters
        M.G. Battalion   24 "
        each Field Company   8 "
        each Field Ambulance   3 "
        1/2 Bn. Monmouth Regt.   8 "

3. **PROVOST ARRANGEMENTS.**

    Straggler Posts and P. of W. Cages will be sited as follows:-

(a)   First phase
        28/H. 3.b.3.5.
        28/H. 3.d.2.3.
        28/H. 9.a.8.7.

        Straggler Collecting Station - WINDWARD HOUSE
                                       28/H. 4.d.2.8.

        Right Straggler Post - Division on Left - 28/B.27.e.9.3.
        Left   "   "   -   "   " Right -28/H. 9.a.7.6.

        Divisional P. of W. Cage - 28/H.4.d.2.8.
        Corps   P. of W. Cage - 28/H. 1.c.7.1.

(b)   Second phase.
        Straggler Posts
            28/I. 7.c.4.7.
            28/I.13.a.7.4.
            28/I.13.c.5.9.

        Straggler collecting Post - The BARRACKS, YPRES -
                                    28/I.7.d.9.8.

        Divisional P. of W. Cage -   -do-   -do-

(c)   Change from First to Second phase will be notified.

(d)   Personnel for Straggler Posts and Prisoners of War Cage will be provided by 87th Inf. Bde. and report to WINDWARD HOUSE 28/H.4.d.2.8. on "Y" Day not later than 5.0 p.m. and bring rations with them for consumption 2 days. They must be provided from numbers "surplus to 900" Col. A Strength or Section XXX. Total required for above purpose 6 N.C.Os, 24 men.

4. **REAR HEADQUARTERS.**

    Rear Headquarters will be located as follows :-

        ✕ 86th Inf. Bde.   BRAKE CAMP   A.30.c.7.1.
        ✕ 87th Inf. Bde.   do   do
        ✕ 88th Inf. Bde.   do   do
        29th Bn. M.G.C.   ORILLIA Camp H. 2.a.7.9.
        1/2 Bn. Mon. Rgt.   FOSTER Camp   H. 1.c.5.9.

✕ Accommodation will be allotted by Division "A".
/ Rear Brigade Headquarters will move into BRAKE CAMP on night Y/Z.

STRETCHER BEARERS.

    Extra stretcher bearers will report for duty under A.D.M.S. as follows on "Y" Day at the PRISON, YPRES, and will bring rations for consumption 2 day with them and all their kit.

                                                      /cont.

5. STRETCHER BEARERS (cont).

   86th Inf. Bde.   3 N.C.Os. 45 men
   87th Inf. Bde.   1 N.C.O. 15 men
   88th Inf. Bde. 1 Off, 4 N.C.Os. 60 men
   Div. Emp. Coy. and
   Band.   5 N.C.Os. and 80 men

  The above personnel provided by Brigades to be taken from those "surplus to 900" Col. A Strength and Section XXX.

6. BLANKETS AND PACKS.

(a) 86th Inf. Bde. will store their blankets, great-coats and packs in huts to be allotted by Staff Captain 86th Inf. Bde in BRAKE CAMP.

(b) 87th Inf. Bde. will store their packs, great-coats and blankets under guards in the billets or camps occupied by them on "Y" day.

(c) 88th Inf. Bde. will store their blankets, great-coats and packs in   their present transport lines before moving into assembly position.

(d) M.G. Battalion will store their packs, blankets and great-coats in ORILLIA CAMP into which camp the three forward companies will be moving on X/Y night to double up with a battalion of 88th Inf. Bde. The Rear Headquarters and remaining company will be moving into ORILLIA Camp on Y/Z night into accommodation vacated by the three forward companies.

7. RATIONS.

(a) Rations are to be delivered early on "Y" day for consumption "Z" day, sufficient hard rations being issued to allow all troops going into action to carry one hard ration for consumption "Z" day in addition to his iron ration.

  Sufficient hard rations must also be made available for issue on "Z" day for consumption Z+1 day as required by Units. Brigades and Formations must inform their respective supply officers of their requirements in hard rations as early as possible so as to avoid delay when "Z" day is definitely settled.

(b) A full issue of rum will be made to all R.A., R.E. Infantry M.G.C. and 1/2 Monmouth Regt. early on "Y" day for consumption Y/Z night.

(c) O.C., Divisional Train must arrange to make as large an issue of solidified alcohol as possible to each Infantry Brigade and M.G. Battalion on "Y" day for use on "Z" day and on "Z" day for use on Z+1 day.

(d) Sterilizing tablets for water bottles will be issued on demand to O.C. Divisional Train Companies who should arrange to procure a plentiful supply to meet demands.

VETERINARY.

  M.V.S. will be established at G.5.a.5.4.

               Lieut-Colonel
24th September, 1918   A.A. & Q.M.G., 29th Division

S E C R E T.

1st BN. ROYAL DUBLIN FUSILIERS.

GENERAL INSTRUCTIONS.

1. TRACKS.

Tracks for Pack Transport will be opened up as follows:-

(a) MENIN ROAD - I.18.a.9.6.- I.18.b.2.8.- I.18.b.5.7.- I.18.b.8.6.- J.13.a.0.9.- JARGON cross roads - S.E. to J.14.a.4.6.- through GLENCORSE WOOD - along BLACK WATCH TRACK.

(b) I.17.c.00.35.- I.17.c.5.2.- I.17.c.9.1.- thence along tramway to I.24.a.6.6.- thence N.E. along SANCTUARY TRACK.

11. SIGNAL COMMUNICATIONS.

1. TELEPHONES.

   (a) "Y" and "Z" Coys. will be provided with telephones and cable, and "X" Coy. also if supply permits for communication with Battn. Headquarters.

   (b) Brigade cable laying party will be picked up from Headquarters, Lancs. Fusiliers, as the Battn. passes RED Line to lay line from BUZZER BOARD, 1st Lancs. Fusiliers, to BUZZER BOARD, 1st Royal Dublin Fusiliers.

2. VISUAL STATIONS.

   There will be Visual Stations at:-

I.16.b.0.4.	Brigade.
J.7.c.6.8.	"
J.14.c.1.7.	"
About J.14.b.2.4.	Battalion.

3. WIRELESS.

   A forward Loop Set will accompany Battn. HdQrs. for transmission to Rear Portion with 1st Lancs. Fusiliers.

4. PIGEONS.

   1 pair each with "X", "Y", and "Z" Coys.
   1 pair at Battn. HdQrs.

5. MESSAGE DOGS.

   3 message dogs will be at Battn. HdQrs.

6. RELAY RUNNERS.

   Yorkshire Cyclists will form relay posts along route HOOGE - CLAPHAM JUNCTION - GLENCORSE WOOD.

(Contd.)

GENERAL INSTRUCTIONS. (2).

111. CONTACT AEROPLANES.

1. **SIGNALS TO 'PLANES.**

    (a)   Red Flares.   These will be issued later.

    (b)   "X", "Y", and "Z" Coys. will send Riflemen with respirators to Q.M. Stores tomorrow at 2.30 p.m., for white flaps to be sewn on the latter as follows:-

    "X" Coy........ 15.
    "Y" Coy........ 20.
    "Z" Coy........ 15.

    (c)   Coys. will each draw 20 Vigilant periscopes from Q.M. Stores tomorrow, and issue 5 to each platoon.
    Above signals will be used to denote positions to contact 'planes at following times:-

    (a) ZERO plus 2 hours 15 minutes.
    (b) ZERO plus 4 hours.
    (c) When called for by plane giving following signals:-
    Dropping White Lights.
    Sounding KLAXON HORN.

2. **AEROPLANES.**

    (a)   Contact aeroplanes will carry two black rectangular flags attached to and projecting from lower plane, and a trailing streamer.   All troops must know these marks.

    (b)   Counter-attack 'plane will watch Corps Front from ZERO plus 1 hour onwards, and will signify imminent hostile attack by dropping Red Smoke Parachute Very Light.

3. **AMMUNITION FROM AEROPLANES.**

    Should the shortage of ammunition be very serious, aeroplanes will drop ammunition on Battn. HdQrs. showing a triangle made of white strips.

25.9.1918.   Major & A/Adjutant.

SECRET.

XXXX
1st BN. ROYAL DUBLIN FUSILIERS.

GENERAL INSTRUCTIONS.

1. TRACKS.

Tracks for Pack Transport will be opened up as follows:-

(a) MENIN ROAD - I.18.a.9.6.- I.18.b.2.8.- I.18.b.5.7.- I.18.b.8.6.- J.13.a.0.9.- JARGON cross roads - S.E. to J.14.a.4.6.- through GLENCORSE WOOD - along BLACK WATCH TRACK.

(b) I.17.c.00.35.- I.17.c.5.2.- I.17.c.9.1.- thence along tramway to I.24.a.6.6.- thence N.E. along SANCTUARY TRACK.

11. SIGNAL COMMUNICATIONS.

1. **TELEPHONES.**

   (a) "Y" and "Z" Coys. will be provided with telephones and cable, and "X" Coy. also if supply permits for communication with Battn. Headquarters.

   (b) Brigade cable laying party will be picked up from Headquarters, Lancs. Fusiliers, as the Battn. passes RED Line to lay line from BUZZER BOARD, 1st Lancs. Fusiliers, to BUZZER BOARD, 1st Royal Dublin Fusiliers.

2. **VISUAL STATIONS.**

   There will be Visual Stations at:-

I.16.b.0.4.	Brigade.
J.7.c.6.8.	"
J.14.c.1.7.	"
About J.14.b.2.4.	Battalion.

3. **WIRELESS.**

   A forward Loop Set will accompany Battn. HdQrs. for transmission to Rear Portion with 1st Lancs. Fusiliers.

4. **PIGEONS.**

   1 pair each with "X", "Y", and "Z" Coys.
   1 pair at Battn. HdQrs.

5. **MESSAGE DOGS.**

   3 message dogs will be at Battn. HdQrs.

6. **RELAY RUNNERS.**

   Yorkshire Cyclists will form relay posts along route HOOGE - CLAPHAM JUNCTION - GLENCORSE WOOD.

(Contd.)

GENERAL INSTRUCTIONS. (2).

111. CONTACT AEROPLANES.

1. **SIGNALS TO 'PLANES.**

    (a) Red Flares. These will be issued later.

    (b) "X", "Y", and "Z" Coys. will send Riflemen with respirators to Q.M. Stores tomorrow at 2.30 p.m., for white flaps to be sewn on the latter as follows:-

    "X" Coy......... 15.
    "Y" Coy......... 20.
    "Z" Coy......... 15.

    (c) Coys. will each draw 20 Vigilant periscopes from Q.M. Stores tomorrow, and issue 5 to each platoon. Above signals will be used to denote positions to contact 'planes at following times:-

    (a) ZERO plus 2 hours 15 minutes.
    (b) ZERO plus 4 hours.
    (c) When called for by plane giving following signals:-
        Dropping White Lights.
        Sounding KLAXON HORN.

2. **AEROPLANES.**

    (a) Contact aeroplanes will carry two black rectangular flags attached to and projecting from lower plane, and a trailing streamer. All troops must know these marks.

    (b) Counter-attack 'plane will watch Corps Front from ZERO plus 1 hour onwards, and will signify imminent hostile attack by dropping Red Smoke Parachute Very Light.

3. **AMMUNITION FROM AEROPLANES.**

    Should the shortage of ammunition be very serious, aeroplanes will drop ammunition on Battn. HdQrs. showing a triangle made of white strips.

G. Heffernan

25.9.1918.   Major & A/Adjutant.

SECRET   Copy No... 6.

Addendum No 1 to 86th Inf.Brigade Operation Instructions No.3.

Reference para 4, 86th Inf.Brigade Operation Instructions No. 3 dated 24th Sept 1918.

The following provisional instructions are issued for your guidance:-

The Field Artillery barrage will come down on the North and South Line I.22.b.68.20. - I.10.d.68.20.

It will stand there for four minutes and then advance due east by lifts of 100 yards per 3 minutes to 1,500 yards, six-minute pauses being made at 500, 1,000 and 1,500 yards.

It will then advance by lifts of 100 yards per 5 minutes to 2,500 yards, where it will dwell for 14 minutes, advancing thence at 100 yards per five minutes to 3,500 yards.

It will dwell at 3,500 yards (the final Field Artillery Barrage Line) for twenty minutes and then cease.

26th September 1918.

P. Cuddon
Captain,
Brigade Major,
86th Inf.Brigade.

Copies to:- All Recipients of 86th Inf. Brigade Operation Instructions No. 3.

SECRET

Copy No. 6

86th INFANTRY BRIGADE OPERATION INSTRUCTIONS No. 7.

26th September 1918.

Reference Special Operation Map "B", 1/10,000.

APPROACH MARCH. 1. On Y/Z night the 2/Royal Fusiliers and 1/Royal Dublin Fusiliers will move up by light railway from TAILOR, FOLLY and DRAKE CAMPS respectively to IPRES. On detrainment, the 2/Royal Fusiliers will concentrate in the vicinity of, and east of THE SCHOOL, I.9.c., and the 1/R.Dublin Fusiliers in the Support Line between I.9.d.8.4. and I.15.a.7.3. where a hot meal will be served to the troops under arrangements to be made by Commanding Officers. The 1/Lancs.Fusiliers will be concentrated in the Front Line by dusk, on Y/Z night, where a hot meal will be served to the troops.

Detraining Point at IPRES for the 2/Royal Fusiliers and 1/Royal Dublin Fusiliers will probably be either GODRICH or MACHINE GUN SIDING.

Routes to be followed from detraining point to Concentration Areas will be notified later. On receipt of instructions as to these routes, Officers Commanding 2/Royal Fusiliers and 1/Royal Dublin Fusiliers will ensure that these routes are thoroughly reconnoitred by guides, who, on Y/Z night, will meet troops at detraining point and guide them to concentration areas. Train arrangements for Y/Z night will be notified by the Staff Captain.

ASSEMBLY. 2.(a) At Zero minus 30 minutes, the 1/Lancs.Fusiliers will be assembled on a line 300 yards in rear of the BLUE LINE.

(b) At Zero, the 1/Royal Dublin Fusiliers will be assembled in the present front line.

(c) At Zero, the 2/Royal Fusiliers will be assembled in the Support Line, between I.15.b.7.3. and I.9.d.8.4..

The 1/Royal Dublin Fusiliers and 2/Royal Fusiliers will not move from the Support Line and the vicinity of the SCHOOL, respectively, before Zero minus one hour.

Commanding Officers will send an Officer to Advanced Brigade Headquarters, I.16.a.0.6. to report completion of assembly.

This is on the assumption that the attack will commence at dawn.

HEADQUARTERS. 3. Headquarters will be established by Zero as follows:-

86th Brigade Headquarters	I.14.b.1.8.
Advanced Bde H.Q.	I.16.a.0.6.
H.Q. 1/Lancs.Fusiliers.)	
H.Q. 1/R.Dublin Fusiliers)	I.16.a.4.7.
H.Q. 2/Royal Fusiliers	I.15.b.75.70.

CONSOLIDATION ON CAPTURE OF OBJECTIVES. 4. It will be impressed on all ranks that objectives when captured, will be held at all costs. Commanding Officers will ensure that consolidation and organization for defence is carried out immediately their objectives are captured.

/ 5. CAPTURED

— 2 —

CAPTURED GUNS. 5. All troops will be warned that in the event of any guns being captured, no parts of them will be removed, but Brigade Headquarters will be informed of their location, so that, artillery personnel can be sent up to bring these guns into action against the enemy. Owing to the condition of the ground, it is probable that our own supporting artillery may not be able to get up for 24 hours.

OCCUPATION OF DUGOUTS. 6. All troops will be warned that no dugouts are to be occupied unless previously occupied by the enemy, to guard against losses from booby traps.

MOPPING UP. 7. Commanding Officers will ensure that all ground up to their objectives is thoroughly mopped up. When the 1/Royal Dublin Fusiliers have passed through the RED LINE, specially detailed parties from the 1/Lancs. Fusiliers will follow up, assisting in the mopping-up of the ground up to the BLACK LINE, and remain there until the 1/R.Dublin Fusiliers have gained their final objective.

COMPASS PARTY. 8. The Brigade Intelligence Officer with two Brigade Observers, each with broad RED Patches on their backs and carrying a RED Flag, will advance throughout the attack in the Centre of the Brigade Front, — all ranks will be warned that the RED Flag denotes the Centre of the Brigade Front.

ADVANCE OVER FLOODED AREA. 9. Commanding Officers will ensure that their troops do not bunch over the flooded area around HOOGE. The attacking troops should work round this area taking advantage of the German, and our own, old tracks.

PRISONERS' CAGE. 10. The Brigade Prisoners' Cage will be established by Zero in the Railway Cutting, I.16.a.4.7.

11. A C K N O W L E D G E.

Issued at 12-30 a.m.

P. Cudden
Captain,
Brigade Major,
86th Inf. Brigade.

Copies to:- 1 - 3 Staff.
4 2/Royal Fusiliers.
5 1/Lancs. Fusiliers.
6 1/R. Dublin Fusiliers.
7 86th T.M. Battery.
8 'A' Coy. 29th Bn M.G. Corps.
9 87th Inf. Brigade.
10 9th Division "G".
11 29th Division "G".
12 88th Inf Brigade.
13 No. 7 Squadron R.A.F.
14 29th Div. Artillery.
15 Bde Signal Officer.
16 Diary.
17 File.

S E C R E T 29th DIVISION

AMENDMENTS TO
ADMINISTRATIVE INSTRUCTION NO. 13.

Para 1 (d)   Divisional Dump is at SCHOOL HOUSE I.9.c.1.0. NOT at I.9.d.2.0.

Para 5.   Section XXX personnel who are not detailed for work under Division, will remain with Transport Lines and will not concentrate at BRAKE CAMP. Surplus personnel to 300 Col. "A" not detailed for other duties will proceed to Reception Camp on 27th inst.

Lieut-Colonel.
A.A. & Q.M.G., 29th Division.

26th September, 1918.

SECRET.   1st Battalion Lancashire Fusiliers.   Copy No: 10

OPERATION INSTRUCTIONS No: 1.

Ref Maps Sheet 28 N.W.4
              28 N.E.3

1. **INTENTION**.
   At a date and hour to be notified later the 29th Division will attack in conjunction with troops on the RIGHT and LEFT.

2. **DISPOSITIONS**.
   This Battalion will be the leading battalion of the 86th Brigade and they will be followed in the attack by the 1st Royal Dublin Fusiliers who will be followed by the 2nd Royal Fusiliers.
   The units on the flanks of the Battalion will be notified later.

3. **BOUNDARIES**.
   These are as shown on map shown to O.C. Companies.

4. **ATTACK**.
   This battalion will seize the first objective the RED LINE, after which the 1st Royal Dublin Fusiliers will pass through this battalion to seize the second objective.
   The 2nd Royal Fusiliers will follow the 1st Royal Dublin Fusiliers.

5. **ACTION BEFORE ZERO**.
   Tapes will be laid out by Captain P.D.W.Dunn during the hours of darkness before ZERO and the Battalion will be in position with the leading lines of "A" and "D" companies on the tapes, the remainder disposed in rear one hour before ZERO. The line of tapes will be approximately 300 yards in rear of Blue line. (The whole battalion will be assembled in our present front line at dusk).

6. **FORMATIONS**.
   "A" Company on the RIGHT and "D" Company on the LEFT will lead the attack with "B" Company in support on the RIGHT and "C" Company in support on the LEFT. The formation will be in accordance with diagram already issued to companies.

7. **LIAISON**.
   "A" company's RIGHT leading section and "D" company's LEFT leading section will respectively be instructed to keep touch with the flank units.

8. **ACTION OF LEFT SUPPORT COMPANY**.
   After the battalion has reached its objective and when the 1st Royal Dublin Fusiliers pass through, "C" company will come under orders of O.C. 1st Royal Dublin Fusiliers and will follow in rear of the left support company of the 1st Royal Dublin Fusiliers forming flanking party for protection of left flank. This company may be used to assist in taking objective of 1st Royal Dublin Fusiliers.

(1)

9. MACHINE GUNS.
   ~~Two~~ One machine guns will be attached to "B" Company and will move on RIGHT flank under orders of O.C. "B" Coy.
   ~~Two~~ One machine guns will be attached to "C" Company and will move on LEFT flank under orders of O.C. "C" Company.
   These latter guns will be handed over to O.C. "D" company when "C" Company moves forward in support of 1st Royal Dublin Fusiliers.

10. STOKES GUNS.
    One Stokes gun will be attached to and move with each of "A" and "D" Companies.

11. MOPPING UP.
    During the advance the rear platoons of "A" and "D" companies will be responsible for mopping up, but all sections of "B" and "C" Companies must be particularly on the alert owing to the broken nature of the ground and the long grass.

12. BATTALION HEADQUARTERS.
    Three hours before ZERO, Battalion H.Q. will be established in railway cutting in I.16.a. and will remain there until the Battalion has taken its objective when it will be moved to the neighbourhood of HOOGE I.18.b.2.6.

13. COMMUNICATION.
    The Officer i/c Signals will move forward with the support companies and will establish a temporary visual and message station as soon as possible at BIRR Cross roads I.17.B.2.8. He will, as soon as the objective has been taken, establish a visual and message station at I.18.b.2.6. and and Advanced Battalion H.Q.
    When this has been done, remaining Battalion H.Q. will move forward from I.16.a.

14. CENTRAL RUNNER ROUTE.
    YPRES - MENIN Road.

15. GENERAL BEARING.
    The line of the advance is on a magnetic bearing of 102°

16. ADJOINING UNITS.
    In the event of a unit on either flank of the Division or within the Division being held up, adjoining units will not check their advance but will carry on and if necessary detail a party to watch their exposed flank.

17. SYNCHRONIZATION OF WATCHES.
    O.C. Companies will send one officer to Battalion H.Q. two hours before ZERO to synchronize watches.

18. ACTION AFTER OBJECTIVE TAKEN.
    After objective has been taken and as soon as the 1st Royal Dublin Fusiliers have passed through followed by "C" Company, "A", "B" and "D" Companies will at once reorganize into platoons. Companies will then remain in diamond formation of platoons in the best cover available, will fill up with ammunition Lewis gun magazines, water etc and then rest their men. They will report to Battalion H.Q. as soon as this reorganisation is complete stating location, strengths etc.

19. **INFORMATION TO THE ENEMY.**
All ranks are to be warned again about giving information to the enemy should they become a prisoner and only the necessary maps are to be carried and all documents which might give information to the enemy must be destroyed before ZERO.

20. **YUKON PACKS.**
The Demonstration Platoon will act as a YUKON PACK squad in accordance with details already issued.

21. **DUMP.**
A Brigade Dump is being formed at I.9.d.5.5. and a Battalion Dump will be formed in I.16.a. in the railway cutting.

22. **TEA.**
Tea for the Battalion will be made at ~~Company~~ Batt H.Q. at I.15.b.8.9. [School] and will be issued to the men about three hours before ZERO at which time the Battalion will be in our front line prior to moving to assembly tapes.

23. **SILENCE.**
It is vitally important that during the forming up before ZERO and the hours of darkness previous, absolute silence should be maintained.

24. **MISCELLANEOUS.**
Barrage tables, medical instructions, S.O.S., Contact aeroplanes etc will be notified later.

25. **A C K N O W L E D G E.**

[signature]
Lieut. Colonel.
Commdg 1st Lancashire Fusiliers.

24. 9. 1918.

ISSUED AT

Copies to:- No: 1   C.O.
              2   Adjt.
              3   "A" Co
              4   "B" Co
              5   "C" Co
              6   "D" Co
              7   86th I.Bde
              8
              9
            10   1st R.D.F.
            11   File
            12   War Diary
            13   O.C. Signals
            14   Asst Adjt
            15   Q.M.
            16   T.O.
            17   Reserved.
            18

SECRET   Copy No...... 6

86th INFANTRY BRIGADE OPERATION INSTRUCTIONS No. 9

26th September 1918.

Ref. Special Operation Map "B" 1/10,000.

1. Ref. para 2 86th Inf.Bde Operation Instructions No. 3 dated 24-9-18

The 28th Inf. Brigade (9th Division) is attacking on the Left of the 86th Inf. Brigade. The 28th Inf. Brigade will attack on a two Battalion Front - the 9th Scottish Rifles on the Right and the 2/Royal Scots Fusiliers on the Left. The R.Newfoundland Regt will be in reserve.

The 9th Scottish Rifles will attack on a one-Company Front and will pass over the RED and BLACK LINES and capture the GREEN LINE.

O.C. 1st Royal Dublin Fusiliers will detail a liaison officer to report to O.C. 9th Scottish Rifles at ARRIVAL FARM, 28/B.28.d.6.3. on 27th Instant.

2. Ref.para 7, 86th Inf.Bde Operation Instrs No.3 dated 24-9-18.

Sections of "A" Coy, 29th Battalion M.G.Corps will report to Commanding Officers on Y/Z night as arranged between Commanding Officers and Section Officers concerned.

Machine Guns, during the attack, will move with Battalions' Headquarters.

3. Ref.para 8, 86th Inf. Bde Operations Instrns No. 3 dated 24-9-18.

Trench Mortar Teams to be attached to 1/R.Dublin Fusiliers, will move with that Battalion from BRAKE CAMP on Y/Z night.

When the 2/Royal Fusiliers pass through the RED LINE, the Trench Mortar Teams attached to the 1/Lancs.Fusiliers, will move forward with the 2/Royal Fusiliers, coming under the orders of the Officer Commanding 2nd Royal Fusiliers.

4.   ACKNOWLEDGE.

                                          Captain.
                                          Brigade Major,
                                     86th Inf. Brigade.

Copies to:- All Recipients of 86th Inf.
             Brigade Operation Instructions
             No. 3.

SECRET.
                2nd Bn. Royal Fusiliers.
                Operation Order No. 70.

Copy.No. ____

Ref. Map. YPRES. 1/10.000.   26/9/18.

1.   Operation Order No. 69 dated 24/9/18 is cancelled and the following substituted.

2.   The 86th Infantry Brigade will attack on a date and at an hour to be notified later, in conjunction with the 87th Brigade on the right, and the 9th Division on the left.
      The day of the attack will be known as Z day, and the day previous to the attack as Y day.

3.   Boundaries and objectives are as shewn on maps issued to Companies.

4.   The attack will be made under an intense field artillery barrage up to the Black line, which will be the final field artillery line. Details of the barrage will be issued later. The remainder of the attack up to the line marked "approximate objective" will be supported by heavy artillery.

5.   The plan of the attack is as follows:-
      The 1st Lancashire Fusiliers with the 2nd South Wales Borderers on their right, will attack up to the Red line.
      The 1st Royal Dublin Fusiliers, with the 1st Border Regt. on their right, will move forward close behind the 1st Lancashire Fusiliers at zero, keeping 500 yards behind them after passing the Blue line, and attack up to the Black line, making good the ground up to the line marked "approximate objective".
      As the 1st Royal Dublin Fusiliers pass through the Red line, the left support Company of the 1st Lancashire Fusiliers will follow in rear of the left support Company of the 1st Royal Dublin Fusiliers, as a flanking party for the protection of the left flank.
      The 2nd Royal Fusiliers, with the 1st Kings Own Scottish Borderers on their right, will move about 300 yards in rear of the 1st Royal Dublin Fusiliers, and will be prepared to support them at any time if necessary. If hostile resistance is easily overcome, the 2nd Royal Fusiliers will exploit the success and capture the line POLDERHOEK SPUR and CAMERON HOUSE in conjunction with the 1st Kings Own Scottish Borderers on the right, who will capture TOWER HAMLETS and VELDHOEK.
      Upon the capture of their objectives by the 86th and 87th Brigades the 88th Brigade will pass through and continue the attack with a view to establishing a line on the high ground GHELUVELT and KRUISECKE. It is essential however that the high ground GLENCORSE WOOD and STIRLING CASTLE be captured, and if necessary the whole of the Division will be employed for this purpose.

6.   (a) The Battalion will be disposed as follows: W and X Companies in the front wave, with W Company on the right. Y and Z Companies in the second wave, with Y Company on the right. A distance of 150 yards will be maintained between waves. Companies will move in diamond formation of platoons as far as possible, shaking out into sections when necessary.
      (b) The inter-Company boundary (inclusive to X Company) will be as follows: Farm I.15.b.8.9. - Bend in road I.17.b.2.5. - HOOGE. N. of Menin Road. - FORT MACLEOD J.14.a.6.5. - CARLISLE FARM (approx) - JUT FARM (approx).
      (c) Very careful liaison must be kept between waves and with the Battalion in front by means of connecting files. This is especially important owing to the bad condition of the ground.

(2)

(d) Battalion H.Q. at zero hour will be at I.15.b.75.70 it will then, as the attack progresses move to the vicinity of HOOGE, and on the capture by the 1st Royal Dublin Fusiliers of the line marked "approximate objective", to the vicinity of CLAPHAM JUNCTION. If the Battalion is able to exploit the success by the capture of CAMERON HOUSE and POLDERHOEK RIDGE, Battalion H.Q. will finally be established at NORTHAMPTON HOUSE J.15.c.85.70.
(e) The Regimental Aid Post will be at the ECOLE at the beginning of the attack, and will later move to a position somewhere on the MENIN Road.

7. On Y/Z night, the Battalion will move by train to YPRES, and will assemble in the vicinity of the ECOLE. Further instructions re march to assembly, and assembly, will be issued later.

8. The Battalion Scouts will move to Battalion H.Q. and be used (a) if the occasion demands during the attack (b) for the exploitation of success.

9. Communications.
(a) Cable. A line will be laid by Brigade to Battalion H.Q. via the 1st Lancashire Fusiliers and the 1st Royal Dublin Fusiliers H.Q. Battalion H.Q. will lay a central line forward into which Companies will tap from their H.Q. Companies will be responsible for the upkeep of this line to their central line. Only Fullerphones will be used before zero hour.
(b) Visual. (Lucas lamps). Battalion Visual Stations will be established, first at I.15.b.75.70, next at I.16.a.4.8. next in the vicinity of HOOGE, and next in the vicinity of CLAPHAM JUNCTION.
(c) Runners. Brigade are establishing relay runner posts at about I.16.b.1.6., J.13.b.5.0. and J.14.b.0.8. Two runners per Company will report to Battalion H.Q. directly Company H.Q. are established.
(d) Pigeons. Each Company will have two pairs of pigeons and Battalion H.Q. three pairs. Battalion H.Q. will also have two messenger dogs.
(e) Wireless. A loop set will be disposed as follows:- the rear portion will move with the Headquarters of the 1st Lanashire Fusiliers, and the forward portion with the H.Q. of the 1st Royal Dublin Fusiliers. On passing through the 1st Royal Dublin Fusiliers the Battalion will pick up the forward portion of the loop set and take it with them for communication to the rear portion.

10. Contact aeroplanes.
Contact aeroplanes will be marked with two black rectangular flags, two foot x one and a quarter foot, projecting from the lower plane on each side of the fusilage. Each plane will also have a trailing streamer.
Planes will call for signals by sounding Klaxon horns and dropping white lights. Front line troops only will answer the call by red flares, vigilant periscopes, and American cloth on box respirators.
Aeroplanes will be signalled to by these means by front line troops at zero plus two hours and fifteen minutes, and zero plus four hours, and subsequently when called for by aeroplanes.
N.B. All men will be warned how to recognise contact aeroplanes.
A counter attack plane will be in the air from zero plus one hour onwards, to give warning of an impending hostile attack. If hostile infantry are observed moving to the attack, this plane will call for annihilating artillery fire and will also signal to the infantry by dropping a red smoke parachute very light.

(3)

A limited amount of bundle packed S.A.A. will be dropped from aeroplanes if required, if called for by the placing of white strips. These strips will be at Battalion H.Q. and attention will be called to them by the firing of a white flare from the ground.

Ammunition will be dropped from zero plus two hours onwards, as long as these ground signals are displayed.

It will not be possible to drop very much ammunition, so that Company and platoon Commanders must make every effort to collect both ammunition, and enemy rifles and ammunition for use.

Sixteen tin discs are being issued to each Company. These are to be used in addition to other signals for shewing the position of front line troops to aeroplanes.

11. One section A.Company, 29th Battalion Machine Gun Corps will be attached for the operation and will report to Battalion H.Q.on Y day. It will supply two guns with double crews to follow in rear of second wave. The remaining two guns will be brought up on pack transport.

12. Ammunition. etc.
170 rounds S.A.A. per man will be carried. Each man will carry one No.36 Rifle grenade and one smoke grenade. The establishment of ground flares will also be carried.

In addition to this a party of 16 men (4 per Company) with Yukon packs and tump lines will proceed with Battalion H.Q. under the charge of the Regimental Sergeant Major. Twelve of these men will carry six Lewis Gun panniers each, and four men will carry two boxes of rifle grenades each.

Brigade ammunition dump will be at I.9.d.5,5.

13. Rations for one day and the iron ration will be carried on the man. Waterbottles will be filled before leaving Camp. Subsequent rations and water will be brought up on pack animals. 2/Lieut.Martin will be in charge of the Battalion Pack Transport, which will be brigaded under Major RIGG, 1st Battalion Royal Dublin Fusiliers.

14. One red flag 3 foot x 2 foot is being issued to each platoon. These flags will be planted on the objective, or at any point where a platoon is held up for any time.

15. ACKNOWLEDGE.

Issued at _1-0 pm_ _____
Capt. & Adjt.
2nd Bn. Royal Fusiliers.

Distribution:- Nos.1-3. Staff.
       4-7. Companies.
        8. Quartermaster.
        9. Transport Officer.
       10. Signal Officer.
       11. Medical Officer.
       12. O.C.Battalion Pack Transport.
       13. Regtl.Sergt.Major.
       14. 29th Bn.Machine Gun Corps.
       15. 86th Inf.Brigade.
       16.) War Diary.
       17.)
       18. File.

SECRET.   Copy No. _____

2nd. Bn. Royal Fusiliers.
Addendum No.1. to Operation Order No. 70.

26/9/18.

1. <u>To para 6.</u> The following provisional instructions are issued.
   The field artillery barrage will come down on the north and south line I.22.b.68.20 - I.10.d.60.20 at zero minus 5 mins. Detailed barrage maps are being issued to-night.

2. <u>To para 7.</u> (a) Approach march. The Battalion will probably detrain at GODRICH or MACHINE GUN SIDING. Further instructions with reference to routes to assembly position will be issued.
   The Battalion will have a hot meal before moving from Camp, and hot tea in hay packs, and rum, will be taken up to the assembly position for consumption before moving forward from there.
   (b) Assembly. At zero minus one hour, the Battalion will move into the support line between I.15.d.7.3 and I.9.d.3.4. where Companies will be formed up ready for the attack by zero minus 30 minutes. Companies will each report to Battalion H.Q. at I.15.b.75.70 directly they are in position.

3. <u>To para 11.</u> This section of A. Company, 29th Bn. Machine Gun Corps, will report at the ECOLE on Y/Z night and will assemble at I.9.d.1.2. where the O.C. Section will arrange for hot food for his section.

4. <u>To para 12.</u> 170 rounds of S.A.A. per man, and the establishment of red ground flares will be carried up from this Camp. On arrival at the assembly position, each Company will send a party from their position of assembly to the Brigade Dump at I.9.d.5.5. where the Regtl. Sergt-Major will issue out to each Company 7 boxes No.36 Rifle grenades and 7 boxes No.27 Rifle grenades, 8 packets of white very lights, 3 S.O.S. rockets, 5 large wire cutters, and lanyards.
   The 16 Yukon Pack men (4 per Coy) will entrain with Battalion H.Q. under the Regtl. Sergt-Major. The 12 men of the 16 detailed to carry Lewis Gun Panniers will have their packs loaded before starting. The remaining 4 men will proceed with the Regtl. Sergt-Major to the Brigade Dump, where they will load their packs with rifle grenades.

5. <u>Captured Guns.</u> All men will be warned that in the event of any guns being captured, no parts are to be removed. Battalion H.Q. will be informed at once of the location of any guns captured.

6. <u>Direction.</u> The Brigade Intelligence Officer with two Brigade Observers, with large red patches on their backs, and carrying a red flag, will advance throughout the attack along the centre of the Brigade front. All ranks will be warned that this denotes the centre of the Brigade front.

7. <u>Prisoners.</u> Any prisoners taken will be used as long as they are wanted, as stretcher bearers, etc. When they are finished with they will be sent to the Brigade Prisoners cage at I.16.a.4.7.

8. <u>Anti-Aircraft Lewis Gunners.</u> One Anti-Aircraft sight will be issued to each Company, and one gun of each Company with the reserve platoon will be told off to look out for, and deal with, low-flying enemy aircraft.

9. ACKNOWLEDGE.

                                                    Capt. & Adjt.
                                                    2nd Bn. Royal Fusiliers.

Distribution as for Operation Order No.70.

SECRET

29th DIVISION

AMENDMENTS TO
ADMINISTRATIVE INSTRUCTION NO. 14.

Para 4   Rear Headquarters 87th and 88th Infantry Brigades will be in respective transport lines as follows :-

87th Inf. Bde.	FOLLY CAMP	28/G.3.d.7.4.
88th Inf. Bde.		28/A.21.a.8.4.

The other Rear Headquarters will be as stated.

O.C., Signals is to ensure telephonic communication between all rear Headquarters and Division "Q" who will be at BRAKE Camp.

26th September, 1918.

Lieut-Colonel.
A.A. & Q.M.G., 29th Division.

SECRET   29th DIVISION.

AMENDMENTS TO
ADMINISTRATIVE INSTRUCTION NO. 14.

Para 1 (a)   for Field Company transport location
             Map sheet should read 28 and not 27.

Para 5.   Stretcher Bearers to report at HOP FACTORY
             (HOUBJONS) 28/H.2.c.3.1. at 4.0 p.m. "Y" day NOT
             to PRISON, YPRES.

                                            R.C. Crawfurd
                                            Lieut-Colonel.
                                   A.A. & Q.M.G., 29th Division.

25th September, 1918.

SECRET.   Copy No. _____

1st BN. ROYAL DUBLIN FUSILIERS.

OPERATION ORDER NO. 14.

26th September, 1918.

(Reference Sheets 28 N.W.4. and N.E.3.)

1. INTENTION.

   On "Z" day the 29th Division will attack, in conjunction with the 9th Division on Left and 35th Division on Right, as follows:-

   86th Brigade......... On Left.
   87th Brigade......... On Right.
   88th Brigade......... In Reserve.

2. ASSEMBLY.

   (a) On Y/Z night the Battn. will proceed by Train and March Route, and concentrate in the SUPPORT LINE between I.9.d.8.4. and I.15.a.7.3., as follows from Left to Right:-

   "Y", "X", "Z", "W".

   (b) On arrival in concentration area Coys. will at once cook hot tea and arrange to serve rum.

   (c) One Section will be sent to report to 2/Lt. ROSS at Battn. Dump 200 yards E. of PINK CHATEAU on MENIN ROAD, to draw Stores for issue.

   (d) At ZERO minus 1 hour "Y" and "Z" Coys. will move forward to the present Front Line vacated by the 1st Lancs. Fus.

3. OBJECTIVES AND BOUNDARIES.

   These have been issued on a map to all concerned.

4. GENERAL PLAN OF ATTACK.

   (a) The Brigade will attack in depth on a one-Battn. front on an initial frontage of 700 yards.

   (b) The 1st Lancs. Fus. will capture the RED LINE.

   (c) The 1st Royal Dublin Fus. will pass through the Lancs. Fus., and establish themselves on the RED DOTTED LINE.

   (d) If the BATTLE goes well the 2nd Royal Fus. will pass through the 1st Royal Dublin Fus. and capture POLDHOEK SPUR and CAMERON HOUSE.

   (e) The 88th Brigade will pass through the 86th and 87th Brigades, and endeavour to capture the high ground at GHELUVELT and KRUISEECKE.

   (f) The objective of greatest importance is the RED DOTTED LINE, and the whole strength of the Division will be used, if necessary, to capture it.

(Contd.)

OPERATION ORDER NO. 14. (2)

5. METHOD OF ATTACK.

   (a) The Battn. will attack on a two-Coy. front ("Z" on right, "Y" on left), and 3 Coys. in Support ("W" Coy. on right, "X" Coy. in centre, and "C" Coy., 1st Lancs. Fus., on left).

   (b) Each Coy. will operate in depth on a three-Platoon front.

   (c) As soon as the right flank of "Y" Coy. moves awar from the left flank of "Z" Coy., in order to move on their portion of the objective "X" Coy. will at once fill the gap so formed, and align itself with the two Front Coys.

   (d) "C" Coy., 1st Lancs. Fus., and "W" Coy., 1st Royal Dublin Fus. will be prepared to carry out either of the following roles:-
   (1) Protect the flanks.
   (2) Support the assault on the RED DOTTED LINE.

   (e) Battn. Scouts (Lt. BLACKWELL) will precede the advance. They will creep as near to the objective as possible, open fire, and keep Coys. informed of the situation. They will not participate in the assault.

6. DIRECTION.

   (a) Magnetic bearing of the advance is 102°.

   (b) Each Platoon Commander will be pointed out by his Coy. Commander definite landmarks to march on.

   (c) The Brigade Intelligence Officer will move with a RED flag in the centre of the advance.

7. LIAISON.

   (a) 2/Lt. NOLAN will keep in touch with the Right Flank of the 9th Division.

   (b) 2/Lt. CASSIDY will keep touch with the 1st BORDER Regt. on the Right.

   (c) Leading Coys. will push out Officer's Patrols to keep touch with the 1st Lancs. Fus. until the RED LINE is passed.

8. DISTANCE.

   (a) As far as BLUE LINE Battn. will follow 200 yards behind 1st Lancs. Fus., and afterwards 500 yards will be maintained.

   (b) "X" Coy. will follow 100 yards behind centre of "Y" and "Z" Coys. The other two Support Coys. will follow at 150 yards distance.

9. REORGANIZATION AND EXPLOITATION OF SUCCESS.

   As soon as the RED DOTTED LINE is reached -

   (a) Battn. Scouts will move out in front to positions whence they can fire on fugitives.
   (b) Fighting Patrols will be pushed out to seize any tactical localities in front which may delay subsequent advance.
   (c) Coys. will be reorganized in depth in a formation ready to follow the 2nd Royal Fus.

(Contd.)

OPERATION ORDER NO. 14. (3).

(d) Ammunition will be collected from casualties and distributed. Lewis Gun Magazines will be refilled.
(e) Estimate of casualties and available strength will be notified to Battn. HdQrs. by runner.
(f) Men must be rested and some rations consumed.

10. MOPPING UP.

(a) Support Coys. will mop up as they follow the leading Coys., but their advance is not to be delayed by this. Advantage should be taken of the pauses in the barrage to do this.
(b) Detachments of the Lancs. Fus. are following the Battn. to mop up any places passed over.

11. ARTILLERY.

(a) The Field Artillery barrage will come down on the N. and S. line I.22.b.68.20 - I.10.d.68.20. for 4 minutes.
(b) It will then creep due E. at the rate of 100 yards in 3 minutes, with pauses of 6 minutes at 500 yards, 1000 yards, and 1500 yards.
(c) After 1500 yards it will lift 100 yards in 5 minutes up to 2500 yards, where it will dwell for 14 minutes.
(d) It will then creep at same rate to 3500 yards (BLACK LINE), dwell there for 20 minutes, and then cease.

12. VICKERS GUNS.

(a) Two sections of Vickers Guns are attached to the Battn.
(b) One section (2 guns only) will follow close behind each of the flank Support Coys.
(c) The section on the right will, after passing the BLACK LINE, take up a position and fire in enfilade to cover the advance of "Y" Coy.
(d) As soon as the objective is gained the left section will take up a position to guard the Left Flank, and the right section will face to protect the Right Flank.
(e) The remaining two guns of each section will come up after the objective is gained.

13. TRENCH MORTARS.

Two Trench Mortars, with double teams, will move directly in rear of the left flank of "W" Coy.

14. BATTALION HEADQUARTERS.

On arrival at assembly position, HdQrs. will be at I.16.a.4.7 in conjunction with HdQrs., 1st Lancs. Fus. It will subsequently move in rear of "X" Coy. to a position in vicinity of FORT MACLEOD.

15. SYNCHRONIZATION OF WATCHES.

The Officer i/c Signals will send a watch round the Coys. at 12 midnight and 2.0 a.m.

16. MESSAGE TO TROOPS.

The Commanding Officer is confident that the Battalion will acquit itself in accordance with the world-wide fighting traditions of the Irish race. Everyone must go forward with one object - to kill and spread terror in the enemy ranks, and so take revenge for March 21st.

Major and A/Adjutant,
1st Royal Dublin Fusiliers.

OPERATION ORDER NO. 14. (4)

DISTRIBUTION.

1. 86th Inf. Bde.
2. O.C. "W" Coy.
3. "   "X" "
4. "   "Y" "
5. "   "Z" "
6. Intelligence Officer.
7. Signal Officer.
8. 1st Lancs. Fus.
9. 2nd Royal Fus.
10. File.
11. War Diary.
12.   "

SECRET   29th DIVISION

ADMINISTRATIVE INSTRUCTION NO. 15

1. **DIVISIONAL DUMP.**

    The contents of the Divisional Dump are as follows :-

    ```
            8 sets of Pack Saddlery
    300,000 rounds S.A.A. (ord.)
    274,600   "    do   M.G. bundle packed.
      1,002   "    T.M. All-ways
      3,037   "    Ground Flares "RED"
        604   "    No. 31 Green and Red, Smoke
      2,376   "    No. 36              Grenades
        336   "    No. 37                       grenades complete
        204   "    No. 32 G.G.R. S.O.S.
        600   "    No. 31 BLUE SMOKE
            8 sets carriers - water tins.
          900 petrol tins full of water.
    ```

2. This dump is reserved for use by 88th Inf. Bde. Group and no other units will be allowed to draw on it except under very special circumstances and on the signature of a Field or Staff Officer.

3. 86th and 87th Inf. Bdes. have their own dumps and must rely on them, demanding by wire on Division "Q" for any additional ammunition etc. required to be sent up by Decauville or delivered to units transport lines.

4. The Divisional Dump is located at SCHOOL HOUSE I.9.c.1.0. and can be approached by pack or limber through main entrance to SCHOOL at I.9.c.6.6. Notice boards will be erected to mark the route and also at entrance to SCHOOL grounds I.9.c.6.6

                                                Lieut-Colonel.
                                        A.A. & Q.M.G., 29th Division.

26th September, 1918.

SECRET   COPY No: 10.

1st Battalion Lancashire Fusiliers.

OPERATION INSTRUCTIONS No: 2.

1. **COMPANY BOUNDARY**
    The inter-company boundary from West to EAST will be, Road from I.16.b.1.5. to I.17.a.7.6. thence light railway to I.17.b.8.5.- WING HOUSE - MENIN ROAD at I.18.a.7.6.- thence along MENIN ROAD to Red Line.
    "A" Company must have one section North of the MENIN ROAD when passing through HOOGE.

2. **CONTACT AEROPLANES**
    (a) The most forward troops will carry RED FLARES, American Cloth on Box Respirators, and Vigilant periscopes for the purpose of signalling to Contact Aeroplanes.
    (b) These, and every other means of signalling their position, will be used by the attacking troops at :-

        ZERO plus 2 hours 15 minutes.
        and at
        ZERO plus 4 hours
            and at such other times as called for by the
    Contact Aeroplane.
    (c) Contact aeroplanes will call for signals from the attacking troops by sounding the Klaxon Horn and dropping WHITE Lights.

    (d) Contact aeroplanes will be marked with two BLACK RECTANGULAR FLAGS (2 feet by 1 foot 3 inches) attached to and projecting from the lower plane on each side of the fusilage. Each contact plane will also have a TRAILING STREAMER
        All troops will be warned how to recognise contact aeroplanes.

3. **COUNTER ATTACK AEROPLANE.**
    A counter attack aeroplane will be in the air on II Corps Front from Zero plus one hour onwards for the purpose of giving warning of an impending hostile attack.
    On perceiving hostile Infantry moving to the attack the counter attack aeroplane will call for annihilating artillery fire by wireless and will also signal the fact that a hostile attack is impending by dropping a RED SMOKE PARACHUTE VERY LIGHT

4. **DROPPING OF AMMUNITION FROM AEROPLANES.**
    (a) Arrangements have been made with the R.A.F. to drop ammunition from aeroplanes, if required.
    (b) Two kinds of ammunition will be dropped :-
        (a) bundle packed S.A.A.
        (b) M.G. Ammunition packed in belts (4 belts per box)
    The ammunition prepared for dropping will be in the proportion of two of bundle packed ammunition to one of M.G. Ammunition in belts.
    (c) Infantry will signal that ammunition is wanted as follows :-

   =   Machine Gun Post requiring M.G. Ammunition.

   =   Bundle packed ammunition required.

(1)

(2)

Each signal will be made up of strips of white cloth 12 feet by 1 foot and in each case attention will be called to the signal by the firing of a white flare from the ground. Two strips per Battalion and one per Machine Gun Coy will be carried The Brigade Signalling Officer will make arrangements for supplying them.

(d) The aeroplanes will be ready to drop ammunition from ZERO plus two hours onwards and will continue to do so as long as the ground signals are displayed.

Once the signals are removed no more ammunition will be sent by aeroplanes unless a report is received from a contact machine that more is required.

(e) It is probable that each ammunition dropping aeroplane will be able to drop about two boxes of ammunition per hour and possibly at the outside three machines can be made available for the purpose on the Divisional Front.

It will not be practicable with these aeroplanes to continue dropping ammunition for a longer period than about four hours and during the day it is calculated that the maximum number of boxes which can be dropped will be 6 boxes of M.G. Ammunition and 16 boxes of bundle packed ammunition.

(f) It is of very great importance, therefore, that ammunition should not be called for except when really required Platoon and Company Commanders will make every endeavour to collect enemy rifles machine guns and ammunition and bring them into use against the enemy.

(g) As many parachutes as practicable must be recovered and returned to Division.

5. **MEDICAL.** The R.A.P. will be with Advanced Battalion H.Q. in the Cutting in I.16.a.

6. A C K N O W L E D G E.

                                      Lieut. Colonel.
                        Commdg 1st Lancashire Fusiliers.

ISSUED AT 2 p.m.
26/9/18.

Copies to:-
All recipients of
Operation Instructions No: 1.

SECRET.   Copy No. _____

2nd Bn. Royal Fusiliers.
Addendum No.2 to Operation Order No.70.
                                                             27/9/18.

1. Z. day will be 28th September 1918. Zero hour will be notified later.

2. To para 4.
   (a) The field artillery barrage will open at zero minus 5 minutes on the north and south line I.10.d.68.20 to I.22.b.68.20.
   (b) At zero the barrage will lift 100 yards and advance due east at the rate of 100 yards every 3 minutes up to a line 1500 yards east of the opening line. Thence it will advance to the final line at the rate of 100 yards every 5 minutes, with the exception of extra pauses as follows:-
       A pause of 6 minutes at line of 500 yards.)
       "   6   "   "   " 1000 "   ) East of opening line.
       "   5   "   "   " 1500 "   )
       "   15   "   "   " 2500 "   )
   (c) On arrival at 2500 yards line, all guns will fire Thermit for 2 mins. to indicate that the Red line has been reached. Thermit will not be fired on the final line.
   (d) At zero plus 158 minutes the field artillery barrage will reach the black line, and will remain on this line until zero plus 177 minutes, when it will cease. East of this line the advance will be supported by Corps heavy artillery.

3. To para 7.
   (a) The Battalion will entrain at OAKHANGER G.3.b.3.3. on two trains at 6.5 p.m. and 6.15 p.m. Companies will be at the station by 6.0 p.m. Order of entraining W.X.Y.Z. H.Q.
   (b) The Battalion will detrain at MACHINE GUN SIDING H.12.a.8.5. and will march from there to the positions of assembly by the following route:- I.7.a.0.2. - along Railway to I.7.c.4.7. - I.7.c.8.9. I.7.d.2.2. - I.7.d.90.35 - I.8.c.0.0. - I.8.c.6.0. - SALLY PORT (I.8.d.1? YPRES Defence Line - Line of Light Railway. The following intervals will be kept:- 100 yards between Companies and 50 yards between platoons.
   (c) Each Company will send one man to Battalion H.Q. at 2.0 p.m. to report to 2/Lt. W.E.Stokes. These men will proceed forward by road this afternoon, and will reconnoitre the above route, meeting their Companies at the detraining point, and guiding them to the assembly positions.

4. The Signalling Officer will arrange to synchronise watches at 12 midnight and zero minus 1½ hours.

5. The 28th Inf.Brigade, 9th Division are attacking on the left on a two Battalion front, with the 9th Scottish Rifles on the right, the 2nd Royal Scottish Fusiliers on the left, and the Royal Newfoundland Regiment in reserve.

6. ACKNOWLEDGE.

                                                  Capt. & Adjt.
                                               2nd Bn. Royal Fusiliers.

Distribution as for Operation Order No.70.

SECRET.

1st Battn. Royal Dublin Fusiliers.

OPERATION ORDER NO. 15.

27th Sept 1918.

1. **INTENTION.**

    The Battalion will move to-night to concentrate in Support Line by train and march route.

2. **ENTRAINING.**

    The Battalion will entrain at HAGLE, G.6.b.2.2., in the following order and time:-

    "Y" Coy .... 7.20 p.m.
    "X" Coy .... 7.20 p.m.
    "Z" Coy .... 7.25 p.m.
    "W" Coy .... 7.25 p.m.

    Hd. Qrs.   )
    M.G's   )
    T.M's   ) .... 7.30 p.m.
    Medical Staff.)

    Battalion will detrain at GODRICH, I.1.c.3.7., at about 8.10 p.m.

3. **ROUTE TO ASSEMBLY.**

    On detrainment, Battalion will march by following route with 100 yds distance between Companies:-

    I.1.c.3.7.- I.7.d.2.2.- I.7.d.90.35.- I.8.c.0.0.-
    I.8.c.6.0.- I.14.a.95.50.- HOLE IN WALL - MOAT LANE -
    I.15.b.2.4.- RAILWAY - SUPPORT LINE.

    G. Heffernan.

    Major & A/Adjutant.
    1st Royal Dublin Fusrs,

    Copies issued to:-

    O.C., "W" Coy
          "X" Coy
          "Y" Coy
          "Z" Coy
    Medical Officer.
    Signals Officer
    R.S.M.
    Lieut BLACKWELL.

NARRATIVE.

SEPTEMBER 28.

4.30 a.m. "Y" and "Z" Coys. moved forward to Front Line vacated by 1st Lancs. Fusiliers.
"W" and "X" Coys. formed up in the open immediately E. of Support Line.

5.26 a.m. Barrage opened.

5.30 a.m. The Battalion, preceded by Battalion Scouts, moved forward close behind the 1st Lancs. Fusiliers. Meeting little opposition, the 1st Lancs. Fusiliers captured the RED LINE. The Battalion immediately passed through the Lancs. Fusiliers, and with little difficulty captured the BLACK LINE. As soon as the barrage lifted the success was exploited, but some opposition was encountered from machine gun nests in pillboxes. Lieut. McALLEN and Capt. NOBLETT especially distinguished themselves in rushing two of these nests and killing the defenders. The RED DOTTED LINE was captured at 8.45 a.m., and the Royal Fusiliers passed through the Battalion to exploit the success.

9.0 a.m. Companies were at once reorganized with a view to following up the 2nd Royal Fusiliers, as the situation indicated that the enemy were overwhelmed and in a state of disorder. Battalion HdQrs. were established near FORT MACLEOD. Owing to the fact that the advance was carried out under very adverse atmospheric conditions, considerable delay was caused in reorganizing, as Coys. had got very mixed up. Touch with the flanks was also with difficulty obtained, the 9th Division shewing a tendency to move too far North.

10.45 a.m. Orders were received to form up and march down the MENIN ROAD in rear of the 2nd Royal Fusiliers. The 88th Infantry Brigade had passed through the 86th Brigade and exploited the success as far as GHELUVELT. The 86th Brigade was accordingly allotted the role of protecting the left flank of the 88th Brigade.

12 Noon. The 88th Brigade being held up just W. of KRUISEEKE cross-roads, the Battalion took up a position just N.W. of GHELUVELT, echeloned in rear of 2nd Royal Fusiliers to protect the flank. Four low-flying E.A. crossed our lines, but on one being at once shot down by Lewis Gun and rifle fire the remainder returned home.

4.0 p.m. The Battalion took up a position for the night N. of GHELUVELT, in J.17.c. and 22.b. to maintain touch between 29th Division and 9th Division, left, who had reached BECELEARE, Headquarters being established in pillbox at POLDER HOEK CHATEAU.

SEPTEMBER 29.

5.0 a.m. Orders were received for the Battalion to move forward on the left rear of the 2nd Royal Fusiliers. The 86th Brigade was protecting the flank of the 88th Brigade, who continued to advance.

6.0 a.m. The Battalion moved forward according to the general plan. Some considerable machine gun fire at long range was encountered from the left flank, and progress was slow.

8.30 a.m. The 88th Brigade were checked 1400 yards E. of KRUISEEKE in K.26.c. and 31.a. The Battalion then took up a position in K.25.c. and 19.c. on the left flank of the Royal Fusiliers, in order to protect the flank of the 88th Brigade. Considerable machine gun and Trench Mortar fire was encountered from the direction of K.20.a. and b. This position was maintained until nightfall, Battalion Headquarters being established at J.23.b.7.0. During the afternoon the enemy put down a very heavy concentrated shoot on KRUISEEKE cross-roads.

11.0 pm. "Z" Coy. took over the front of the Royal Fusiliers, who were withdrawn into Brigade Reserve.

SEPTEMBER 30.

8.0 a.m. The 88th Brigade, finding the enemy had withdrawn overnight, pressed on in pursuit. The Battalion moved forward at once to protect the left flank of the 88th Brigade.

10.0 a.m. The 88th Brigade were checked 200 yards W. of GHELUWE, where the enemy held a strongly wired position, and further advance was not possible. The Battalion then took up a position in K.34.a. and d., in touch with the 4th Worcesters, 88th Brigade on the right. Battalion Headquarters were established at K.27.c.1.1. Lieut. WAGNER carried out a daring reconnaisance of the enemy position to find out any means of penetrating it, but found it so strongly wired and supplied with machine guns that no advance was considered possible without Artillery support. In the meanwhile the 1st Lancs. Fusiliers had moved up on the left of the Battalion and established themselves on the road from K.29.central - K.35.central.

7.0 p.m. The Battalion moved to a position in K.27. in support of Lancs. Fusiliers, with Headquarters at 27.b.7.7.

OCTOBER 1.

8.0 a.m. The Lancs. Fusiliers attempted to advance, but met with strong opposition and were unable to progress. The remainder of the day passed without event.

7.0 p.m. Headquarters and 3 Coys. of the Battalion moved into Brigade Support near ZUIDHOEK, leaving "X" Coy. in support of 2nd Royal Fusiliers, who relieved 1st Lancs. Fusiliers, the latter moving into Brigade Reserve. Battalion Headquarters were established at J.24.b.8.5.

Strength 14 O/s. 48 O/rs. 983 O/R.

On Strength		Off Strength

Officers	O/Ranks	Officers	O/Ranks
2/Lt J. Nolan	From Base 23	Capt G.F. Racey	Evacuated 11
" W.P. Spiers	" Hosp. 4	Invalided 15.9.18	Drowned 2
Joined 17.9.18	" Overseas 1		To England 2

Strength 21 O/s. 49 O/rs. 996 O/Rs.

2/Lt E.G. Oswald	From Base 2	2/Lt Green	Evacuated 15
" G.A. Simpson	" Hosp. 2	A/S 20.9.18	
A/Capt in camp P.T	at Hosp in Camp 9	Capt R. Macdonald	
Taken on Strength 20.9.18		Invalided A/S 20.9.18	
2/Lt R.A. Lawrence, Wounded 28.9.18	Killed 1		
Capt G.H. Hobbs	Wounded 25		
Capt W. Blackwood	To Base 2		
	O/R's		
	Wounded		

Strength 30 O/s. 46 O/rs. 983 O/R.

WAR DIARY

OF

1st BN. ROYAL DUBLIN FUSILIERS

FOR

MONTH OF

OCTOBER, 1918.

VOLUME 43.

WAR DIARY or INTELLIGENCE SUMMARY

1st Royal Dublin Fusiliers

Army Form C. 2118.

For month of October 1918

Place	Date	Hour	Summary of Events and Information	Remarks and references to Appendices
ZUIDHOEK K.29.a. (Sheet 28)	1st		Fine day. Operations continued. Rifle & Lewis Gun instruction attended. Strong offensive reconnoitred.	
	2nd		Wet day. Batt. Transport lorries were formed to GHELUVELT J.22.c.1.8 (Sheet 28) no fresh attempt made by 86th Brigade to advance relinquished south.	
YPRES	3rd		2 officers returned by 41st Divn – 86th Bde were they taken over by 122 Bde. Battn. moved back at 4 p.m. to Billets in the old Cavalry Barracks & officers club in YPRES where they arrived about 9 p.m. Casualties. KILLED. 17. O.Rs. Died of wounds Lieut W. BLACKWELL and 2/Lt. J. NOLAN. M.B.E M. wounded Capt R.V. RYAN, a/Capt C.H. NOBLETT. M.C. Lieut D.P. WAGNER M.C. (seriously at duty), 2/Lt W.F. SQUESS, 2/Lt W.A. STEWART, 2/Lt G.A. SEMMENCE and 91 O.R.S. Missing 10. O.Rs.	
"	4th		RESTING & cleaning up. Commanding Officer addressed the Battalion.	
"	5th		Bde moved by Rail to LEDERKHEM area – Battn. entrained troops at the 107th Bde at 3.50 p.m. Batt. Transport bivouacked at J.5.a.3.1	
LEDERKHEM	6th	8 p.m.	Fine day. Some rain at night – Battn. held line – very heavy enemy shell fire at intervals on expectation of a	

1st Royal Dublin Fusiliers

Army Form C. 2118.

WAR DIARY
or
INTELLIGENCE SUMMARY.
(Erase heading not required.)

Instructions regarding War Diaries and Intelligence Summaries are contained in F. S. Regs., Part II. and the Staff Manual respectively. Title pages will be prepared in manuscript.

For month of October 1918

Place	Date	Hour	Summary of Events and Information	Remarks and references to Appendices
LEDEGHEM			Continued Von advance.	
"	9th		86th Bde relieved by 88th Bde on Divisional front. Batt relieved by 4/5 Batt Worcester Regt. Moved to BECELAERE – 88th Bde now in Support.	
			Casualties. Killed S.O.Rs wounded Lieut M. LAYTON, Lieut J. BURKE-SAVAGE M.C. 2/Lt C.J.G. CONERNEY. 37. O.Rs.	
BECELAERE 10th 11. 12. d.79.			Batt move back by march route to YPRES	
YPRES	11th – 12th		Batt Resting at YPRES Divisional Reserve. YPRES intermittently shelled on night of 13th inst. by rail.	
	13th		Batt move forward at 1 PM to assembly positions near LEDEGHEM for attack on the morrow by the 29th Division in conjunction with the 9th Div on its left & 36th Div on its Right – The 29th Div will attack in a Two Bde front 88th Bde on Right. 86th Bde on Left – Battalion Transport lines move forward to BECELAERE.	
LEDEGHEM	14th		Attack commenced at 5.35 AM. Approx. forming up Jog greatly enhances difficulty Mountainous direction. Lt. Col. A. Moore D.S.O. killed by shell fire. He had been in Command of Battalion Since October 1917 & his loss is felt on	

Army Form C. 2118.

1st Royal Dublin Fusiliers

WAR DIARY
or
INTELLIGENCE SUMMARY.
(Erase heading not required.)

Instructions regarding War Diaries and Intelligence Summaries are contained in F. S. Regs., Part II. and the Staff Manual respectively. Title pages will be prepared in manuscript.

month of October 1918.

Place	Date	Hour	Summary of Events and Information	Remarks and references to Appendices
ZUIDHOEK K.29.a (Sht 28)	1.		Fine day. Operations continued vide Narrative attached. Strong opposition encountered.	
	2.		Wet day. Batt Transport lorries unable to proceed to GHELUVELT J.22.c.1.6 (Sht 28) no fresh attempt made by 86th Brigade to advance & improved position.	
YPRES	3.		2/Lt Grimmer relieved by 41st Div - 86th Bde having been taken over by 122 Bde. Batt moved back at 4pm to Billets in the old Cavalry Barracks & Officers Club in YPRES where they arrived about 9pm. Died of wounds Lieut W. BLACKWELL Canadian. KILLED 17.ORs. and 2/Lt J. NOLAN H.R.Dr.M. Wounded Capt K. RYAN, A/Capt G.H. NOBLETT.M.C. Lieut D.P. WAGNER M/C (remained at Duty), 2/Lt W.F. SQUIRES, 2/Lt W.A. STEWART, 2/Lt G.A. SEMMENCE and 91.O.R's. Missing 10. ORs.	
-,,-	4th		RESTING & cleaning up. Commanding Officer addresses the Battalion.	
-,,-	5th		Batt moved by Rail to LEDERGHEM area - Batt where trains to J.5.a.3.1. 36.9.J. Batt Transport have moved to J.5.a.3.1.	
LEDEGHEM.	6th - 8th		Fine days. Some rain at night - Batt. held line - Very heavy shelling, still fire at intervals in expectation of a	

1st Royal Dublin Fusiliers.

Army Form C. 2118.

Instructions regarding War Diaries and Intelligence Summaries are contained in F. S. Regs., Part II. and the Staff Manual respectively. Title pages will be prepared in manuscript.

WAR DIARY
or
INTELLIGENCE SUMMARY.
(Erase heading not required.)

for month of October 1918.

Place	Date	Hour	Summary of Events and Information	Remarks and references to Appendices
LEDEGHEM			Continuation from advance	
"	9th		86th Bde relieved by 88th Bde on Divisional front. Batt. relieved by 4th Batt. WORCESTER Regt. Move to BECELAIRE – 86th Bde now in Support. Casualties Killed S.O.Rs wounded Lieut M. LAYTON, 2Lieut J BURKE-SAVAGE M.C. 2/Lt. C.J.G CONERNEY. 37. O.Rs.	
BECELAIRE	10th–12th d.7.9		Batt move back by march route to YPRES.	
YPRES	11th–12th		Batt Resting at YPRES Divisional Reserve. YPRES intermittently shelled on night of 13th inst.	
	13th		by Train Batt moves forward at 1 PM to assembly positions near LEDEGHEM for attack on the morning of the 29th. 29th Divisions in conjunction with the 9th Divs. on its left & 36th Divs on the Right – The 29th Div will attack on a Two Bde front 88th Bde on Right – 86th Bde on Left – Battalion Transport lines move forward to BECELAIRE.	
LEDEGHEM	14th		Attack commenced at 5.35am Ypres–Roulers Roulers formed by – fog great, advances difficult & visibility direction. Lt Col. A. Moore D.S.O. killed by shell fire. He had been in command of Battalion since October 1917 & his loss cast a	

(A10266) Wt W5300/P713 750,000 2/17 Sch. 52 Forms/C2118/16 D. D. & L., London, E.C.

WAR DIARY
or
INTELLIGENCE SUMMARY.

(Erase heading not required.)

Army Form C. 2118.

1st Royal Dublin Fus.

Instructions regarding War Diaries and Intelligence Summaries are contained in F.S. Regs., Part II. and the Staff Manual respectively. Title pages will be prepared in manuscript.

Place	Date	Hour	Summary of Events and Information	Remarks and references to Appendices
			month of October 1918.	
	14th	(Continued)	a gloom over what was otherwise a Splendid day for the Battalion. At 6pm Batt. withdrew to Billets in Ypres LT2a. L.I.4th (Sheet 28.)	
	15th		Batt. in Billets. Enemy S.E. of ROLLEGHEM CAPPEL — Transport at DADIZEELE — Some horses killed by shell fire. Casualties. Killed Lt Col. A. Moore D.S.O. Wounded 2/Lt J.F. BREAKWELL. 2/Lt T.A. CHADWICK, 2/Lt E.G. COLDWELL. Killed 8 ORs. Wounded 47 ORs. Missing 1 OR.	
HEULE G.11.c.93 (Sheet 29)	16th		Batt. move forward to Support near HEULE G.11.B.53. in billets by 5pm. Transport move forward to L5.d. Sheet 28. Large number of bombs dropped during night by E. aeroplanes. Lt Col. A. Moore D.S.O. buried in graveyard near Prison at YPRES. As to Many 9 Batt. attend as possible.	
HEULE	17th — 18th		Batt. clean up. reorganize. Baths. Also change of underclothing. Weather fine	
—do—	19th		Transport move from HOTTE to E. — Raining. Orders received that advanced parties be entrained in the morning the 88th Lgt Rail. forming HQ Transport 9 Bn. LYS on the divisional front.	

Army Form C. 2118.

1st Royal Dublin Fusiliers

WAR DIARY
or
INTELLIGENCE SUMMARY.
(Erase heading not required.)

Instructions regarding War Diaries and Intelligence Summaries are contained in F. S. Regs., Part II. and the Staff Manual respectively. Title pages will be prepared in manuscript.

Place	Date	Hour	Summary of Events and Information	Remarks and references to Appendices
			October 1918	
HEULE	20		Batt. move from billets at 5. am Marched by march route to position	
			on assembly in 29/H.14.a. Barrage opened at 6.am. 88th Inf.Bde	
			cross Lys. Batt. move forward at 8.30 am. Batt cross the Lys	
			in Spares 29/H.23 a.b. Vide narrative of operation	
			Bde assembles in CUERNE area 29/H.21.a.	
			Wheeled Transport lines move to CUERNE area 29/H.21.a.	
	21st		Batt. relieved outpost position in support in ST. LOUIS area	
			29/H. & I.34.C. & later to BILLETS near STEENBRUGGE 29/F.25 central.	
			CASUALTIES wounded. Major W. T. RIGG (in command) 2/Lt	
			M.F. O'Donnell. M.C. 2/Lt. E.E. HAWTREY 2/Lt. W.A. STEWART (slightly)	
			wounded operations 28/9/18) Killed 7 OR Wounded 50 ORs	
STEENBRUGGE	22nd		Transport & Tran H.Q. join Battalion. was under command of Capt.	
			C.M. McFEELY. D.S.O. M.C. Enemy artillery active on forward zone; 7.7H & 9mm on back area	
CUERNE	23		Batt. move back by march route to CUERNE 29/H.S.d. area	
			dated in convent.	
	24th		Batt. resting.	
	25th		Batt moved by march route to RONCQ x 28 a (Lys Valley 1/40000)	
			marched off 5.40 a.l. arrive about 11 a.m. division pass from II to XV corps	

Army Form C. 2118.

1st Royal Dublin Fusiliers

WAR DIARY
or
INTELLIGENCE SUMMARY.
(Erase heading not required.)

Instructions regarding War Diaries and Intelligence Summaries are contained in F. S. Regs., Part II. and the Staff Manual respectively. Title pages will be prepared in manuscript.

For month of October 1918.

Place	Date	Hour	Summary of Events and Information	Remarks and references to Appendices
RONCQ	26.		Batt. moved to BONDUES. move off at 10.45 a.m arrive 12. Midday. Billetted in N° Hospice. Fine day.	
BONDUES	27.		Church services for all Denominations. Fine day	
B/E 17.C	28.		Lt. Col. J.A. MELDON assumed command of the Battalion. Batt engaged working parties first day. Working parties as before. Weather fine.	
"	29.		Baths. Inspection of Rifles, steel, helmets, gas, by A.D.m.s. Sgt. + Praris of Demanding.	
"	30.		Parade in afternoon. Fine day	
"	31.		Inclined to Rain. Company training etc.	

Attached :-
Administration Instructions dated 17/10/18
Operation order No 16 " 13/10/18
 Relief   " L.5. " 18/10/18
  "   " L.6. " 19/10/18
 Operation " L.7. " 21/10/18
 Narrative operations 28/9/18 — 31/10/18 Marked "Y"
    "   "   14/10/18   " "L".
    "   "   28/10/18 - 29/10/18 " "S".
 Captures Statement of, about operations   " "C"
 Battalion Strength chart   " "R"

J.A. Meldon Lt Col.
Commanding 1st Bn Royal Dublin Fusiliers

1st BN. ROYAL DUBLIN FUSILIERS.

RELIEF ORDER. NO. L. 5. 18.10.1918.

1. The 86th Infantry Brigade will relieve the 88th Infantry Brigade in the Line on the Divisional Front tomorrow, 19th inst.

2.
   (a) 1st Royal Dublin Fusiliers will relieve the 2nd Hampshire Regt. and 4th Worcester Regt. in the Line.
   (b) 2nd Royal Fusiliers will move into Support in G.18.
   (c) 1st Lancs. Fusiliers will move into Reserve.

3. On completion of relief 1st Royal Dublin Fusiliers will be disposed as a Battalion in Outpost, with sentry groups and picquets. Coys. as follows:
   "W" in Right Front, and "X" in Left.
   "Y" in Right Support and "Z" in Left Support.

4. "W" and "Y" Coys. meet guides at 5.0 p.m. in H.18.a.2.6.
   "X" and "Z" Coys. meet guides at 6.0 p.m. in H.8.b.3.0.

5. M.G. and T.M. will be under arrangements of their O.Cs.

6. Divisional Boundaries as follows:-
   Southern: H.21.a.0.0. - WATERMOLEN CH. - HOULE STN. G.17.d.0.7.- G.15.& 16.central.
   Northern: HOOGEBURG (H.11.a.8.4.) - H.9.c.9.0. along grid line to G.1.d.0.0.

7. Headquarters of Units will be as follows:-
   1st Royal Dublin Fusiliers: H.9.c.60.80.
   2nd Royal Fusiliers: G.18.a.70.50.
   1st Lancs. Fusiliers. G.12.a.50.40.
   86th T.M. Battery: H.13.a.70.70.

8. On our Left: 26th Infantry Brigade (9th Division); immediate Left Battalion, 7th Seaforth Highlanders.
   On our Right: 123rd Infantry Brigade (41st Division); immediate Right Battalion, 11th Queen's.

9. 86th Infantry Brigade Headquarters will close at G.10.d.3.3. at 3.0 p.m., 19th, and open at H.1.c.9.1. at same hour.

10. Rations for the 20th will be issued tomorrow (19th) and will be carried on the man.

(sd) G. LORD, Lieut.
A/Adjutant, QIVI.

SECRET.   Copy No.

1st BN. ROYAL DUBLIN FUSILIERS.

OPERATION ORDER NO. 16.

                                                   13th October, 1918.

(Ref. Sheets: 28 S.E. 1/20000 & 20 N.E. 1/20000).

1. **INTENTION.**
   On "J" Day the 29th Division will attack in conjunction with 9th Division on Left and 36th Division on Right as follows:-

           86th Brigade......... On Left.
           88th Brigade......... On Right.
           87th Brigade......... In Reserve.

2. **ASSEMBLY.**
   On "J" - 1 night the Battn. will proceed by Train and March Route, and concentrate behind front line between L.2.a.5.5. and L.3.a.4.5.

3. **OBJECTIVES & BOUNDARIES.**
   These have been issued on a map to all concerned.

4. **GENERAL PLAN OF ATTACK.**
   (a)   Brigade will attack in depth of one-Battn. front on an initial frontage of 630".
   (b)   2nd Royal Fus., in conjunction with 2nd Leinsters, will capture RED LINE N. and S. between Squares "L" and "Q".
   (c)   1st Royal Dublin Fus. will pass through the Royal Fus. and capture the BLUE LINE, DADIZEELE - STEENBEEK Road.
   (d)   1st Lancs. Fus. will pass through 1st Royal Dublin Fus., and capture the GREEN LINE running along Railway line N. from COURTRAI in 0.18.b. and 0.12.d.
   (e)   One Coy. of 1st Lancs. Fus. will be detailed to mop up LEDEGHEM.
   (f)   Battalions will be prepared to support one another in the capture of their objectives where strong opposition is met.

5. **METHOD OF ATTACK.**
   (a)   The Battn. will attack on two-Coy. front ("Y" on Right, "Z" on Left), and two Coys. in Support "W" on Right, "X" on Left).
   (b)   Each Coy. will operate on two-platoon front.
   (c)   A platoon "X" and "W" Coys. will act on Right and Left for liaison.
   (d)   Scouts will precede the advance and keep Coys. informed of the situation.

6. **APPROACH MARCH.**
   Battn. will move by train from YPRES to detraining point in vicinity of WATER DAM, HOEK, where tea will be served. After tea Battn. will move to assembly positions.

7. **DIRECTION.**
   Magnetic bearing of the advance is 102°.

8. **DISTANCE.**
   As far as RED LINE Battn. will follow 200 yards behind 2nd Royal Fus.

9. **REORGANIZATION & EXPLOITATION OF SUCCESS.**
   As soon as BLUE LINE is reached Coys. will reorganize in depth, and send out fighting patrols to seize any tactical localities in front which may delay subsequent advance.

10. **ARTILLERY.**
    Barrage maps have been issued to all concerned.

1st R.D.F. Operation Order No. 16. (2)
----

11. **VICKERS GUNS.**
    Two Guns are attached to the Battn.
    Four Machine Guns of the Machine Gun Coy. in the line will barrage from ZERO minus 3 minutes to ZERO plus 2 minutes the N.E. outskirts of LEDEGHEM.

12. **TRENCH MORTARS.**
    Two Mortars will be attached to the Battn., and will move with "W" Coy.

13. **ROYAL ENGINEERS.**
    Thirty bridges have been dumped at the STATION, LEDEGHEM. One platoon, 1/2nd Mon. Regt. will carry these bridges and place them over the WULFDAMBEEK to enable the attacking troops to cross this stream.

14. **PRISONERS.**
    All prisoners will be sent back to Brigade Advanced HdQrs.

15. **SYNCHRONIZATION OF WATCHES.**
    O.C. Signals will send a watch round Coys. at 1.0 p.m.

16. **BATTALION HEADQUARTERS.**
    On arrival at assembly position Headquarters will be at L.8.a.6.7.

17. **CONTACT AEROPLANES.**
    (a) Contact aeroplanes will be marked with BLACK RECTANGULAR FLAGS attached to and projecting from the lower planes on each of the fuselages; also a TRAILING STREAMER.
    (b) Attacking troops are supplied with RED FLARES and DISCS for the purpose of shewing their position when called for by 'planes
    (c) Contact 'Planes will call for attacking troops to shew their positions by:-
        (1) Sounding a KLAXON HORN.
        (2) Dropping WHITE FLARES.
    (d) A counter-attack 'plane will be in the air from ZERO plus one hour, and will signal hostile counter-attack by dropping a RED PARACHUTE VERY LIGHT.
    (e) Aeroplanes will drop S.A.A., pigeons, food, and rations if urgently required, by parachutes. As many as possible of these parachutes must be returned to Brigade Headquarters.

18. **ACKNOWLEDGE.**

            P. Lod.
            Lieutenant & A/Adjutant,
            1st Bn. Royal Dublin Fusiliers.

Copies to:-
1. 86th Inf. Bde.
2. O.C. "T" Coy.
3. "   "X" "
4. "   "W" "
5. "   "Z" "
6. Intelligence Officer.
7. Signal Officer.
8. 1st Lancs. Fus.
9. 2nd Royal Fus.
10. File.
11. War Diary.
12. "   "

1st BN. ROYAL DUBLIN FUSILIERS.

19.
OPERATION ORDER. NO. L.6.   XX.10.1918.

(Ref. Sheet 29. 1/40000.)

1. The 86th Infantry Brigade tonight will force the passage of the River LYS, and will establish a general line: H.28.c.5.7. - H.23.c.0.0. - H.18.b.2.3.

2. The 88th Infantry Brigade will advance from this line at 06.00 tomorrow, 20th inst., in conjunction with 9th Division on Left and 41st Division on Right.

3. Objectives for the 20th inst:- Line O.9.central - O.4.central - ST. LOUIS - I.35.central.
   Alternative objective of the 29th Division:- Line of the River ESCAULT from V.5.a.5.0. to P.30.b.5.0.

4. Boundaries. Southern: COURTRAI - BOSSUYT CANAL from H.26.b.4.9. to O.9.central; thence to V.5.a.5.0. Northern: H.11.a.5.5. - h.18.b.2.3. - P.30.b.5.0.

5. 86th Infantry Brigade will move to concentration point in accordance with orders already issued. It will be prepared to cross the LYS at 06.00, 20th inst. Coys. will assemble in concentration area, H.14.a., in the following order:-
   In Artillery Formation of Coys.
   "W" on Right; "X" on Left.
   "Y" Right Support; "Z" Left Support.

6. Ferries will be at:-
   H.21.c.85.60.
   H.21.b.95.20.
   H.16.c.00.10.
   Barrelpier Inf. bridges at:-
   H.21.c.95.65.
   h.16.c.0.0.

7. One section of Machine Guns with double teams will be with 1st Royal Dublin Fusiliers.

8. Two Trench Mortars will be with Headquarters of 1st Royal Dublin Fusiliers.

9. The 28th Infantry Brigade on the Left and the 122nd Infantry Brigade on the Right will be operating in conjunction with the 86th Infantry Brigade tomorrow, 20th inst.

10. 86th Infantry Brigade Headquarters will close at G.10.d.4.4. at 06.00 tomorrow, and open at H.1.c.9.1. at the same hour.

11. Battalion Advanced Headquarters will be in rear of "Y" Coy.

(sd) G. LORD, Lieut.
A/Adjutant, QIVI.

1st BN. ROYAL DUBLIN FUSILIERS.

OPERATION ORDER. NO. L.7. 21.10.1918.

(Reference Sheet 29. 1/40000).

XX The 87th Infantry Brigade will continue the advance tomorrow, 22nd inst., on the Divisional Front, in conjunction with troops on either flank.

87th Infantry Brigade will pass through 86th Infantry Brigade at 9.0 a.m., and attack under cover of an Artillery barrage.

When the 87th Infantry Brigade has passed through, Battalions of the 86th Infantry Brigade will accomodate themselves in billets in vicinity of areas at present occupied by them, and will hold themselves in readiness to follow up in Support to 87th Infantry Brigade.

(sd) G. LORD, Lieut.
A/Adjutant,
1st Royal Dublin Fusiliers.

SECRET.

1st BN. ROYAL DUBLIN FUSILIERS.

ADMINISTRATIVE ORDER.

12th October, 1918.

1. **SUPPLIES.**

    Rations for consumption on "J" Day will be Preserved Rations for all ranks. Each man will carry rations for "J" Day with him, in addition to his Iron Ration, and water bottle filled.

    Dinners will be served at 12 noon. Tea will be provided at detraining point and also at point of assembly. Two cookers, with one cook per Coy., under 2/Lieut. HAWTREY, will proceed to detraining point, E.14.d.8.8., and will select a place in the vicinity where tea will be served to the Battalion. Cookers will afterwards return to new Transport Lines at K.7.c.8.8.

    Two cooks per Coy., with camp kettles, will proceed to the vicinity of point of assembly with the Battalion, and will serve tea to the Battalion on the morning of "J" Day.

2. **TRANSPORT.**

    First Line Transport will move to K.7.c.8.8. on "J" - 1 day, and may afterwards move to K.6.s. They will be clear of MENIN GATE by 3.0 p.m.

3. **KITS, ETC.**

    All surplus Q.M. Stores and Officers' kits will be stored at BARRACKS, YPRES, in the same place as before.

    Blankets and packs will be stored in the same place, and will be moved forward on "Y"-1 day with First Line Transport and such extra Transport as may be required. All kits, blankets, and packs to be stored by Coys. by 11.0 a.m. tomorrow, 13th inst.

4. **AMMUNITION.**

    An Advanced Brigade Dump has been formed at K.6.c.4.5. of S.A.A., No. 36 Grenades, Verey Lights, reserve tins of water, and shovels. Battalions should clear their own dumps on "J" Day before drawing on this.

Lieutenant & A/Adjutant,
1st Bn. Royal Dublin Fusiliers.

1ST BN. ROYAL DUBLIN FUSILIERS.

YPRES OPERATIONS, 28.9.1918 - 3.10.1918.

1. ORDER OF BATTLE.

    In Command............. Lt.Col. A. MOORE, D.S.O.
    Acting Adjutant........ Major J.G.P. HEEFERNAN, M.C.
    Signal Officer......... 2/Lieut. C.G.C. FISHER, M.C.
    Battn. Scout Officer.... Lieut. W. BLACKWELL.

    Comdg. "W" Coy......... Capt. K. RYAN.
    "   "X" Coy......... Capt. G.H. NOBLETT, M.C.
    "   "Y" Coy......... Capt. J.F.J. CARROLL.
    "   "Z" Coy......... Capt. C.St.L. WEBB.

2. GENERAL PLAN.

    The Battalion attacked as Support Battalion of the 86th Infantry Brigade as part of a general operation involving the Second British Army and the Belgian Army. The Infantry plan of attack is given in Battalion Operation Order No. 14. Objectives and Boundaries are shewn on Map "A" attached (Appendix 1).
    ZERO hour for the attack was fixed at 5.30 a.m., Septr. 28.

3. ASSEMBLY.

    At 7.10 p.m., September 27th, the Battalion left BRAKE CAMP to concentrate in Assembly area in olf British Support Line between I.9.d.8.4. I.15.a.7.3. (Battalion Operation Order No. 14). The Assembly was carried out without incident, and was completed at 11.30 p.m. Owing to the original Headquarters selected being burnt out a new location was established at I.15.b.8.8.

OCTOBER 2.

No fresh attempt was made to advance, and the day passed quietly.

8.0 p.m. "X" Coy., on relief by 1 Coy., Worcestershire Regt., rejoined the Battalion.

OCTOBER 3.

4.0 p.m. On relief of Division the Battalion marched back to billets at YPRES.

---

5. ## GENERAL REMARKS.

(a) <u>ARTILLERY.</u> On the first day, September 28, the barrage was very good. One gun appeared to be firing very short, and 80% of the casualties incurred came from this short shooting.

(b) <u>VICKERS GUNS.</u> Once off good roads Vickers Guns are very immobile. They cannot keep up with advancing Infantry. Their best role appears to be:

    (1) To come into action when advance is definitely checked, and enfilade hostile T.Ms. and pillboxes.
    (2) Cover reorganization and give Infantry an opportunity to rest when objectives have been gained.

(c) <u>TRENCH MORTARS.</u> It is only a waste of ammunition for T.Ms. to fire unless they are cooperating in an actual operation. Retaliation fire is worthless.

(d) <u>LEWIS GUNS.</u> Platoon Commanders need greater training and experience in bringing their guns into action rapidly. The question of supply of ammunition and magazines requires attention. An automatic supply of Lewis Gun magazines should be sent up with rations nightly.

(e) <u>RIFLE GRENADES.</u> Only Smoke Grenades are of any use, and it is doubtful if these are of any real assistance.

(f) <u>DIRECTION.</u> The entrance upon undevastated areas where landmarks are plentiful will simplify.

(g) <u>POSITION OF HEADQUARTERS.</u> The position of the Battalion Commander is well forward, so that opportunities can be seized at once. A Report Centre must be maintained well in rear.

(h) <u>COMMUNICATIONS.</u> The safest means is by runner. When advance is rapid and far it is not feasible to use double runners for every message, as numbers prohibit.

(i) <u>STRETCHER BEARERS.</u> As long as open warfare lasts no extra stretcher bearers for operations are required. German prisoners and personnel following in rear are sufficient to deal with casualties.

(k) MORAL. The operations again demonstrated the great truth of the Napoleonic axiom that victory is 90% moral. This does not appear to be sufficiently grasped. Officers must husband and look after their men. It is useless to attack if men are not in good heart and fit condition, for failure is almost certain and the resultant damage to moral hard to remedy. The infantryman is above everything a human being, and there are limits to his endurance and capabilities.

6.

CONCLUSION.

In conclusion I can only place on record my very keen appreciation of the splendid manner in which all ranks fought and endured. The attack was carried out under as adverse weather conditions as ever experienced. Measured by the gain of ground alone the success attained was remarkable, apart from the capture of prisoners and material which there was no time to count.

The Battalion had suffered heavy losses and experienced ill fortune on the SOMME earlier in the year, but the great success attained, at comparatively light cost, has raised the hearts of Officers and men to an unprecedented degree and restored the former fighting prestige of the Regiment, and this is certain to have a great influence on all subsequent operations.

(sd) G. HEFFERNAN, Major & A/Adjutant,
For Lieut.Col. A. MOORE, D.S.O.
Commanding 1st Bn. Royal Dublin Fusiliers.

1st BN. ROYAL DUBLIN FUSILIERS.

OPERATIONS, 14.10.1918.

13th. The Battalion moved at 1.0 p.m. from YPRES, and proceeded by March Route and Train to Position of Assembly, which was taken up as follows:-
Along line of Railway from L.2.c.70.50 to L.8.a.70.60.

14th. At 5.35 a.m. attack was opened, 2nd Royal Fusiliers leading, closely supported by 1st Royal Dublin Fusiliers in following order:-
Leading Coys: "Y" on right, "Z" on left, with "W" in right support and "X" in left support.
Shortly after ZERO a thick fog, caused by ground mist and smoke shells, made visibility difficult and led to loss of direction.
The first objective was reached by parties of all three Battalions at 9.0 a.m. There heavy M.G. and T.M. fire was met with, which temporarily held up the advance. Orders were received for the reorganization of the 1st Royal Dublin Fusiliers and 2nd Royal Fusiliers, which were withdrawn from the line, leaving the 1st Lancs. Fusiliers to hold it.
At 12.30 p.m. the advance was continued to the BLUE LINE, 1st Lancs. Fusiliers leading, followed by 1st Royal Dublin Fusiliers in close support, with 2nd Royal Fusiliers in reserve.
The advance was pushed forward as far as a line running from about G.8.a.80.60. to G.8.c.80.80. At this line heavy enemy M.G. and T.M. fire was met with, and further progress was very slow.
The 1st Royal Dublin Fusiliers took up a position in Support from G.8.a.40.00 to G.8.a.10.80, where they remained until 6.0 p.m., when they were withdrawn to billets in squares in L.12.a. and L.11.b.

(sd) G. LORD, Lieut. & A/Adjutant,
For O.C., 1st Bn. Royal Dublin Fusiliers.

1st BN. ROYAL DUBLIN FUSILIERS.

OPERATIONS, 20 - 21.10.18.

(Reference Sheet 29).

1. **ORDER OF BATTLE.**
   - "W" Coy., Right Front.
   - "X" Coy., Left Front.
   - "Y" Coy., Right Support.
   - "Z" Coy., Left Support.

2. **OBJECTIVES.** Assembly Position: H.14.a.
   Objective: I.35.a.5.4, road running S. through ST. LOUIS, I.4.b.5.0; W. to cross-roads at I.4.c.8.6; S. to T-road at I.4.c.6.4; along road S.W. to Canal bank (BLUE LINE).
   Divisional Boundaries: N.- Line running from H.11.d.9.5. to I.35.a.5.4. South.- Line running H.21.d.2.2. to H.29.c.3. and then along the Canal bank to line of objective.

3. **PRELIMINARY ARRANGEMENTS.** Bridges had obeen thrown across the LYS at H.21.c.8.7., and on arrival at the Assembly Position the Intelligence Officer, with Battalion Scouts, reconnoitred the route to this bridge.

4. **PLAN.** The advance was to be carried out on a one-Battalion front of about 3000 yards, narrowing to about 1000 yards at Square I.25., and to a depth of 8000 to 9000 yards. The 88th Brigade made good the advance up to a line from H.18.b.5.4. running S. to H.28.c.9.5. (RED LINE) during the night 19th - 20th, where the 1st royal Dublin Fusiliers were to pass through them and make good the objective given above, i.e. BLUE LINE.

5. **NARRATIVE.** The Battalion moved from billets at HEULE at 5.0 a.m. to the Assembly Position, and moved from there at 8.30 a.m., 2½ hours after the barrage put down for the 88th Infantry Brigade had commenced. The Battalion crossed the River without hitch, and re-assembled in Square 23.a. Having previously heard that the 88th Infantry Brigade had not waited for us to pass through at the RED LINE, the Battalion rested here until the Officers' patrols which had pushed out returned, having got into touch with the rear Battalion of the 88th Infantry Brigade.
   The Battalion moved forward on orders from Brigade at 9.0 a.m. by road to I.33.a.0.5. The Left Coy. passed through 88th Infantry Brigade, and reached some buildings at I.34.d.2.4., where they were held up by machine gun fire from hill at O.4.d.5.3., the Right not having come up as fast. They were exposed to a great deal of shell fire, being more or less under observation. The Left Coys. maintained these positions until early the following morning, the 21st.
   The Right Coy. pushed on slowly, and by very clever manoeuvring outflanked the enemy position which had held up the advance of the Left Coy. and secured the position and held it during the night 20th-21st. It was then arranged that the 1st Lancs. Fusiliers and 2nd Royal Fusiliers would attack in the morning as soon as the Divisions on our right and left had completed the advance that they were attempting in conjunction with us on the 20th. The Battalion was to go over in Support of the 1st Lancs. Fusliers (on right) and 2nd Royal Fusiliers (on left).

21st,
At 4.30 a.m./the Battalion withdraw and took up Support positions at O.4.b. and I.34.c., approximately 500 yards in front of the 1st Lancs. Fusiliers, who were to pass through us when the barrage came down in front of road running O.5.a.8.3. S. to about O.10.c.8.8. The Order of Battle was changed, "Y" Coy. being in front of "W" Coy. on the Right, and "Z" Coy. in front of "X" on the Left.

Owing to a change of orders the advance did not take place, but the 2nd Royal Fusiliers, at about 4.30 p.m. attacked on a short front under a barrage, and made good the road running on the E. side BANHOUT BOSCH (O.11.a.&c.)

6. RELIEF. The Battalion was ordered to withdraw to billets at ST. LOUIS, where it arrived at about 8.30 p.m.

7. GENERAL REMARKS. A section of "A" Coy., 29th Battn. M.G. Corps, was attached to the Battalion - two guns to "W" Coy. and two to "Y" Coy., but they did not get much opportunity.

A gun of the 86th Trench Mortar Battery was attached to "Z" Coy., but it was unable to get any targets.

(sd) G. LORD, Lieut. A/Adjutant,
For O.C., 1st Bn. Royal Dublin Fusiliers.

1ST BATTN. THE ROYAL DUBLIN FUSILIERS.

SUMMARY OF STRENGTH FOR MONTH OF OCTOBER 1918

	Officers	O.R.
Strength of Battn. 1st October	47	976

Casualties from Oct 1st - 13th:

	O.	O.R.		
Killed		22		
Wounded	7	124		
Missing.		10		
Evacuated.		8		
Struck off strength	2		9	164
			38	812

Joined Battn Oct 1st - 13th
From Base	2	68		
From hospital		4	2	72
Strength at 13th Oct.			40	884

Officer Casualties.

Wounded: Lieut W. Blackwell, (Died of Wds)
2/Lt J. Nolan, M.C., D.C.M"   )
Capt J. V. Ryan,
2/Lt W.F. Spiess
"   W.A. Stewart.
Lieut M. Layton.
2/Lt C.J.G. Conerney.

S. O. S. Major J.G.P. Heffernan, M.C., (G.S.O.3, 29th Divn)
Lieut A.H. Weir, (M. G. Corps)

Hospital. Capt C. St. L. Webb. (Invalided 13-10-18)
Capt J.F.J. Carroll, (Invalided 3-10-18)
Capt F. L. Chadwick, (Invalided 19-10-18)

Joined. Capt F. L. Chadwick, 5-10-18
2/Lieut W. F. Williamson, 5-10-18

	O.	O.R
Strength of Battn 13th October	40	884

Casualties Oct 13th - 31st

	O.	O.R		
Killed	1	16		
Wounded	8	110		
Missing		38		
Struck off strength	2	11		
Evacuated		27	11	202
			29	682

Joined Battn. Oct 1st/31st.

	O.	O.R		
From Base	9	39		
From Hosptl		15	9	54
Strength at 31st Oct.			38	736

Officer Casualties.

Lieut-Colonel A. Moore, D.S.O. Killed 14-10-18
Major W. T. Rigg, wounded 20-10-18.
2/Lieut T.A.H.Chadwick, wounded 14-10-18
" J. F. Breakell. " "
" I. Burke-Savage " "
" E. G. Coldwell, " "
" M. F. O'Donnell " "
" W. A. Stewart, " 21-10-18
" E.E.H.Hawtrey, " 20-10-18

Joined:

Lt-Col J.A.Meldon, 28-10-18
Capt W.P.Oulton,M.C. 18-10-18
2/Lieut C.J.G.Connerney,
" W. A. Stewart, 18-10-18
Lieut L. R. Elliott, 19-10-18
" A. R. Holman, "
2/Lt M. J. Sheehan, "
" D. S. Norman, "
" W. Martin, "
" M. Dunden, 23-10-18

S. O. S.

Capt C. St. L. Webb, Invalided

Hospital.

2/Lieut N. H. Hamilton.

1st BN. ROYAL DUBLIN FUSILIERS.

STATEMENT OF CAPTURES (APPROXIMATE) DURING OPERATIONS IN BELGIUM, 28.9.1918 - 21.10.1918.

28.9.1918 - 3.10.1918.
Prisoners.................. 200.
4.2. Guns.................. 6.
5.9. Howitzer.............. 1.
Large number of Field Guns,
"   "   " Trench Mortars.
Very many Machine Guns.

14.10.1918.
Prisoners.................. 100.
4.2. H.V. Guns............. 2.
Field Guns................. 18.
Machine Guns............... 16.

---

20 - 21.10.1918.
Prisoners.................. A few wounded.
Machine Guns............... 5.

WAR DIARY

OF

1st BATTALION ROYAL DUBLIN FUSILIERS

FOR MONTH OF NOVEMBER. 1918.

WAR DIARY
of
1st Royal Dublin Fusiliers
for month of
November 1918
Volume. 44

Army Form C. 2118.

1st Royal Welsh Fusiliers

WAR DIARY
or
INTELLIGENCE SUMMARY.
(Erase heading not required.)

Instructions regarding War Diaries and Intelligence Summaries are contained in F.S. Regs., Part II. and the Staff Manual respectively. Title pages will be prepared in manuscript.

for month of November 1918

Place	Date	Hour	Summary of Events and Information	Remarks and references to Appendices
BONDUES 36/E.17.c	1st		Batt. practice "cerémonial" & company training	
"	2nd		Company training.	
"	3rd		Church service for all denominations – Batt. attended service at 5pm given by Revd Royal Fusiliers	
"	4th		Bde ceremonial Parade. Inspection by XV Corps Commander Lt. GEN. Sir BEAUVOIR DELISLE K.C.B. D.S.O. at 5.30pm Batt attend concert by divisional concert troupe.	
"	5th		Wet-day. interior & exterior with training. Inter-coy Platoon Futbol carried on in doors.	
"	6th		Full day inclusive training. Coy training	
"	7th		very wet-day	
"	8th		Batt move to LUIGNE 29/S.23.d. Vide Note no 3 attacked. Batt arrived about 2pm. 1 accommodation Billets - Division passed from XV to II CORPS.	
LUIGNE 29/S.23.d.5.6.	9th		Batt move at short notice to 29/T.6.a.22 to Billets vacated by 2nd Batt. South Wales Borderers - Move commenced 2.30 (am) Batt arrived near 5pm. Enemy reported returning rapidly on 2 ARMY Front area	
(near) RUDDERVOORDE T.6.a.22	10th		Batt move at 8.5.am. moved to SAINT-GENOIS 29/H.16.a arrive 10.45am village greatly damaged about by enemy shell fire. Take over Billets vacated by 1st BORDER REGT (87th Bde) = 88th Inf Bde in LINE - Enemy shell re-training - KAISER officially reported as having abdicated.	

Army Form C. 2118.

1st Royal Dublin Fusiliers

WAR DIARY
or
INTELLIGENCE SUMMARY.
(Erase heading not required.)

Instructions regarding War Diaries and Intelligence Summaries are contained in F. S. Regs., Part II. and the Staff Manual respectively. Title pages will be prepared in manuscript.

Place	Date	Hour	Summary of Events and Information	Remarks and references to Appendices
			For month of November 1918.	
SAINT GENOIS 29/u.16.a	11th		Following wire received at 10.15 a.m. from 86th Brigade:- "29th Div. wire begins AAA. 88th Brigade. Hostilities will cease at 11.00 AAA. 87th & 86th will stand fast in present positions on line of River DENDRE. AAA. 88th Brigade will establish outposts on line of River DENDRE. AAA. Defensive precautions will be maintained AAA. There will be no intercourse with enemy AAA. C.R.E. will concentrate all energies on communication including in this office for army infantry required AAA". ———— ENDS. Strong rumours that the enemy had accepted our terms to an "AR- MISTICE" were current all last night - News received with tre- mendous calm by the Battalion - No one able to realize that the fighting has really ceased.	
POTTES 29/u.30.a.8.8/17	12th	9.50 AM	Orders received at 2.50AM the Battalion were to move at 8am to POTTES - where Battalion arrived 9.45 a.m. Village much damaged by shell fire but good billets obtained for all.	
near BAIVRENX 37/E17.C.08.	13th		Batt. moved about 10.45am march to BAIVRENX 37/E.17.C.0.8. Batt arrived 2.45pm. Billetted in farms scattered round the locality. Weather very fine.	
FLOBECQ 36/E.17.C.0.8 30/T.27.	14th		Batt moved at 8.30 am to FLOBECQ arrived 3.30 pm Dinners en Route. Comfortable Billets - Very fine weather.	

Army Form C. 2118.

1st Batt. Royal Dublin Fusiliers

WAR DIARY
or
INTELLIGENCE SUMMARY.
(Erase heading not required.)

Instructions regarding War Diaries and Intelligence Summaries are contained in F.S. Regs., Part II. and the Staff Manual respectively. Title pages will be prepared in manuscript.

November 1918

Place	Date	Hour	Summary of Events and Information	Remarks and references to Appendices
FLOBECQ 39/T.27	15th	to month if	Inspection cleaning of kit.	
"	16th		Church Service. Fine weather but cold.	
"	17th		Batt. march from FLOBECQ at 6.55 a.m. with views to proceed to Billets in GHISLENGHIEN 38/S.26.a. Batt. arrive at this late place at former miles & 55th Div. already occupying all billets in the village – Batt.	
FOU LEN G. 38/P.17.a.r.d	18th		further march to GONDREGNIES & FOU LENG [?] & after delay served orders meanwhile Billets H.Q's in Château at 38/R.24.c.4.0. Batt. quietly settled. Men settled down at 4.p.m. Day very cold. Some snow turning to Rain about 4.30 p.m.	
"	19th		Fine day but foggy damp. Companies spend day dealing cleaning up – Conference at Batt. H.Q. C.O's & 2nd i/c. Very foggy all day.	
"	20th		Batt. move by march route to RERECQ-ROGNON a distance of about 10 MILES. Mov't off 9-20 a.m. arrive 2 p.m. Nice village – Batt. comfortably billetted.	
RERECQ-ROGNON 31/E	21st		Very fine day – Lieut D.R.WAGNER M.C. & 15 O.R's proceed to BRUSSELS to represent Batt. at State entry of King of the BELGIANS. Lt. Col. J.A. MELDON + Capt. A.S. DELANY also attend.	
LILLOIS-WITTERZÉE	23rd		Batt. move at 9-55 a.m. march to LILLOIS-WITTERZÉE arrive 2-45 p.m. billeted for night	
COURT STETIENNE	24th		" " " 9-50 " " " COURT-STETIENNE " 2-pm " " "	

Batt. billeted by Curé in bounds & given an enthusiastic reception.

Army Form C. 2118.

1st Bn. Royal Dublin Fusiliers

WAR DIARY
or
INTELLIGENCE SUMMARY.
(Erase heading not required.)

Place	Date	Hour	Summary of Events and Information November 1918	Remarks and references to Appendices
WILHAIN ST PAUL	25th		Batt. move at 10.50 am. March to WILHAIN ST PAUL arrive 2.15 pm – Billets not good. Villages dirty. Slight rain all day – Batt. not cleaned up.	
ECHEZEE	26th 27th		Batt. move at 9.15 am by usual route to ECHEZEE arriving 2.15 pm. Day wet – Road uneven & bad for marching distance about 13½ miles.	
MOHA	28th		Batt. move at 9.20 am by usual route to MOHA about 4 miles N.W. of HUY on the MEUSE River – arrive about 3.15 pm. Wet day.	
WARZÉE	29th		Batt. move at 7.10 am – marched to WARZÉE arriving about 2.15 pm – nice day.	
AYWAILLE	30th		Batt. move off at 8 am but after marching 3 kilos orders are received that move is cancelled Batt. therefore return to WARZÉE, on arrival there fresh orders received that move will take place as arranged. Batt. therefore move off again at 10.15 am & march AYWAILLE at 5 pm. Men have dinners en route. Trying march roads being very muddy. Billets very good.	
			*Headed operation order No 3 dated 7. nov. 18. Batt. slightly chest.	

Commanding 1st Royal Dublin Fus.

1st BN. ROYAL DUBLIN FUSILIERS.

MOVE ORDER NO. 3.

7th November, 1918.

1. INTENTION.
   The Battalion will move into billets in LUIGNE Area S.E. MOUSCRON, tomorrow, the 8th inst.

2. ADVANCE PARTIES.

   will be detailed later.

3. STARTING POINT: TIME.
   The Battalion will be on road into BONDUES, ready to move off, at ~~09.55~~. Head of column at corner of "X" Coy's Office. 10.05.

4. ORDER OF MARCH.

   Band.
   Headquarters.
   "W" Coy.
   "X" "
   "Y" "
   "Z" "
   Transport.

5. DISTANCES.
   Distances on line of march will be as follows:-

   100 yards between Coys.
   100 yards between last Coy. and Transport.
   25 yards between every 6 vehicles.

6. REAR PARTY.
   O.C. "W" Coy. will detail a rear party of 1 Officer 1 N.C.O. and 3 men to collect stragglers. This party to move 30 yards behind Transport.

7. TRANSPORT.
   (a) All blankets to be at Q.M. Stores by 08.30.
   (b) All Stores and Officers' kits to be at Q.M. Stores by 09.00.

8. DRESS.
   Full Marching Order, soft caps to be worn. Waterproof sheet to be shewing only 2 inches below flap of pack. Steel helmets to be strapped on pack.

9. SMOKING.
   No cigarettes to be smoked while marching, but allowed at 10 minutes' halt.

10. ACKNOWLEDGE.

2/Lieut. & A/Adjutant,
1st Royal Dublin Fusiliers.

On Strength

Officers	O/Ranks
Lt. J. Riordan joined 2/5	2
2/Lt. J. Benn " "	8
Capt J.C. Bonner " 7/5	27
Major L.W. Dickie " 16/5	Reception Camp
" J.G.P. Hoffman 17/5 16/5	
Lt. E.A. Stark joined 24/5	
2/Lt. D.W. Stark " "	

Off Strength

Officers	O/Ranks	
Lt. J.G.P. Bonner died 13/5	Evacuated	3-5
2/Lt. K.J. Hamilton invalided 14/5	To Base	1 2
Capt E. Barclay M.C.	S.O.S.	1 1
To Infy. Base 27/5	" Deserters	6

Strength 31/75   O/Ro   O/R's
                     38   736

Strength 30/5   42   716

Army Form W.3091.

Cover for Documents.

Nature of Enclosures.

1st Battn Royal Dublin Fusiliers

War Diary

For

December 1918.

Notes, or Letters written.

Army Form C. 2118.

WAR DIARY
or
INTELLIGENCE SUMMARY.
(Erase heading not required.)

WAR DIARY
of
1st Bn. Royal Dublin Fusiliers
:- for :-
Month of
December 1918
Volume 45.

Army Form C. 2118.

WAR DIARY
or
INTELLIGENCE SUMMARY.
(Erase heading not required.)

1st Royal Dublin Fusiliers

Instructions regarding War Diaries and Intelligence Summaries are contained in F. S. Regs., Part II. and the Staff Manual respectively. Title pages will be prepared in manuscript.

December 1918.

Place	Date	Hour	Summary of Events and Information	Remarks and references to Appendices
BASSE-DESNIÉ	1		Batt. move at 11 am to BASSE-DESNIÉ - arrive at 2.7 pm - Billets very scattered.	
" "	2, 3,		Batt. "Cleaning up."	
STER	4th		Batt. move by march route at 10 am to STER passing through SPA en route - Bad day raining arrive in STER 2 pm Bad billets.	
WEYWERTZ	5th		Batt. move by march route at 8.10 am to WEYWERTZ in Germany Crossing frontier at 8.30 am very nice day, beautiful scenery. Arrive in WEYWERTZ at 1.45 pm - moderate billets - inhabitants friendly -	
SIMMERATH	6th		Batt. move at 8.15 am by march route to SIMMERATH arriving 3.15 pm long march, fine day, beautiful scenery.	
EMBKEN	7th		Batt. move at 9.35 am by march route to EMBKEN - Tea taken en route. Batt. arrive 4.45 pm - Fine day, beautiful country route very hilly - Long march	
LECHENICH	8th		Batt. move at 8.10 am by march route to LECHENICH Tea taken en route. Batt. arrive in billets at 2.30 pm nice day.	
COLOGNE (SULZ Suburb of)	9th		Batt. move at 9 am by march route to the outskirts of COLOGNE arrive in billets 1 pm. People very friendly - Snowy up to 4 pm then raining.	

Army Form C. 2118.

1st Royal Dublin Fusiliers

WAR DIARY
or
INTELLIGENCE SUMMARY.
(Erase heading not required.)

Instructions regarding War Diaries and Intelligence Summaries are contained in F. S. Regs., Part II. and the Staff Manual respectively. Title pages will be prepared in manuscript.

For month of December 1918

Place	Date	Hour	Summary of Events and Information	Remarks and references to Appendices
SHLZ. Suburb of COLOGNE	10th		Fine day, Batt clean up, have baths.	
	11th		Misthful weather. Company inspections clothes fitting etc.	
	12th		Wet day. Commanding Officers Inspection of Companies.	
BENSBERG	13th		March through COLOGNE - Army Commander (2nd Army), General Sir HERBERT PLUMER. G.C.B. G.C.M.O. G.C.V.O, A.D.C, taking the Salute Agreed near the HOHENZOLLERN BRIDGE as the Brigade was about to cross the RHINE. Weather very bad, heavy rain all day. Large move forward in Motor troops marching through - Very orderly crowd no outward expression of approval or disapproval - Batt arrived Willichhat 8.30 a.m. Tarmed BENSBERG by 1.15 p.m whole Brigade in large Military College - (Cadet School)	
			27td SA. HELDON, Commanding Brigade present - company inspections, cleaning up, inspection. Weather had. Church Service for all denominations on Sunday 15th inst -	
"	14th 15th			
"	16th		Memory day - Field-Marshal Sir DOUGLAS HAIG. KT. G.C.B, G.C.V.O, K.C.I.E c.in.c British Armies in France visits BENSBERG. Pays a Short Visit to this Cadet School - He inspects the impudent Battalions drawn up around the Square to receive him -	

Army Form C. 2118.

1st Royal Dublin Fus.

WAR DIARY
or
INTELLIGENCE SUMMARY.

(Erase heading not required.)

Instructions regarding War Diaries and Intelligence Summaries are contained in F. S. Regs., Part II. and the Staff Manual respectively. Title pages will be prepared in manuscript.

For month of December 1918

Place	Date	Hour	Summary of Events and Information	Remarks and references to Appendices
BENSBERG.	17–20		Wet weather – usual Routine.	
BERG-GLADBACH	21st		Batt. move by route march at 10.10 am to BERG-GLADBACH distance of about 8 kilos from BENSBERG. Battalion accommodated in Billets, a bit scattered but comfortable. Day fine.	
"	22nd		Fine day. Church Services for all Denominations. Lectures, inspection, football – the power concert.	
"	23 & 24.			
"	25th		Roman Catholics attend Midnight Mass in village church celebrated by Rev. D. POWE R.C.F. (Batt. Chaplain). C of E. Service 9-45 am Recreation Room. Men's dinner 1 o'clock. Whole Battalion dine together in Recreation Hall. Brig. Gen G.R.M.C. HEAPE D.S.O. M.C. & Major S.Gt. P. HEFFERNAN M.C. (Commanding in absence of Lt Col. J.A. MELDON on leave) address the men & get convivial reception. Officers dine together in village Hotel, reserved for the occasion. Orchestra from COLOGNE play during traffic dinner – This is the first Xmas in which the Officers of the Batt. have all dined together in service.	
"	26th		Paper chase for the men – Sergeants dinner at 7.30 pm.	
"	27th		Training in morning – Boxing competition in afternoon.	
"	28th		Wet day.	

1st Batt. Royal Dublin Fusiliers

Army Form C. 2118.

WAR DIARY
or
INTELLIGENCE SUMMARY.

(Erase heading not required.)

Instructions regarding War Diaries and Intelligence Summaries are contained in F. S. Regs., Part II. and the Staff Manual respectively. Title pages will be prepared in manuscript.

Place	Date	Hour	Summary of Events and Information December 1918	Remarks and references to Appendices
KURTEN	29"		Battalien 1st LANCASHIRE Fus. in "outpost area" - Move by march Route at 9. a.m. on arrival Battalion disposed as follows:— Batt. H.Qrs. KURTEN— "X" Coy on the Right at FORSTEN— "Z" Coy in the centre at JUNKERMUHLE + "W" Coy on the left at WIPPERFELD, "Y" Coy in support at BECHEN. Bad day very heavy rain - country very pretty, wooded + hilly. Training; Educational classes + Lectures. Games. Unsettled weather.	
	30+31st		Many men, Continuing on Cadre left, have in part few days been sent home to be demobilized — what a connection with Demobilization is now so large that a separate staff under 2/Lt. J. CASSIDY M.C has been set aside to deal with it.	

Attached Batt. Strength shewn [variations]

B. Jefferson
Major
Commanding 1st Royal Dublin Fusiliers.

On Strength

Officers

2nd Lr. Fitzpatrick N. Nolan
Taken on Strength 10.12.15

5th Can. Rangers
youin Intrepido attached
2nd Army. H.Q5.

Others

Hamilton Hosp'l 13
" Base 92

Strength 30.11.15 Offrs. 42 Others 716.

Strength 31.12.15 Offrs. 42 Others 763

Off Strength

Officers

2 Lt. J.S. Clarke M.C.
to England on munition fake 25.12.15

Others

Evacuated 29
Deserted 1
Committed to Prison 1
To England
on munitions 23
To Canada
to Agricultural +

Southern Div.

Vol 34

32 X
6 sheets

Wt. W3905/P1607 2,500,000 7/18 McA & W Ltd (E 3591) Forms W3091/4.

Army Form W.3091.

Cover for Documents.

Nature of Enclosures.

1st Battalion Royal Dublin Fusiliers.

WAR DIARY

FOR

JANUARY. 1919.

Jan – Dec
1919

Notes, or Letters written.

X WAR DIARY X
of
1st Royal Dublin Fusiliers.
for
Month of
"JANUARY"
1919.
Volume 46.

1st Batt. Royal Dublin Fusiliers.

WAR DIARY or INTELLIGENCE SUMMARY

Army Form C. 2118.

Instructions regarding War Diaries and Intelligence Summaries are contained in F.S. Regs., Part II. and the Staff Manual respectively. Title pages will be prepared in manuscript.

(Erase heading not required.)

Place	Date	Hour	Summary of Events and Information January 1919.	Remarks and references to Appendices
KURTEN (GERMANY)	1st		Fine day. Games etc for the men.	
"	2nd–6th		Weather fine. Training, lectures, Educational classes, games, "W" Company Boxing Competition. Inter-Company Fire day – In afternoon some very amusing movies.	
"	7th		Fine fighting – Some very amusing movies. Inhabitants quiet & amenable Fine days – Training etc as before.	
"	8–9th		Must confirm cases by the new cheaper Rules regulating the issue of PASSES.	
"	10–12		Must confirm. Some snow in the night 11th/12th. Since that time weather frosty. Battalion practically daily for demobilization. Men leave Battalion daily for demobilization. Men on ant: two (2) years more extra service to complete. Also men sent to England for 28 days leave – there is no doubt in order to have men ready to proceed to Germans abroad being detained – consequent upon the important fees on Peace and promises made by prospective M.P's prior to the speech of General Election false hopes as to early Demobilization have been raised in the Army – Much difficulty therefore is now experienced in making Men understand that a state of War continues to exist and that an Army has to be maintained in the field.	
"	13th		In view of difft: tommus advance parties proceed to BERG-GLADBACH to arrange about taking over Billets of 2nd R. Fus. 2nd R. Fus send advance party to take over from us.	

1st Batt Royal Dublin Fusiliers

Army Form C. 2118.

WAR DIARY
or
INTELLIGENCE SUMMARY.
(Erase heading not required.)

Place	Date	Hour	Summary of Events and Information	Remarks and references to Appendices
BERG-GLADBACH	14th		Batt. relieved in outpost area by 2nd Batt. Royal Fusiliers - Battalion moves by companies to BERG-GLADBACH all in by 2 p.m. Billetes in large paper factory - comfortable - Day fine but dull.	
"	15th		Cleaning up, Inspections. Educational instruction, C.O's conference. Football Target practice.	
"	16		Batt. ceremonial Parade - COLOURS officially received back by Battalion	
"	17		Batt. inspected on ceremonial Parade by Brig. Gen. G.R.H. CHEAPE. D.S.O. M.C. (Commanding 86. Infy. Bde) - Lt. Col. J.A. MELDON reports from leave & assumes command of the Battalion.	
"	18th		Training, Recreation, Games as before	
"	19th		Church Service for all Denominations - Afternoon C.O's conference	
"	20th		Batt. inspected on ceremonial Parade by Divisional Commander Major Genl. D.E. CAYLEY. C.B., C.M.G. - afterwards in Batt. Dining Hall this Commander presents Decorations for Gallantry in action to Officers men of the Batt. He also presents Silver Bugle. 1st Prize in the Divisional "Drums" competition - won by the Batt in July 1918.	

Army Form C. 2118.

1st Batt. Royal Dublin Fusiliers

WAR DIARY
or
INTELLIGENCE SUMMARY.
(Erase heading not required.)

Summary of Events and Information for month of January 1919.

Place	Date	Hour	Summary of Events and Information	Remarks and references to Appendices
BERG-GLADBACH	21st-23rd		Usual daily Routine - Training lectures etc.	
"	24th		In afternoon association football Match Officers v. L.A.N. First Round drawn.	
"	25th		Inter Platoon Shooting Competition - "½" Coy Win. In afternoon Inter Coy Cross Country Run won by "W" Coy. Batt. Boxing Competition - Church Service for all denominations.	
"	26th		Preliminary Rounds in afternoon - good fighting.	
"	27th		Weather cold - snowing. Lecture in morning. In afternoon Batt boxing finals. A saw very keen fighting.	
"	28th		Usual Training etc	
"	29th		Usual Training - lecture in morning by Capt. A.S. DELANY.	
"	30th		Usual Routine	
"	31st		Lecture in morning by Capt. M.F. HEALY R. Dub Fus (Armoured Salvage Offr.). In afternoon Bde Boxing Competition - won by 1st Battalion again - Special Contest between Pte RONAN 1st the Batt. v. Cpl. DELANEY 2nd Batt being dispatched for front LEINSTER Regt. RONAN won. DELANEY fighting.	

M. Melden Lt. Col.
Commanding 1st Royal Dublin Fusiliers.

Appendix I

On Strength January 1918.

Officers		O/Ranks	
Reported O.M. Madura January 7th	45	Reported from Base	45
Lieut. S. Sesser Forage	8/9	" Leave	9
		" Hospital	1
		" No reason	1

Strength 31.12.18

Officers	O/Ranks
42	76 3

Strength 31.1.19

Officers	O/Ranks
42	65 3

Off Strength

Officers		O/Ranks	
Lieut. R. E. Taylor		Sick to Hospital	110
To England to part H.O. 17.52		" 2 yrs Colour Service	40
Capt. J. One to 2nd Bn H.S.e. unit.		" Discharge	35
To 2 nd on Off. Course	6/9	" Service Offrs Course	1
		" 86 S.N. 3	3
		" No reason	2

ORDERLY ROOM
FEB 1919
1st Bn. ROYAL DUBLIN FUSILIERS

M 35

War Diary
of
1st Bn Royal Dublin Fusiliers
for
Month of February
Volume. 47.

Army Form C. 2118.

WAR DIARY
or
INTELLIGENCE SUMMARY.
(Erase heading not required.)

1st Batt. Royal Dublin Fusiliers

Instructions regarding War Diaries and Intelligence Summaries are contained in F.S. Regs., Part II. and the Staff Manual respectively. Title pages will be prepared in manuscript.

for Month of February 1919.

Place	Date	Hour	Summary of Events and Information	Remarks and references to Appendices
BERG-GLADBACH (Germany)	1st		Weather fine & frosty. Inter-Coy Shooting competition in morning. won by "C" Coy. Inter-Coy Cross Country Race in afternoon won by "A" Coy. "Z" Coy being 2nd.	C.F.
" "	2nd		Weather fine but cold. Church Parades for all Denominations - Cold day inclined to snow.	C.F.
" "	3rd 4th		Musical Routine - weather fine but cold - place still.	C.F.
" "	5th		Snow fell during night. Chance during day - place still.	C.F.
" "	6th 7th		Usual Training - Companies firing on the Range. Band arrive. The Batt. Band from the Depot NAAS Co KILDARE under Bandmaster Mr. L.E. CAULFIELD and are taken in strength of Battalion.	C.F.
" "	8th		Inter-Coy Shooting won by "I" Coy. Inter-Coy Sergeants Shooting competition also won by "Z" Coy. In afternoon "Z" Coy won Inter-Coy Cross Country Race "W" Coy being 2nd beaten only by 10 points.	C.F.
" "	9th		Church Service for all denominations. Band Play parties do church - just returns since beginning war that the Batt. Band has done duty with Batt.	C.F.
" "	10th 11th		Usual Training etc. Goodbye - the Rev. D. POWER C.F. leaves Batt. for good. He has been Confession Priest Batt. for 3 years more or less period Batt. where in 1st Div. He is succeeded by Chpt- the Rev. E. KELLY M.C. C.F. together very fine - Plenty Skating to be had.	C.F.

WAR DIARY
INTELLIGENCE SUMMARY

1st Royal Dublin Fusiliers

Army Form C. 2118.

February 1919

Place	Date	Hour	Summary of Events and Information	Remarks and references to Appendices
BERG-LADBACH	12-13		Usual Routine	C.F.
— do —	14.		do. Weather Mild, much mud owing to thaw. CAPT	C.F
— do —	15th		J.C. BONNAR & Lieut D.P. WARNER leave Battalion for Demobilization. Inter Coy Football final X Coy beat W Coy 4 goals - 2 goals.	C.F.
— do —	16th		Church Service for all Denominations - Comdg. Officer Lt-Col. T.A. MELDON admitted to Hospital with Influenza, Major W. POWITON M.C. assumes command - Batt made orders to move forward nar - Advance parties proceed at 11.30 am	C.F
BATT H.Q. KURTEN (MAPS 2L & 12K)	17th		Batt. relieve 1st Lancashire Fus in forward area. Move at 9.30am by march Route. well en-cy - on completion of move Batt disposed as follows:- Batt HdQrs KURTEN, W Coy-WIPPERFELD, X Coy-FORSTEN & DELLING, Y Coy-INKER MUHLE, Z Coy-BECHEN. BOLSHEVISTS reported to be giving trouble in NEUTRAL ZONE between our Army & the GERMANS -	C.F
— do —	18th		Showery day. Comdg. Officer visits Companies & outposts.	C.F
— do —	19th		Corps engineers wiring Defended localities - Dull day. Some rain &	C.F
— do —	20 & 21st		do Weather uncertain -	
— do —	22nd		Work as before. Batt badly beaten at football by 1st LAN. Fus at BERG-LADBACH 2nd Round Divisional football Competition.	C.F

1st Batt. Royal Dublin Fusiliers

WAR DIARY
or
INTELLIGENCE SUMMARY

Army Form C. 2118.

for month of February 1919

Place	Date	Hour	Summary of Events and Information	Remarks and references to Appendices
KURTEN Batt HQrs	22nd	continued	MAJOR J.C.P HEFFERNAN M.C. returns from leave & assumes command of the Batt. Vice a/Major W.POULTON M.C.	
" "	23rd		Church service for all Denominations - weather unsettled, much rain	
" "	24th		Companies engaged in wiring defences at WIPPER FELD, LANDENBERG (new Def. Plan) and BILSTIN (between JUNKERMUHLE & FORSTEN) very dull day & misty.	
" "	25		Commanding Officers attend Brigade Conference - Very wet day - No wiring done	
" "	26		Commanding Officers conference with Gen. PLUMER - Drier day - defence entrenches	
" "	27		Work on defences continues - dull day - Coxes 9 GLADBACH for final Coy & Batn. football Competition	
" "	28		Work continues - ry day Drill. Boxing Competition Battalion Competition	

G. Heffernan ar Major
Cmdg IRDF

Appendix II

On Strength   February 1919

Officers   Officers   Off Strength
Major A Dawton not   O/Ranks   Capt J.K Bonner   Officers
taken on Strength 13/2/19 Joined from depot 31   Lt Col K.J.P. Dunn d. 15/2/19 Comm into R.S. un   1
                         Draughton   3   Lieut OP Burgess nor   wounded   2
                         Hospital   1   taken P Strength 15/2/19   Evacuated   2   20
                         Base   2   S.U.S. prisoner   6
                                                                                  Demob. on Leave   3   3

                                                  O/Ranks
                                                   653

                                                   657

                 Officers
                    42

                    41

Strength 31.1.19
Strength 28.2.19

APRIL INTELLIGENCE SUMMARY 1937

of the

1st Royal Dublin Fusiliers

VOLUME 49

Army Form C. 2118.

1st Bn Royal Dublin Fusiliers.

WAR DIARY
or
INTELLIGENCE SUMMARY.

(Erase heading not required.)

Summary of Events and Information for the month of April 1919

Place	Date	Hour	Summary of Events and Information	Remarks and references to Appendices
MÜLHEIM	1st 2nd 3rd		Usual daily routine — weather bad. CF.	
			Capt T.F. CONSIDINE leaves the battalion for good deserving weather fine. CF	
	4th		All released men of the Battalion proceed to Concentration Camp KÖLN for demobilisation. Capt A.K. HOLMAN, Lieut D. WALLIS, 2/Lt MA.CONDRON, proceed Lt. S. MORRIS MC. 2/Lts J. CASSIDY MC. I.W. MARTIN proceed to U.K. in turlough. Major WP. DOLTON MC. proceed for demobilisation. Rev. F. KELLY C.F. proceeds to 5th R. IRISH REGT and to SOUTHERN DIVN ARTILLERY. CF	
	5th		D.W. CADRE of the battalion 4 offrs. 80 OR's leaving the bands proceed to KÖLN by lorry and entrain for CHARLEROI. Train leaves 0950 and arrives CHARLEROI 0200 high morning. CF	
LE QUESNOY	6th		The chief trouble in knowing the Cadre is the volume of kit clothing trans stores. Lt (Quar Mas) proceeds by lorry at 0900 G/E QUESNOY (5 hours journey) to take over the Mühlheim equipment	

1st Bn R.D.F. CF

Army Form C. 2118.

1st Bn Royal Dublin Fusiliers WAR DIARY or INTELLIGENCE SUMMARY.

Instructions regarding War Diaries and Intelligence Summaries are contained in F. S. Regs., Part II. and the Staff Manual respectively. Title pages will be prepared in manuscript.

(Erase heading not required.)

Place	Date	Hour	Summary of Events and Information	Remarks and references to Appendices
Le Quesnoy	6th (continued)		Billets both enjoyed as in GERMANY in the town have been taken up by shell-fire, & its every forty most of the houses shelled and settled down by 1100 hours. C.F.	
	7th 8th Sun		Talking over 1st M.O.C. equipment & transport from the 2nd R.D.F proceeded with. C.F.	
	9th		Football match v. Engine 1st 2nd R.D.F result draw one all - hard contain - weather fine. C.F.	
	10th 11th		Dull days of hard daily work - covered in Hotel de Ville in the evening. C.F.	
	12th		Carry out every day work. C.F. Cross-country run in afternoon - 20 competitors C.F.	
	13th		Sunday - usual services - hockey match in afternoon 1st 2nd R.D.F Casen v 2nd Leinsters & 2nd Munsters Casen - Dublins won 3 - 0. C.F.	
	14th		Cold day - usual daily round. C.F.	

Army Form C. 2118.

1st Bn Royal Dublin Fusiliers WAR DIARY or INTELLIGENCE SUMMARY.

(Erase heading not required.)

Instructions regarding War Diaries and Intelligence Summaries are contained in F.S. Regs., Part II. and the Staff Manual respectively. Title pages will be prepared in manuscript.

Place	Date	Hour	Summary of Events and Information	Remarks and references to Appendices
Le Quesnoy	15th (Continued)		Usual routine. Rain all day. J.M.	
	16th		Cross-Country Run. Good following. B.J.M.	
	17th		Shooting Competition for Cadre – very poor results. J.M.	
	18th		Usual drills. Dark – rotten day. J.M.	
	19th		Cross Country Run in afternoon. Course was in remarkably good time J.M.	
	20th		Usual Services – Sunday. J.M.	
	21st		Cels wet day. Usual drills round J.M.	
	22nd		Practice in the morning for the inter Coln Cadre – not so good results as expected J.M.	
	23rd		Cross Country Race in the afternoon which a team for Corps Sports J.M.	
	24th		Football match in the afternoon v. 2nd Dublins resulted a draw. J.M.	
	25th		Miserable wet day – usual routine. Execution Drill. J.M.	
	26th		Another wet day. Bde Sports postponed on account of continuous of moisture J.M.	
	27th		French Operation afternoon in Cinema. Rain all day. J.M.	
	28th		The Band went on two days leave to LILLE. J.M.	
	29th		Shooting Competition v. 2nd Dublins. Lost by 18 points. Shooting poor.	
	30th		Band returned from LILLE. J.M. Cels wet day – usual routine. J.M.	

G. Heffernan Lt Col
Cmdg 1 R.D.F

WAR DIARY
of the
1st Bn. Royal Dublin Fusiliers
for the month of
MAY
1919

Volume. 50.

Army Form C. 2118.

1st Bn Royal Dublin Fusiliers. WAR DIARY
or
INTELLIGENCE SUMMARY.

(Erase heading not required.)

For the MONTH of MAY 1919

Place	Date	Hour	Summary of Events and Information	Remarks and references to Appendices
LE QUESNOY	1st		Usual routine J.I.N.	
	2nd		Weather still cold & wet. Usual daily round. J.I.N.	
	3rd		A fine day at last. Tug of war against 2nd R.D.F. - won in two successive pulls. J.I.N.	
	4th		Sunday:- Usual Church Service. Weather looks as if it has taken a change for the better. J.I.N.	
	5th		Usual Routine. Weather very good. J.I.N.	
	6		Usual Routine. Weather very good. J.I.N.	
	7th		Competitors for Sports sent to Corbeny Stuk ? 6 to Mm off Battalion very good PM	
	8th		Weather fine - usual routine. J.I.N.	
	9th		Usual daily round. J.I.N.	
	10th		Corps Sports at CAUDRY - 40287 Private O'Hagan came 3rd running the Mile. Rest with 104 yards against the wind. J.I.N.	
	11th		Sunday - usual services J.I.N.	

1st Bn. Royal Dublin Fusiliers **WAR DIARY** or **INTELLIGENCE SUMMARY**

Army Form C. 2118.

For the Month of MAY 1919

Place	Date	Hour	Summary of Events and Information	Remarks and references to Appendices
Le Rhonoy	12th		Weather still keeps fine - usual routine YN.	
	13th		Reception of Cadre to 36 began - two hour Sentry-way for Guard - Dance in Dublin Hall YN.	
	14th		Preparations for moving down to the Reception Camp begun - Officers of French Artillery give dance in Dublin Hall YN.	
	15th		Cadre moved down to the Reception Camp - Billets better as compared to those in College YN.	
	16th 17th		Usual routine - very fine weather OF.	
	18th		Sunday - usual services OF.	
	19th		Daily work carried out OF.	
	20th 21st		Practised a rifle & Musketry competition - lovely weather OF.	
	22		Shooting Competition won in Eagle of 2nd RDF. Ros.1 by 3.9 points. OF.	

Army Form C. 2118.

1st Bn. Royal Dublin Fusiliers WAR DIARY or INTELLIGENCE SUMMARY.

(Erase heading not required.)

Place	Date	Hour	Summary of Events and Information	Remarks and references to Appendices
Is Quetta	23rd		May 1919 For the month of —	
			Rescue competition between officers & R.S.M. 1st & 2nd R.D.F. Won by 17 points — very hot weather. CF	
	24th		Usual daily work. CF	
	25th		Sunday — Memorial Service to the Israeli killed in the war held in the church. CF	
	26th 27th		Usual work carried out — firing practice on the range. CF	
	28th		Shooting competition amongst Cadre — shooting isn't very good. CF	
	29th-31st		Usual daily routine — weather very warm. CF	

C. Bishop.
C/Sergt.
C/Sgt. 1st R. F. Dub. Fus.

www.ingramcontent.com/pod-product-compliance
Lightning Source LLC
Chambersburg PA
CBHW080908230426
43664CB00016B/2752